Ecological Ethics
and the
Human Soul

Ecological Ethics
and the
Human Soul

Aquinas, Whitehead,

and the Metaphysics of Value

Francisco J. Benzoni

University of Notre Dame Press

Notre Dame, Indiana

Copyright © 2007 by University of Notre Dame Press
Notre Dame, Indiana 46556
www.undpress.nd.edu
All Rights Reserved

Manufactured in the United States of America

Library of Congress Cataloging in-Publication Data

Benzoni, Francisco J.
Ecological ethics and the human soul : Aquinas, Whitehead,
and the metaphysics of value / Francisco J. Benzoni.
    p.   cm.
Includes bibliographical references and index.
ISBN-13: 978-0-268-02205-1 (pbk. : alk. paper)
ISBN-10: 0-268-02205-4 (pbk. : alk. paper)
1. Environmental ethics. 2. Metaphysics.
3. Theism—History. I. Title.
GE42.B465   2007
179'.1—dc22
2007030317

To Kim,

for your love and unwavering support

To Nathan and Isaiah,

for your love, boundless energy, and zest for life

Contents

Acknowledgments   ix

Introduction   1

PART I
Created Goodness and Moral Worth: Thomas' Bifurcation   11

Chapter One
The Metaphysical Grounding of Goodness   17

Chapter Two
The Moral Bifurcation of Creation   41

PART II
The Human Soul: Analysis and Critique   75

Chapter Three
Thomas' Conception of the Human Soul   77

Chapter Four
The Soul as an Entity: A Critical Assessment   93

PART III
The Unity and Moral Worth of All Creation   125

Chapter Five
An Alternative Metaphysics   127

Chapter Six
Intrinsic Value and Moral Worth   162

Conclusion   178

Appendix A
Spiritual Change and Materiality   183

Appendix B
God's Nature: The Controversy   188

Notes   191

Bibliography   239

Index   247

Acknowledgments

I wish especially to acknowledge Chris Gamwell, Paul Griffiths, and Kimberly Wade-Benzoni for their generous support and guidance.

Chris Gamwell has provided valuable insights, continuous direction, and critical feedback throughout every phase of this process. His encouragement and dedication have been invaluable, and his thorough embodiment of the intellectual virtues has been inspirational. I am deeply grateful for his contribution to this work, and, more generally, to my intellectual development.

Paul Griffiths' encouragement and critical questioning have helped shape this work at crucial junctures. I have enjoyed and profited from our interaction.

Kimberly Wade-Benzoni has been an inspirational support throughout this project. I have greatly benefited from her love and unwavering faith.

Introduction

This is a work in ecological ethics. For many people, the need for such an ethic has become pressing in our time, yet demonstrating this need can be a surprisingly delicate business. To be sure, one can cite an endless list of existing and looming ecological problems. Let me provide a representative, but by no means exhaustive, list.[1] If today is a typical one on our planet, human beings will destroy 160 square miles of tropical rainforest, create 72 square miles of desert, add 78 million tons of carbon dioxide to the atmosphere, erode 71 million tons of topsoil, and increase our population by 233,000. In the course of a year the numbers will become mind-numbing: between 26 and 30 billion tons of carbon dioxide added to the atmosphere, a total population increase of 85 million, an area of tropical rainforest the size of Michigan lost. The current rate of human-induced extinctions is estimated to be 1,000 times the background rate. This tremendous loss of other life, this simplification of the rich diversity of creation, very likely places us in the midst of one of the great extinctions that have struck our planet only two or three times since life evolved here. The rapid increase in the concentration of carbon dioxide and other "greenhouse gases" almost certainly means that the global temperature will rise over the coming decades with catastrophic effects for some of earth's inhabitants, human and non-human alike. In addition, our use of nitrogen, especially in fertilizers, threatens to overwhelm the natural nitrogen cycle so vital to the proper growth of plants. Human modifications to the natural environment have not only changed the structure of ecosystems (for example, which plants or animals exist, or what portion of the land is "developed") but also, perhaps more fundamentally, the very processing and functioning of these systems. In the past fifty years, carbon, nitrogen, phosphorous, and water cycling have changed more rapidly than at any other period in recorded human history.[2]

The facts and statistics are alarming—but the term "mind-numbing" may be more to the point. We hear the numbers and read the reports about the threat of some ecological problem or other, and we learn simply to filter them out and go on with our lives. After all, the issues seem too large and remote. Besides, we have more pressing problems—bills to pay, sick children, an exam to prepare for, a migraine headache, two reports due by tomorrow, and so on. Macro-scale ecological problems, and the vast majority of more regional problems, simply do not affect our lives as concretely and immediately as do our other concerns. But as we deal with those problems in our daily lives, we contribute to the macro-level problems described above. Our use of fossil fuels to power our increasingly large vehicles and houses, our longer commutes from far-flung suburbs, and our consumption of processed food grown or raised across the globe with tremendous amounts of fertilizers and pesticides all leave an ecological wake, a trail of effects, which is as complex as it is damaging.

In this work, I presuppose that ideas have efficacy; they make a difference in how we live. One complex of ideas that many of us appear to hold as a background belief (that is, without explicitly articulating it) is that human beings are separate from the rest of creation. According to this view, we have a separate destiny (whether worldly or otherworldly) from the rest of nature, which exists to serve us in our pursuit of that destiny. This view of reality rests easily with a consumerist culture in which values such as ease and gratification become the defining metaphors of "the good life." Once we see ourselves as separate from the rest of nature, there is no need to attend to the connection between our consumption of resources and the effects of this consumption on the rest of the natural world. To be sure, it is more difficult to justify this resource use in light of the tremendous want of much of humanity. But this problem is usually answered by the argument that the living standard for all of humanity can be made richer through the further exploitation of nature. This claim reflects the "rising tide raises all boats" mentality, in which the rising tide is the flow of resources from the natural economy to the human economy.[3] If nature itself, if other creatures, are understood to have moral worth—to be worthy of direct moral consideration[4]—then this justification would have no merit.

A Note on Terminology

Before continuing, I want to take a moment to explicate my terminology. I use the term "instrumental value" or "instrumentally good" to designate the value or goodness of worldly creatures that consists solely in their contribution to some other worldly creatures. It is the value or goodness that creatures have as a means to other creatures' ends. Moreover, I use the term "intrinsic value" or "intrinsic goodness" to designate the value or goodness of worldly creatures that does not consist solely in their contribution to some other worldly creatures. On the common usage, the intrinsic value of a creature entails that it is worthy of direct moral consideration by human beings. In this work, I use the term "moral worth" to mean "worthy of direct moral consideration," and so leave open the question of whether intrinsic value entails such moral worth.

I shy away from the term "intrinsic value" or "intrinsically good" in the usual sense (that is, as entailing moral worth) because, in our conversation with Thomas Aquinas, it will be useful to employ the term "intrinsic goodness" to denote the goodness which all creatures have by the very fact that they have actuality or being. Specifically, in Thomas' ontology, all creatures are intrinsically good in the particular sense that they are denominated good by their own intrinsic form rather than extrinsically denominated good by participation in the Form of the Good. Such intrinsic goodness does not, I will argue, entail that all creatures are worthy of direct moral consideration or that they are valuable as ends in and of themselves.

On my usage, the intrinsic goodness of a creature may, *but need not,* entail that this creature has moral worth. Distinguishing "intrinsic value" and "moral worth," then, helps us to better understand Thomas' thought. Further, as we will see, this distinction has some important implications for the current conversation in ecological ethics. This means, of course, that I am using the term "moral worth" in a different sense than it would be applied to things (human actions or characters) that might be immoral. That is, my use of "moral worth" differs from the use on which only human actions (and, by extension, human traits of character and lives as a whole) may be called "morally worthy," because only human actions can be immoral. In contrast, I employ "moral worth" to characterize anything that practical reason or moral assessment must take into account as a moral end.

Toward an Ecological Ethic

Human behavior clearly does negatively impact other life, as evidenced, for example, by the ongoing massive simplification of the diversity of life on earth. To morally justify such destructive activity, an ethic that accords moral worth to all creatures would demand that the well-being of other creatures be weighed alongside that of humans. Though a finely developed ecological ethic would allow for differences in moral worth, it would not sanction any moral bifurcation between human beings and the rest of creation.

My primary interlocutors in this book are Thomas Aquinas and Alfred North Whitehead. Thomas holds that human beings are finally separate from nature; as a consequence, only human beings ultimately have moral worth. By contrast, Whitehead holds that all entities exist along a continuous metaphysical spectrum, so human beings cannot but be continuous with the rest of nature; on this conceptualization, all creatures have some degree of moral worth. These thinkers' diverse metaphysics demand divergent ethics.

What makes Thomas, in particular, an intriguing, fruitful, and relevant conversation partner on the topic of ecological ethics? With some exceptions, Thomas is not usually listed among the culprits in critiques of the historical understanding of the relation between human beings and the rest of creation, even when the discussion focuses exclusively on Christian thinkers. After all, he consistently maintains that all creatures are ontologically good—that is, good in their very being. This is a far cry from a mechanistic view of creation, in which non-human creatures are understood to be mere "things" devoid of value.

Nevertheless, in the work of Thomas, we find the same moral bifurcation that exists in, say, the work of René Descartes. Frequently, what unites the work of those who morally separate human beings from the rest of creation is not so much their view of the rest of creation as their view of the human being, specifically the human soul. The work of Thomas is especially instructive because of the lucidity with which he demonstrates the centrality of a certain understanding of the human soul to the moral bifurcation in question. It is this view of the human soul that ties together at least many of those who seek to justify separating human beings from the rest of creation. And this view, and the separation that it underwrites, are still prominent in contemporary thinking.

By demonstrating the weaknesses in Thomas' account of this relation and offering a viable alternative, I hope to challenge the contemporary bifurcation between humans and the rest of nature. I offer an alternative understanding of human beings as a part of nature, even if the highest part. According to this understanding, all creatures are understood to have moral worth. If this vision, or something akin to it, could be articulated with sufficient force, clarity, and persuasive power to become embedded in the worldview of a significant number of people, then we could begin to change our current destructive patterns of existing in the world.

Organization of the Book

This book is divided into three parts. In Part I, I argue that Thomas' view of the rational soul of the human being so separates humankind from the rest of creation that non-rational creatures can only be understood as instrumental to the human good. In the first chapter, I examine the metaphysical basis of creaturely goodness in Thomas' understanding of reality. This examination concerns: first, Thomas' explanation of the convertibility of being and goodness; and second, Thomas' understanding of the participated goodness of creatures. The convertibility of being and goodness entails that all creatures are good insofar as they have being, actuality, or *esse*. However, I argue, this ontological goodness does not, in itself, entail that all creatures have moral worth or are worthy of direct moral consideration. Ontological goodness, in Thomas' thought, is a metaphysical or meta-ethical matter, not an ethical one. All creatures are good insofar as they all have, to some extent, what they all desire: actuality. Creatures possess being and goodness partially or to some extent, while God possesses being and goodness universally and completely. Therefore, creatures are said to participate in being and goodness. The fact that creaturely goodness is participatory does not alter the conclusion that creaturely goodness does not entail that every creature has moral worth, though it does set the convertibility thesis within Thomas' larger metaphysical framework.

To understand the moral import of Thomas' ontology, it is necessary to examine his teleology. I undertake this task in the second chapter. I argue that Thomas' conception of the human soul is of a piece with his under-standing of the *telos* of human beings as different in kind from the *telos* of non-rational creatures. Since the human soul continues in existence after the body perishes, Thomas argues, it is suited for the "final perfection" of the universe in which all motion will cease. No other "mixed bodies" (such as minerals, plants, or animals) are suited for this final perfection. Since the "first perfection," or the completion of the world at its creation, exists for the sake of the "second or final perfection," all non-rational creatures can only be understood as instrumental to the human good. That is, the final perfection exists for the sake of human beings, while all material creation exists for the sake of this final perfection. While embodied, human beings require non-rational creatures for survival and for revelation of the Cre-ator. Once the animal existence of human beings has ended—once we re-ceive our spiritual bodies—there is no need for non-rational creatures, and so their existence will cease. This discussion clarifies the distinction be-tween ontological goodness and moral worth by demonstrating, in Thomas' thought, that, even though all creatures have ontological goodness, only human beings have moral worth. Ultimately, non-rational creatures have only instrumental goodness; they are instrumental to the human good and lack moral worth of their own.

I next demonstrate that the moral conclusions reached by these onto-logical and teleological considerations are reflected in Thomas' moral the-ory. Specifically, I demonstrate that his understanding of natural law and the virtues systematically excludes the possibility of according moral worth to non-rational creatures. Natural law is rational participation in the eter-nal law; the eternal law, as God's providence over creation, has ordered na-ture such that non-rational creatures are ultimately merely instrumental to the human good. No precept of natural law, then, could possibly encourage human beings to respect the moral worth of non-rational creatures. With regard to the virtues, the relevant virtue is justice, which properly orders our relations to others. Human justice is modeled on divine justice; divine justice, in giving each creature its due, orders the lower to the higher in a strictly instrumental fashion. Therefore, direct moral consideration of non-rational creatures is positively excluded by Thomas' understanding of justice.

In Part II, I take up the topic of Thomas' conception of the human soul in order to demonstrate that this conception is philosophically untenable. In chapter 3, I present the problem as it presented itself to Thomas: either the soul is a complete substance and survives the perishing of the body, or the soul is the form of the body and so is united in existence with it. The problem with the first position is that it threatens to shatter the unity of the human being, while the second position threatens the immortality of the soul. Thomas attempts to demonstrate that the soul is both subsistent (that is, it exists in itself and so is able to survive the death of the body) *and* the form of the body by maintaining that the soul is an incomplete substance, requiring the body for its own proper operation. To lay the groundwork for addressing Thomas' arguments for the subsistence of the human soul, I examine his understanding of the cognitive powers of the human soul. One important conclusion of this discussion is that the informing of the intellect by intelligible species (by which the intellect knows universals) is an ontological, and not merely representative, matter.

In chapter 4, I turn to Thomas' arguments for the subsistence of the human soul, which is his primary justification for the moral bifurcation of creation. I argue that these demonstrations suffer from the fatal flaw of inferring from the representative qualities of our thoughts (the fact that we represent the world in terms of universals, which are immaterial) to the ontological qualities of our thoughts (the notion that the faculty by which we know must itself be immaterial) without any suitable middle term. This is akin to arguing that because I am thinking of the redness of my wife's car, my thought itself must be red. Insofar as Thomas' conception of the human soul is untenable, then his justification for morally separating human beings from non-rational creatures collapses.

I conclude chapter 4 by sketching the argument that Thomas' philosophy ultimately is marred by his metaphysical distinction between material and immaterial entities. If this distinction could be shown to be viable, then the problems pointed out in chapter 3 would be resolved, because immaterial entities could only know in an immaterial fashion. However, this distinction itself depends on the success of Thomas' arguments for the subsistence of the human soul. Insofar as these arguments fail, the distinction itself is untenable. Alternatively, this distinction can be understood to be justified by Thomas' arguments for God's existence; after all, Thomas argues for the existence of God *as an immaterial entity*. However, I posit that his arguments finally fail because their success depends on his use of analogical language to speak of God, which, in turn, depends on the success of the arguments for God's existence. This vicious circularity undercuts the arguments' effectiveness. Thomas' metaphysical distinction between material and immaterial entities, then, is ultimately untenable. Thus, his primary justification for morally separating human beings from the rest of creation is itself unjustified. Because the ontological bifurcation between material and immaterial entities cannot be sustained, there is no reason to agree with Thomas that non-rational creatures have only instrumental worth.

In Part III, I offer an alternative to Thomas' metaphysics. Drawing on the thought of Alfred North Whitehead, I develop in chapter 5 the foundation for an ecological ethic that accords some degree of moral worth to all creatures. After outlining Whitehead's metaphysics, I argue that his account of subjectivity provides a rationale for according moral worth to all creatures. According to Whitehead, subjectivity "goes all the way down," meaning that all metaphysically fundamental entities have the capacity to experience and are, to some extent, self-creative. This capacity is the basis of moral worth. On this account, all creatures also affect the divine experience; thus, we all share the same *telos,* though we contribute to it according to our own capacities. As contrasted with Thomas, Whitehead rejects any bifurcation of nature; human beings and non-rational creatures are of the same generic type. All creatures are self-creative and contribute directly to the *telos* of the universe—the creation of beauty—and thus have intrinsic value and moral worth. This continuity between creatures, each of which enjoys subjective experience, provides a promising foundation on which to build an ecological ethic. Every creature has value in and for itself because value (and moral worth) is the subjective enjoyment of experience.

In chapter 6, I summarize some of the basic underpinnings of an ecological ethic built on neoclassical grounds. I then demonstrate the relevance of this value theory to the contemporary conversation of ecological ethics. I argue that this theory integrates the best insights of two of the leading theorists of the intrinsic value of non-human entities, environmental ethicists Holmes Rolston III and J. Baird Callicott, while avoiding the problems that plague their theories. Rolston argues that the intrinsic value of non-human creatures, including non-sentient living beings, is independent of human valuation. Callicott maintains that there can be no value without a valuer and that the intrinsic value of non-human creatures depends upon human sentiments. Both thinkers agree that valuation requires consciousness and that consciousness coincides with subjectivity. I argue that both thinkers are right where they take themselves to disagree and both wrong where they agree. That is, Rolston is right to maintain that the intrinsic value of non-human creatures is independent of human consciousness, and Callicott is right to hold that value requires a valuer. How is it possible to hold two positions simultaneously? By insisting that subjectivity, and thus valuation, "goes all the way down." This position challenges the agreement between these thinkers that valuation requires consciousness and that consciousness coincides with subjectivity. In Whitehead's metaphysics, valuation requires subjectivity, but subjectivity does not require consciousness. The value theory developed on the basis of this metaphysics helps to resolve a number of difficult problems of concern to today's environmental ethicists.

PART I

Created Goodness and Moral Worth

Thomas' Bifurcation

For Thomas, the world is suffused with goodness. It is good in each of its parts and especially as a whole. It is good literally to the very core of its being; it comes from the Good and is ordered to the Good. Further, all species of creatures are necessary, on Thomas' account, for the perfection of the universe.

This account seems to offer the promise of a much more robust ecological ethic than a thoroughgoing, mechanistic worldview would allow. For example, this understanding of the created order suggests that Thomas would morally oppose the wholesale destruction of species, rainforests, watersheds, and wetlands. Yet a robust ecological ethic does not find fertile soil in Thomas' thought. His ethic accords strictly instrumental value to non-rational creation; any argument against the wholesale destruction of creation would have to find its rationale in the human good. This is not an accidental feature of Thomas' ethic: his accounts of the human soul and of divine providence describe the relation between human beings and non-rational creatures in a way that cannot but instrumentalize such creatures.[1]

Although I will argue that Thomas' ontology (which holds all creatures to be intrinsically good) and moral theory (which accords only instrumental value to non-rational creatures) are consistent and systematically interwoven, one might also argue that a chasm exists between them. For Thomas, what makes a thing ontologically good is actuality or being, but what makes a thing worthy of direct moral consideration is the capacity to consciously relate to universals (and thus enjoy rational freedom, possess an immortal soul, know God, and so on). To be sure, this capacity means that whoever possesses it has greater actuality and greater ontological goodness than something that does not. Yet this sliding scale of ontological goodness gives way to a moral bifurcation, for reasons I will clarify. It is in this shift from a sliding scale of goodness to a bifurcated morality where a disjunction can be discerned. Interestingly, however, in the end, the bifurcation is, in fact, an ontological one. Despite the sliding scale of ontological goodness, ultimately an ontological divide separates human beings (with our immaterial subsistent souls) from other material creatures (who lack such souls). It is this divide that is reflected in the moral bifurcation of creation.

Recent works in the Christian tradition on the relation between human beings and the rest of material creation elucidate the history of this divide.[2] Anna Peterson, in particular, echoes certain themes in this portion of the book when she argues, "The soul links humans' origins, capacities, and ultimate destiny to God and, thus, forever divides them from the 'non-spiritual' part of creation. The soul performs the same function that other human qualities, notably conceptual thought and language, fulfill for secular thinkers: the soul is not just an added piece of equipment but a singular dimension that transforms the meaning of humanness."[3] Peterson traces both the history and the tensions of this understanding of the human soul, as separating people from the rest of material creation, to the Christian tradition.[4] While the notion that differences among human beings imply superiority or inferiority has been broadly rejected, the notion that there is a qualitative difference between human beings and the rest of creation has been left intact.[5] It is this separation that I seek to explore and critique, and to which I ultimately want to offer an alternative.[6]

As alluded to above, it is possible to distinguish two relevant strands in Thomas' thought. On the one hand, he clearly states that all creatures are ontologically good in their very being and that all species are necessary for the perfection of the universe. On the other hand, he also clearly states that lower creatures are "ordered to" or "for the sake of" higher ones. These two features of Thomas' thought have given rise to divergent assessments of the

moral status he accords to non-rational creatures. A number of contemporary interpreters argue that Thomas' ethic accords only instrumental value
to non-rational creatures.[7] Others, however, hold that his ethic is amenable
to according moral worth to at least some non-rational creatures.[8] One
author has even attempted to show that, at least in some circumstances,
Thomas' ethic prescribes vegetarianism.[9]

Notably, modern interpreters of Thomas on the issue of ecological ethics, however much their interpretations may vary, share the opinion that
a strictly instrumental view of non-rational creatures is wrong and that
moral theory should accord moral worth to at least some non-rational
creatures. Because ecological ethics per se is largely a modern concern, one
might ask why we are interrogating Thomas on this issue if it is not a concern for him. First, the issue is not simply whether or not he explicitly accords moral worth to non-rational creatures. Rather, the issue is whether
or not his moral theory can accommodate the accordance of moral worth
to other creatures. It may simply be that Thomas' statements about the
strictly instrumental value of non-rational creatures reflect his personal
view on the matter, but that this view is accidental rather than systematic
to his comprehensive view of reality.[10] Thus, our concern is whether Thomas' system as a whole allows for the possibility of non-rational creatures
being accorded moral worth or whether, as I argue, he systematically excludes such worth.

One might press the issue, however. So what if some modern-day interpreters of Thomas believe that a moral theory should accord moral worth
to at least some non-rational creatures? Why should we care about their
attitudes toward any given moral theory? In fact, the question before us is
whether according moral worth to non-rational creatures is an issue with
which Thomas ought properly to have been concerned.

Thomas' accordance of only instrumental worth to non-rational creatures is problematic for a number of reasons. First, this strictly instrumental value raises an internal tension in at least one area of Thomas'
project. He argues that the diversity of creation is necessary for the perfection of the universe, an argument that might seem to indicate the possibility of building a case for according moral worth to non-rational
creatures.[11] But Thomas' view is that the "first perfection" of the universe
(that is, the universe in its changeable state) is provisional and will give way
to the "final perfection," in which non-rational creatures will not exist

because they are no longer needed to further the human good. Thus, on the one hand, he argues that all (types of) creatures are directly necessary for the perfection of the universe, and, on the other hand, that non-rational creatures are solely instrumental to the human good.

Second, the rationale for Thomas' moral separation of human beings from the rest of creation largely rests on his conception of the rational soul. In Part II, I argue that this conception is philosophically untenable. If we assume the success of that argument, Thomas is left without a rationale for the moral separation. And, in Part III, I offer an alternative that finds untenable Thomas' moral separation of human beings from non-rational creatures based on a freedom/slavery dichotomy. Once all creatures are understood to be, in some sense, related to universals and so in some measure free, then there is a positive reason for according moral value to all creatures.

Third, although the point is a contentious one, there is at least an argument to be made that, properly understood, the Christian tradition demands that all of God's creatures be considered not merely as instruments but also as having moral worth, whether such worth be based on their own value and/or their value to the universe and/or to God.[12] And finally, as a practical matter, if our understanding of ourselves in relation to the rest of creation influences our behavior, then, arguably, an instrumental view of non-rational creation results in ecologically destructive behavior. If my argument is successful, then Thomas' thought would be saddled with the unenviable burden of sanctioning the destruction of God's handiwork.

In this first part, I address only the first of these four points, concerning the tension within Thomas' account caused by his instrumentalization of non-rational creatures. The second point will be central to the later portions of the book. There is not space here to deal with the third and fourth points (though I believe that, in the end, all creatures are properly accorded moral worth in the Christian tradition and that our idea of ourselves in relation to the rest of creation does have efficacy). My primary goals for this first part are to demonstrate that Thomas systematically excludes the accordance of moral worth to non-rational creatures and to examine his rationale for that exclusion. Ultimately, I side with those who hold that Thomas' moral theory accords only instrumental value to non-rational creatures. I demonstrate the consistency of this theory with his larger metaphysical project and thus show the systematic nature of Thomas' denial of moral worth to non-rational corporeal creatures.

Those who hold that Thomas' metaphysics does, or can, support an ecological ethic that accords moral worth to non-rational creatures often support their view with one of two basic lines of reasoning. The first is founded on the notion that the ontological goodness of all creatures means that all must be worthy of direct moral consideration. At its core, this line of reasoning confuses ontological goodness with moral worth. By contrast, I argue that Thomas' understanding of ontological goodness does not translate directly into moral worth. When this ontology is considered in light of Thomas' teleology, the notion that non-rational creatures are worthy of direct moral consideration is positively excluded. The justification for this exclusion rests, finally, on Thomas' understanding of the human soul and his correlative account of divine providence.

The second line of reasoning depends upon Thomas' clear and numerous statements to the effect that all creatures or, more precisely, all types of creatures are necessary for the perfection of the universe. Because the perfection of the universe is God's primary goal in creation and because it is definitive of Thomas' understanding of morality to bring the human will into alignment with the will of God, it seems to follow that human beings are morally bound to respect the diversity of life on earth. This line of reasoning can be argued independently of the previous one. That is, one might argue that, regardless of the moral worth of individual creatures, species ought to be given moral consideration because they are necessary to reflect God's glory to the greatest extent possible in the universe. It is worth noting that, although the modern classification of creatures into "species" originated with Aristotle and the precise meaning of the term is still debated, it is nevertheless clear that Thomas' sense of "species" is not equivalent to that meant by the term today. Still, for the purposes of this book, sufficient overlap exists to allow us to bypass this complex and contentious matter. Specifically, it seems safe to say that if we confine our attention to living creatures, both Thomas' and the modern understanding of species would entail that the greater the number of species, the greater the diversity of life. That is all the overlap we need.

On its face, this second line of reasoning seems plausible. Yet it only holds true if we jettison Thomas' conception of divine providence and, with it, his conception of the divine nature; because of these conceptions, God directly and infallibly preserves each and every species in existence; each is necessary for the perfection of the universe.[13] Further, this line fails to take into account Thomas' understanding of the difference between the first and final perfection of the universe and the fact that the first perfection (the completion of the world at its founding) is for the sake of the final perfection (the final state of the universe when all motion will cease).

In the first chapter, I examine Thomas' metaphysical grounding of the goodness of creatures. I begin with a cursory overview of his general metaphysics and then consider creaturely goodness as convertible with being and as participated goodness. After examining these notions with some care, I conclude that the ontological goodness of creatures does not, in Thomas' account, directly entail moral worth because such goodness does not entail human moral responsibility toward non-rational creatures. In the second chapter, I consider Thomas' teleology in order to bring out the moral import of this ontology. I conclude that, according to Thomas, the rational soul of the human being—specifically, the human capacity to consciously relate to universals—so separates people from non-rational creatures that these creatures can only be instrumentally good. For instance, only human beings are truly free. Other material creatures are "slaves" to be used as "instruments" by the free. Again, only human beings are suited for the end times, when all motion and all time shall cease. Other creatures will cease to exist at that point because they will no longer be useful to human beings. In order to support this conclusion of the strict instrumentality of non-rational creatures to the human good, I briefly examine Thomas' moral theory. In it, I argue, non-rational creatures are beyond the moral pale.

Chapter One

The Metaphysical Grounding
of Goodness

In this chapter, we ask how the goodness of creatures is related to their moral worth. This is not Thomas' question. Rather, Thomas' concern is to demonstrate both that the goodness of creatures is intrinsic (and, properly understood, substantial) rather than merely extrinsic and accidental *and* that this intrinsic goodness of creatures does not confuse the creature with the Creator. Precisely how the goodness of creatures is related to their moral worth is not directly addressed because Thomas' concerns are metaphysical or meta-ethical. Still, from his discussion of the ontological goodness of all creatures, it is possible to show that there is no direct entailment of their moral worth.

Before turning to Thomas' account of goodness, it is helpful to gain clarity on some basic concepts in his general metaphysics. This cursory overview will be sufficient to set up the conversation in this chapter as well as in subsequent chapters. In Thomas' metaphysics, the most basic existent is a substance, or "first substance,"[1] a particular thing that exists in itself and not in another. Thomas' term for the kind of existence enjoyed by a first substance is "subsistence," which simply means that it exists in itself and not in another. To say that it exists in itself and not in another means that it is the ultimate subject that is not predicated of another. And an "entity" is "an individual in the category of substance,"[2] a *hoc aliquid*, an individual something. It is that which exists in a complete sense; all other things exist in a dependent sense, as having their existence in a first substance. A dog, a tree, a person, an ant, an angel would all be examples of entities or first substances or individuals in the category of substance. Things that exist in a dependent sense, such as "white" or "tall," exist only as instantiated in a primary substance and are termed "accidents."

Thomas, following Aristotle, distinguishes the category of "substance" from nine categories of "accidents." Thomas understands these ten categories to be the most comprehensive genera or classes of things: substance, quantity, quality, relation, place, time, position, state, action, affection. Each category is a supreme genus; nothing higher or more general could be predicated univocally of whatever is being classified. For example, if we start with an individual, Socrates, we can list predicates that apply to him with ever-increasing generality. We can start by predicating "man" of Socrates, then predicate "animal" of "man," "living thing" of "animal," and so on until we reach the highest univocal predicate in this series, "substance." We could do the same with the whiteness of Socrates, first predicating "white" of Socrates, then "color" of "white," until we reach the highest univocal predicate in this series, "quality."

The fundamental difference between substance and the nine categories of "accidents" concerns their mode of existence or being. The being of a substance is independent, while the being of an accident is dependent upon a substance. The accidents "white" and "tall," for example, exist only as instantiated in a primary substance such as a man or a tree. In other words, a substance exists in itself and not in another; it is not predicated of anything else. Accidents, however, exist only in a substance; their existence is derivative and dependent. As we will see, Thomas claims that the human soul is a substance, albeit a unique sort of substance.

In the respect that a substance is or does something, it is in act or is actual. In the respect that a substance can be or can do something, it is in potency or has potentialities. This distinction between actuality and potentiality is central in Thomas's metaphysics. To oversimplify, actuality is that which is or is being done, and potentiality is that which can be or can be done. Whether something is in act or in potency may depend upon one's perspective. For example, an intellect that actually understands something is in act with regard to the thing understood but in potency to further understanding.

The distinction between form and matter can be considered an instance of the general contrast between act and potency.[3] Material substances are composites of matter and form.[4] Matter is closely associated with potentiality; it is that which is in potentiality to substantial change. Moreover, matter is the subject of substantial change, which takes place when one substance is corrupted and another generated; for example, a tree is burned and becomes ashes. That which remains the same through the substantial change, that which provides the continuity through change, is the underlying matter, which first takes one form ("tree-ness") and then another ("ashes-ness"). Technically, this understanding of matter is what Thomas calls prime matter,[5] "something which is in the genus of substance as a kind of potency, which is understood as excluding every species and form, and even as excluding privation, and yet is a potency capable of receiving both forms and privations."[6] As a pure potentiality, prime matter has no existence but is posited to account for continuity between things that either undergo substantial change or change in substantial form. (Without positing prime matter, substantial change would be a new creation on Thomas' metaphysics.)

In contrast to matter, form is the intelligible structure or pattern that makes a material thing be the kind of thing that it is; so form is associated with act. It is the defining principle of a thing, "the principle by which things have being."[7] The form is universal since it is the principle of the *species* or *type* of thing. The matter is what makes a thing be just *this* thing and not another. "[M]atter is the principle of individuation of all inherent forms, because, since these forms, considered in themselves, are naturally in something as in a subject, from the very fact that one of them is received in matter, which is not in another, it follows that neither can the form itself thus existing be in another."[8] Just as the form is the principle of specific diversity, so matter, as subject to the accident of quantity and its dimensions, is the principle of individuation or numeric diversity. For instance, Samuel is a man by the substantial form of humanity, but Samuel is *this* man by the particular matter that is so informed and that differentiates him from all other things.

In order to continue, we must distinguish between two types of forms: substantial and accidental. A substance is said (formally) to be or to exist in a determinate mode, as a particular type of thing or species, by its substantial form. "Substantial forms of their very nature constitute species."[9] It is from the substantial form that the substance has whatever actual existence it has. And the substantial form is the act that constitutes the substance as such. The intrinsic substantial form exercises formal causality, not efficient causality,[10] with regard to the act of being of the substance it informs.[11] Thus, a thing's being or *esse* can be said to come from its form in the order of formal, but not efficient, causality. (Otherwise, in generation, a thing would be the efficient cause of its own species, which is impossible.)[12] It is by the substantial form that, formally speaking, a thing is and is the determinate kind of thing that it is. It is by its accidental forms that a thing has those attributes that are not essential to or definitional of that kind of thing. Thomas summarizes the difference between substantial and accidental forms as follows: "The substantial form differs from the accidental form in this, that the accidental form does not make a thing to be 'simply,' but to be 'such,' as heat does not make a thing to be simply, but only to be hot. . . . Now the substantial form gives being simply [again, formally speaking]; therefore by its coming a thing is said to be generated simply; and by its removal to be corrupted simply."[13] For example, a man is white by the accidental form "whiteness," but a man is a man by the substantial form "humanity" or "rational soul." The subject of substantial change is prime matter, while the subject of accidental change is a particular substance.

The forms of material things do not subsist or have being per se; they are not entities in their own right.[14] (The human soul will be the exception to this rule.) This is true of accidental forms, which, by definition, exist only in a substance, but it is also true of substantial forms. As Thomas puts it, "[B]eing is not predicated univocally of the form and the thing generated. A generated natural thing is said to be *per se* and properly, as having being and subsisting in that being: whereas the form is not thus said to be, for it does not subsist, nor has it being *per se;* and it is said to exist or be, because something is by it."[15] Substantial and accidental forms of material things are abstract. They are that *by which* something exists, either as an accident or a substance. Only primary substances subsist. Neither the substantial form nor the prime matter has any separate existence apart from the material substance of which it is a part—again, with the singular exception of the human soul.

A primary substance is not simply a group of accidents bound together by a copula, but, rather, it is a unit of existence, all of whose constituent elements *are,* by one and the same act of existing that is that of the substance.[16] Substances subsist or exist in themselves in that whatever is in them belongs to them by a single act of existing. This single act accounts for and causes that which is in them to be.

With that cursory look at Thomas' general metaphysics, let us now turn to a brief overview of his account of the goodness of creatures with its Aristotelian and Platonic influences. Thomas seems to have become increasingly aware of a tension between the claim that a creature is good by its own intrinsic form and the claim that a creature is good by participation in God. He wrote the only known commentary from the thirteenth century on Boethius' *On the Hebdomads*.[17] In this work, the tension noted above is put into stark relief. Boethius poses the problem "as to the way in which [creatures] might be good: whether by participation or by substance."[18] He argues that, given his presuppositions, either solution results in a contradiction. Boethius' presuppositions are that all things seek the good and that all things seek their like. Since, then, all things must be good, he proceeds to ask how they are good. If, by participation, then they are not good in themselves. But then they do not seek the good, because all things seek their like, and this contradicts what the many and the wise agree upon. If creatures are good by their substance, then they can indeed seek the good, but they must also be substantially good like the first good. Indeed, they must be the Good-itself. Boethius concludes that, therefore, they must be good *by relation* to the first good rather than good by participation or by their substance.

While Thomas does not go this route, he takes the question that Boethius asks with great seriousness. He seeks to forge an answer that ensures both that creatures are intrinsically good *and* that creatures are not confused with the Creator. He does this by reformulating Plato's understanding of participation to include efficient, and not only formal, causality. It is clear from his commentary on Boethius' work and from his own formulation of the problem in *Disputed Questions on Truth*, question twenty-one (which was written at about the same time as the commentary on Boethius), that he believes that Boethius took a too-restricted view of participation. For Boethius, it only makes sense to speak of participation when something already exists. Thomas seeks to expand the notion of participation to the very being of a created substance.

In attempting to resolve the tension noted above, Thomas synthesizes important features of both Aristotle's and Plato's understanding of goodness. For Aristotle, goodness is a transcendental in the sense that it runs through all the categories and in that sense transcends any one of them. For Plato, goodness is transcendent in the sense that it is above all the categories and that all things are formally good by virtue of their participation in this first good rather than by virtue of any inherent goodness. Aristotle's conception is attractive to Thomas because it makes goodness and being convertible; all creatures are good by their own formal goodness and are not merely extrinsically thus denominated by virtue of their participation in the first good. This seems to be demanded by the biblical account of creation. The complication for Thomas, however, is that the transcendentals—goodness, being, one, and truth—are also divine names. God is goodness-itself, being-itself, supremely simple, truth-itself. So, while Thomas echoes Aristotle in rejecting Plato's claim that there are separate forms of natural things, he agrees with Plato that there is a separate form of the transcendentals of being, truth, one, and goodness, which we call "God." Since God is goodness-itself, creatures must be good by virtue of their participation in this first good. Thomas, then, needs to explain how all things are good by virtue of their own goodness as well as how all things are good by virtue of their participation in the first good.[19]

I start this discussion by considering the Aristotelian aspect of Thomas' thought: his demonstration of the convertibility of being and goodness. Through this discussion, I seek not only to unfold Thomas' understanding of the convertibility of goodness and being but also to demonstrate that ontological goodness does not, of itself, directly translate into moral worth, as it does not have any direct entailments for how human beings ought to interact with non-rational creatures. I then turn to the Platonic aspect of Thomas' thought: his understanding of participation and creaturely participation in the first good. In this discussion, I argue that the participation of creatures in the first good does not alter our earlier conclusion that only human beings have moral worth. Rather, this Platonic notion of participation simply contextualizes the Aristotelian thesis of the convertibility of being and goodness, in the sense that the being that is convertible with goodness is, in creatures, participated being. Thus, creatures are completely different from, and utterly dependent upon, the Creator.

Goodness as Convertible with Being

"All arts and all teaching, and similarly every act and every choice seem to have the attainment of some good as their object. For this reason it has correctly been proclaimed that good is what all desire."[20] So begins Aristotle in his *Nichomachean Ethics,* an exploration of the human good. Thomas, in his commentary on this work, examines the definition of the good as "what all desire." His interpretation goes beyond the literal content of Aristotle's text by considering the good properly so considered, or metaphysically.

The usual way of defining something on Thomas' (and Aristotle's) metaphysics is to reduce it to something more general (genus) and then add that which differentiates it from other members of the same genus (difference). The genus and the difference together constitute the species of a thing and comprise its definition. The good, however, cannot be reduced to anything more general because it is a *prima,* a first thing. Like being, true, and one, the good is a transcendental. It transcends such categories as substance, quality, quantity, and relation, not in the sense that it refers to a reality beyond these categories, but in the sense that it goes through or characterizes all entities in these categories. The categories, in contrast, are determinations of what exists, and none of them extends to every being or mode of being that exists. Goodness, like being, extends to everything that is; it cannot be reduced to anything more general. "[P]rimary things cannot be understood by anything anterior to them, but by something consequent, as causes are understood through their proper effects."[21] So Aristotle defines the good, as he must, by its effect. The good is "what all desire" because it is the moving principle of the appetite.[22]

Against Plato, Thomas follows Aristotle in arguing that there is no separate, subsistent form of the good *that is formally the goodness of all things.* Thomas explains, "In regard to this we should bear in mind that good is enumerated among the primary entities to such a degree— according to the Platonists—that good is prior to being. But, in reality, good is convertible with being."[23] Good is common to all being.

In addition to some helpful remarks in his commentary on Boethius' *On the Hebdomads,* Thomas deals most systematically with the goodness of creatures in question twenty-one of *Disputed Questions on Truth* and questions five and six of the first part of the *Summa Theologiae.* In the *Summa Theologiae,* the topic of question five is "Of Goodness in General." It is here that Thomas addresses the basically Aristotelian conception of goodness. In the first article of this question, he asks whether goodness differs really from being. His answer, of course, is that goodness and being are convertible. He is seeking to demonstrate that "good" and "being" signify the same reality, that "good" does not add anything to "being." The diversity in the concepts "good" and "being" results only from a diversity of ways in which the same reality is conceived in the intellect. Both concepts signify the same *res*, but under different intelligible aspects; "good" considers this *res* as desirable while "being" considers it simply. Thus, Thomas' argument for the convertibility of goodness and being aims to show that, though these terms are conceived differently by the intellect, they signify the same thing or pick out the same *res*.

> Goodness and being are really the same (*sunt idem secundum rem*), and differ only in idea (*rationem*); which is clear from the following argument. The essence (*ratio*) of goodness consists in this, that it is in some way desirable. Hence the Philosopher says . . . : "Goodness is what all desire." Now it is clear that a thing is desirable only in so far as it is perfect; for all desire their own perfection. But everything is perfect so far as it is actual. Therefore it is clear that a thing is perfect so far as it exists; for it is existence that makes all things actual (*esse enim est actualitas omnis rei*).[24] . . . Hence it is clear that goodness and being are the same really. But goodness presents the aspect of desirableness, which being does not present.[25]

His argument, then, moves as follows:

1) The *ratio* of goodness is that it is desirable.
2) The desirable is what is perfect.
3) The perfect is what is actual.
4) The *ratio* of being is that it is the actuality of all things.
5) Therefore, goodness and being are the same really.

Let us follow Thomas' argument on the convertibility of goodness and being in more detail. He begins with Aristotle's definition of goodness. The *ratio*, or the conception in the intellect,[26] of the good is that "it is in some way desirable."[27] Because good is a transcendental, Thomas follows Aristotle in giving a definition a posteriori; it must be defined through its proper effect. The term "good" designates that toward which the appetite is drawn. Something is desired because it is good (or thought to be good), not vice versa.

Thomas then clarifies what makes something desirable, what it is that one desires when one desires the good: "Now it is clear that a thing is desirable only in so far as it is perfect, for all desire their own perfection."[28] Thus, "desirable" is identified with "perfect." According to Thomas, what all human beings desire when they desire any good is their own perfection: "Whatever good one may desire, one desires a certain perfection and excellence therefrom."[29] Therefore, a thing is desirable insofar as it is perfective of the one desiring. As Thomas puts it in *Disputed Questions on Truth,* "the essence of good consists in being perfective."[30] But something is perfective only insofar as it is itself perfect in some way. So, with these first two steps of his argument, Thomas has maintained that the good is what is desirable, what is desirable is what is perfective, and what is perfective must itself be perfect in some way; thus, what is desirable must be in some way perfect.

"Everything is perfect insofar as it is actual," Thomas continues.[31] In other words, what is perfect is identified with what is in act, and anything is perfect insofar as its substantial or accidental potentialities are actualized. That which is perfect is complete and lacks nothing appropriate to its kind. A thing in potency is imperfect because it has not yet reached its end. For instance, a seed is imperfect insofar as it has not yet reached its end, or goal, of growing into a tree. Perfection demands that potency be reduced to act, and every act is a perfection and a good. "Good" is identified with "desirable," "desirable" with "perfect," and "perfect" with "actual." So goodness and actuality are coincident.

The final step in Thomas' argument is to equate actuality with being: "to be (*esse*) is the actuality (*actualitas*) of all things."[32] He has now reached the metaphysical foundation for the claim that being and goodness are convertible. "Being" refers to the act of being (*actus essendi*). And for Thomas, being is not mere static existence. Being as such is not indifferent to good and bad. Understood as actuality, being is a perfection.[33] To be in act is to be perfect, which is to be desirable and thus good. What makes a thing desirable, its actuality, is the same as what makes it a being. *Actuality* is the *res* signified in different ways by the *ratio* of good and the *ratio* of being. It is Thomas' novel identification of being with actuality that enables him to demonstrate the convertibility of being and goodness.

It is important to see that the novelty of Thomas' understanding of being does not simply mean that being is one perfection among others, as if we might have one perfection of being, another of life, another of wisdom, and so on. On the contrary, being for Thomas includes any and every perfection. Being is the actuality of anything else that is called "act." To illustrate this point, Thomas points out that such goods as life or wisdom are only good insofar as they are actual (or have being) and only desirable insofar as they are to become actual.[34] Again, he states, "every excellence of any being whatsoever is ascribed to a thing in respect of its being, since no excellence would accrue to man from his wisdom, unless thereby he were wise, and so on."[35] Therefore, he maintains, "Being, as we understand it here, signifies the highest perfection of all: and the proof is that act is always more perfect than potentiality. . . . Wherefore it is clear that being as we understand it here is *the actuality of all acts, and therefore the perfection of all perfections.*"[36]

Being is what actualizes and, indeed, is the actuality of all that exists. A dynamic, and elusive, notion at the heart of Thomas' metaphysics, being is the actuality of substantial forms of existing things, the actuality of activities, the actuality of intentional beings, and so on. Insofar as anything is actualized and has being, it is good, according to Thomas. He maintains that "every being, as being, is good. For all being, as being, has actuality and is in some way perfect; since every act implies some sort of perfection; and perfection implies desirability and goodness. Hence it follows that every being as such is good."[37]

Thomas, then, holds that every existing creature is good and that the world is brimming with goodness. Insofar as any creature is actual, and insofar as it has actualized any of its potentialities, it is good. By virtue of the actuality of its substantial form, a creature has being simply and goodness relatively (that is, relative to what it can be). In actualizing its further potentialities, the creature gains being relatively (or accidentally) and, insofar as it becomes perfect in its kind, gains goodness simply. Clearly, then, all creatures are ontologically good.

There is an important distinction in Thomas' thought between essential and accidental being, and a mirrored distinction between essential goodness and accidental goodness. These distinctions help to clarify how creatures are good. An objector argues that goodness differs really from being, for Boethius says: "I perceive that in nature the fact that things are good is one thing, that they are is another."[38] Thomas replies that being and goodness are the same in reality but are not predicated of a thing absolutely in the same way.[39] According to Thomas, "being simply" (*ens simpliciter*) differs from "good simply" (*bonum simpliciter*). Since being (*ens*) signifies something that is in act (*esse in actu*), something is said simply to have being insofar as it is distinguished from that which is only in potentiality. Each thing's substantial being (*esse substantiale*) distinguishes it from what is merely potential, so it is by its substantial being that each thing is said to have being simply. By any further actuality added to the substance, a thing is said to have being in a certain respect. This is accidental being. But good-ness signifies perfection that is appetible, and so something final. There-fore, that which has its ultimate perfection, or has actualized the potenti-alities appropriate to its kind, is said to be good simply. That which does not have the ultimate perfection it ought to attain is not said to be good simply, but only good in a certain respect. In this way, a thing that has sub-stantial being is said *to be* simply but *to be good* in a certain respect, for in-sofar as it is actual, it has some perfection. Viewed in its complete actuality, with all the potentialities of its kind actualized, a thing is said *to be good* simply and *to be* in a certain respect, for the perfections added to substan-tial being are accidental. In its primal actuality, a thing simply exists. In its complete actuality, a thing is good simply.[40] A thing is a being simply by virtue of its substantial being. A thing is good simply by virtue of having actualized those potentialities proper to its kind.

It is tempting at this point to claim that since all creatures are good and since goodness, as what is desirable, has the status of a final cause, then all creatures are worthy of direct moral consideration or are ends in them-selves. That is, it is tempting to claim that since, in Thomas' thought, all creatures are ontologically good, all creatures have moral worth—tempting, but unwarranted. No conclusions regarding the moral worth of creatures can be drawn from the bare fact of ontological goodness.

In Thomas' thought, all existing creatures have some perfection, at the very least the perfection of having substantial existence, and thus are onto-logically good. This is the metaphysical or meta-ethical claim that all crea-tures have some actuality, since goodness has been shown to be identical to actuality. The ontological goodness of creatures does not, of itself, translate directly into moral worth.[41] Thomas has asserted only that all creatures possess, to some extent, what all creatures desire. Or all creatures possess what is good—that is, actuality—and, in that sense, all created things are good.

In the context of our discussion, Thomas' convertibility thesis means simply that every creature possesses some good insofar as it has being or actuality and that all creatures desire being or actuality (and perfections suitable to their type) as an end. This does not mean that they seek this or that creature—which has actuality—as their end or that human beings ought to respect such a creature as an end-in-itself. In other words, all creatures possess what is good—that is, actuality—and, in that sense, all created things are good. For example, a rock is good because it has existence. Although a human being desires existence, this does not imply that the rock is the end for him. It simply means that a rock and a human being resist corruption because they both desire existence, either naturally or willfully. Actuality is what is sought as an end. A human being naturally desires his own existence and not the existence of a rock. Individual creatures have actuality to some extent and thus are good, but they are not thereby themselves final ends or to be morally considered for their own sakes. Every being possesses, to some extent, the good (that is, the actuality) that all creatures seek. In that sense, all creatures are good. But it is not the goodness (or well-being) of this or that creature that another creature seeks as its own end because such an end would not be perfective of the one seeking it.

Further, for Thomas, in the case of material creatures, a creature may be desirable, and thus good, because it is instrumental to some actualization or perfection of the creature doing the desiring. For example, a person may desire a turkey because its meat sustains life. But a thing's desirability need not imply that it is an end—that it is desired for its own sake—because something can be the term of the appetite either absolutely as an end or relatively as a means.[42] There is, in the division of the good, the *useful* that is desired for the sake of some other end, the *virtuous* that is desired for its own sake, and the *pleasant* that rests in the thing desired. A creature may be desirable and good *to another creature* solely as a useful means for acquiring some other good or actuality, just as the desirability of the turkey in the above example is on account of its capacity to sustain human life.

Still, Thomas makes statements such as "goodness has the aspect of the end, in which not only actual things find their completion, but also towards which tend even those things which are not actual, but merely potential."[43] In other words, goodness is that which all human beings seek, that which is desirable as such. So it would seem that the goodness of a thing does directly imply that this thing is a final cause or an end. But when Thomas speaks of goodness as a final cause, he intends that goodness be taken in its transcendental sense as that actuality which all things seek and in which they find their completion. This is the goodness of this or that creature only in the sense that this or that creature possesses actuality to some extent, and actuality is what all desire for themselves.[44] To say that any individual creature is desirable or ontologically good does not in itself say anything more than that it has actuality and seeks actualization. To put it somewhat differently, to say that the perfection of any given creature is desirable as an end for that creature is not to say that it is desirable as an end for human beings; therefore, it does not entail that the creature has moral worth. That any given creature seeks to preserve and augment its own being (that is, is ontologically good) does not entail for Thomas that human beings are likewise morally obligated to care for that creature's well-being.

Participated Goodness

With Aristotle, Thomas holds that every creature is denominated good by its own being; every creature is good insofar as it is. The good is transcendental and, like being, cuts through all categories. Still, Thomas argues that "creatures are not good by their essence but by participation."[45] For Thomas, participation is a way of denoting the absolute distinction between creature and Creator and the complete dependence of the creature on the Creator. It is his way of expressing philosophically the theological notion of creation. Examining Thomas' understanding of participation helps clarify the relation of creaturely goodness to the Creator's goodness and gives a basis for Thomas' account of the hierarchy of being and goodness in creation.

It is tempting to argue that since all creatures participate in the supreme good, according to Thomas, all creatures must be worthy of direct moral consideration. After all, they are good by virtue of the same goodness that causes any and all goodness in creation. However, an examination of Thomas' theory of participation negates this conclusion. His theory does not fundamentally alter the earlier conclusion that the convertibility of being and goodness does not entail the moral considerability of all creatures, though it does contextualize this analysis within Thomas' larger metaphysical framework. Further, by examining his understanding of participation, we are led naturally to consider his conception of the perfection of the universe and the interrelation between creatures. By considering these notions (in the next chapter), we can gain clarity on his understanding of the moral status of all creatures.

Some of the central disagreements among interpreters of Thomas in the last century have focused on his theory of participation.[46] Thus, to enter into a discussion of this theory is to enter murky and unsettled waters. For the most part, we can steer clear of these controversies, entering the discussion only to the modest extent necessary for our purposes—that is, first, to demonstrate that participation does not entail the moral worth of all creatures; and second, to prompt a discussion of Thomas' understanding of the perfection of the universe and the need for diverse species or grades of goodness. In examining his understanding of participation, I will consider simultaneously how the transcendentals as common are related to the transcendentals as divine names.[47] In two of Thomas' most systematic treatments of goodness,[48] he deals with these issues in sequence, first inquiring into the topic of goodness in general and then addressing the goodness of God. The first, which we looked at above, begins with Aristotle's definition of good; the second adopts the Platonic understanding of the good, albeit with important qualifications.

Plato, in Thomas' reading, held that anything that can be separated in thought is separate in reality. Thus, just as "man" can be understood apart from Socrates and Plato, "man" exists separately as "man-in-himself" or "the idea of man." It is by participation in this "man-in-himself" that Socrates and Plato are called men. Likewise with goodness, Plato asserts that there is a separate form of goodness, "good-in-itself" or "the idea of good." By participation in this "good-in-itself," all things are called good. For Plato, "all things are formally good by the first goodness."[49] In the same way that Socrates and Plato are called men by participation in separated man and not by any inherent humanity, so all creatures are called good by participation in the goodness of the first good and not by any inherent goodness.

Thomas' treatment of Plato's conception of separate forms is interestingly different when treating natural forms as well as the form of the good. Following Aristotle, Thomas flatly rejects the notion that there are separate forms of natural things; there is no separately existing "man-in-himself." Thomas argues that natural things are what they are through an intrinsic, rather than a separated, form. But in the case of the form of the good, he follows a different tack. Thomas sees Plato's view—that goodness is a separate form and other things are good from this goodness—as largely correct, even if in need of modification. Thomas summarizes his view on Plato's understanding of separate forms as follows: "Although this opinion appears to be unreasonable in affirming separate ideas of natural things as subsisting of themselves—as Aristotle argues in many ways—still, it is absolutely true that there is first something which is essentially being and essentially good, which we call God."[50]

Even if Plato is correct that a separate form of the good exists, however, he is wrong to ascribe the formal goodness of creatures to their participation in this first goodness, according to Thomas. The goodness of creatures is real, but participated, goodness. Plato's view is unacceptable because it accords creatures no inherent goodness of their own. For Plato, creatures are formally good only by participation in the first goodness, where participation entails sharing a common form. This view is incompatible with the biblical understanding of the created order, notes Thomas, for God calls each and every creature good and all creatures very good.[51] The whole created order and each of its parts have real, inherent goodness. The convertibility of being and goodness establishes this point philosophically.[52]

Thomas holds, then, that Plato was wrong to maintain that the separate form of the good is the formal goodness of all things. Plato's position cannot be correct, according to Thomas, because all things do not have the same formal goodness; all things are not called "good" univocally. But this error of Plato's was part of a larger oversight. Plato's metaphysics, in Thomas' (and Aristotle's) reading, failed altogether to account for change, which is to say that it neglected the efficient and final causes, the source and the end of motion.[53] Thomas corrects this oversight by incorporating a basically Aristotelian conception of efficient causality within a basically Platonic conception of participation.

When participation is concerned solely with formal causation, then Thomas understands a form, such as whiteness or humanity or heat, to be shared by whatever individuals exist with these attributes. These individuals participate in the form as though each possessed it or shared in it partially. When the notion of participation comes to include efficient causality, as it does for Thomas, it can no longer be viewed solely in terms of forms that various individuals share in or partake. This opens up the possibility of speaking of participation in terms of an agent that brings into existence not other beings who share in the same nature but, rather, beings who have an entirely different nature because they only share partially in the nature of their cause.[54] That is, it opens the possibility of speaking of creation in terms of participation, clearly a major concern for a Christian thinker attempting to speak of a Christian doctrine in terms of Greek metaphysical categories. By understanding participation in the first goodness primarily in terms of efficient causality, Thomas attempts to solve the dilemma presented by Boethius in a more satisfactory manner than

Boethius himself was able to do. All creatures are good by virtue of their own goodness and thus are, in a sense, *substantially good*. But this goodness is received from the first goodness and possessed only partially, so all creatures are *good by participation*.

Let us examine more closely Thomas' understanding of participation and the participated goodness of creatures. In his commentary on Boethius' *On the Hebdomads*, Thomas states: "'to participate' is, as it were, 'to grasp a part.'"[55] This is basically an etymological explanation, since participation in Latin means "to take part" (*partem capere*). But Thomas goes beyond etymology when he continues, "therefore when something receives in a particular way that which belongs to another in a universal way, it is said 'to participate' in that."[56] If some quality or perfection is possessed partially rather than completely or universally, then the subject of that quality or perfection is said to participate in it.[57] Thus, a given perfection can be shared by many subjects insofar as none is identical with it or insofar as each participates in it. That which participates is less extended in scope than that in which it participates.

Thomas singles out three major modes of participation, the third of which is most relevant to this discussion.[58] This third mode incorporates the Aristotelian notion of efficient causality insofar as it is, according to Thomas, the way "an effect is said 'to participate' in its own cause, and especially when it is not equal to the power of its own cause, as, for example, if we should say that 'air participates in the light of the sun' because it does not receive that light with the brilliance that it has in the sun."[59] With this third mode, the effect participates in the cause in the sense that the effect receives partially what is in the cause universally. Every causal agent produces its effect according to the form by which it acts, so the effect must have some similarity to the cause. "Since every agent reproduces itself so far as it is an agent," Thomas writes, "and everything acts according to the manner of its form, the effect must in some way resemble the form of the agent."[60] So, for instance, the heat of a fire warms a man on a cold winter's night, but the man does not receive the form of the fire, or heat, in the same manner that it exists in the fire. Insofar as the man becomes warm, the effect (this warmth) is like the cause (the fire). Insofar as the man is not literally burning, he does not perfectly receive the form of the fire. The third mode of participation primarily concerns those effects that cannot perfectly receive the form of the agent. It is this kind of participation that is relevant to the causal relation between creature and Creator, and thus forms the basis for an understanding of how creatures are good by participation.[61]

Creation is a kind of causal relation, albeit a unique one. Insofar as it is a causal relation, it is the source of the similarity between God and creatures. In some way, creatures must be like God because they are made by God. As Thomas writes, "If, therefore, the first goodness is the effective cause of all goods, it must imprint its likeness upon the things produced; and so each thing will be called good by reason of an inherent form because of the likeness of the highest good implanted in it."[62] The degree of similarity between the effect and its cause varies according to the capacity of the effect to receive the form of the agent.

Thomas distinguishes between univocal and non-univocal causes. With univocal causes, the likeness of the cause is found in the effect according to the same specific formality. "When the effect is proportionate to the power of the agent," Thomas writes, "[the] form must be of the same kind in the maker and the thing made: for then maker and thing made are of the same species."[63] A univocal cause is the cause of becoming only and not of being, according to Thomas: "A cause of becoming is that which educes a form from the potentiality of matter by means of motion, such as a cutler who is the efficient cause of a knife."[64] A univocal cause is the cause of "this matter" receiving "this form."[65] The univocal agent causes the effect to participate in a form according to the second mode of participation, the way a subject participates in an accidental form or matter participates in a substantial form. The cutler (efficiently) causes the knife to receive the same form as the planned knife had in his intellect.

Non-univocal agents are universal causes and bring about effects that do not share in the same species. Indeed, "the non-univocal agent is the universal cause of the whole species," according to Thomas.[66] Still, even if they do not share in the same species, the cause and effect must be, in some sense, similar. They may be similar in a remote fashion, insofar as they are alike in genus rather than species, as is the case, according to Thomas' physics, with things generated by the sun or other heavenly bodies.[67] For example, that which is generated by the sun is not itself another sun, but it receives something of the sun's heat so that the generated nature has some likeness to the sun. The effects of all creaturely causes participate in the likeness of the agent's form according to the same specific or generic formality. The similarity between cause and effect grows more remote as we move from sharing the same specific formality to sharing the same generic formality.

In moving to the most universal of causes, Thomas argues that "if there is an agent not contained in any 'genus,' its effect will still more distantly reproduce the form of the agent."[68] The effects will not participate in the agent's form according to some specific or generic formality, but only according to a certain analogy. Thomas continues, "[I]n this way all created things, so far as they are beings, are like God as the first and universal principle of being."[69] God is being by his essence, being *per essentiam, ipsum esse.*

All things caused by God participate in a certain likeness of God not because of any specific or generic similarity, Thomas holds, but insofar as *esse* is common to all. Thomas moves with increasing universality of what is similar between cause and effect, from species to genus to *esse.* So even though the similarity is increasingly remote, each creature is somehow similar to God insofar as each proceeds from the first being. It is because of this reduced similarity that creatures are said to participate in their cause. They receive partially what is universally or wholly present in the cause. The likeness of creatures to God is affirmed solely according to analogy because of the fundamental difference between God and creatures (which I seek to clarify below): God is being by virtue of his essence and creatures are beings by virtue of participation. The same is true of goodness. Thus, because of this analogical relation, we can already see how Thomas can hold with Plato that the good is a separate form without holding that all things are good by the same formal goodness.[70]

A non-univocal cause is not merely a cause of becoming but also a cause of being. An effect is said to participate in its cause when the effect receives partially what is in the cause universally, and, with a non-univocal cause, this cause is the cause of the very existence of the effect. As such, *on-going participation* is necessary for the very existence of the effect. That is, since the effect depends upon the cause for its continued existence, it must continuously participate in this cause. This is not the case with an effect of a univocal cause because such an effect relies on its cause to become but not to be.[71] Although some creatures (such as heavenly bodies) may play a role in the causation of being, they act only as instruments of God; no creature can create *esse.*[72]

The following metaphysical principle of causality plays a pivotal role in Thomas' account of creation: "That which is said to be essentially so and so is the cause of all that are so by participation: thus fire is the cause of all things ignited as such."[73] Two related notions help to clarify this principle. First, according to Thomas, "whatever perfection exists in an effect must be found in the effective cause: either in the same formality, if it is a univocal agent . . . ; or in a more eminent degree, if it is an equivocal agent."[74] This notion follows from Thomas' understanding that every agent seeks to produce its like insofar as it acts according to its own form. Second, the causal question "Why?" comes to an end if an attribute belongs to something essentially. The issue becomes definitional or self-evident; this thing is essentially thus-and-so, and the attribute is essentially identical with the formal cause. To ask why "fire" is "hot" is, for Thomas, to ask why fire is fire; to ask why a "human being" is a "rational agent" is to ask why a human being is a human being.

When we consider these two notions together, we gain insight into the causal principle outlined above. That is, if any perfection in an effect must preexist in the cause, and if the causal question only terminates when a perfection is essentially identical with the formal cause of a thing, then it follows that any caused perfection must be traced back to an efficient cause in which this perfection preexists essentially as its own formal cause. So, for instance, a thing warmed by fire traces its warmth to the fire, which is essentially hot. To put the matter another way, any perfection that is not part of a thing's essence or an effect of a thing's essential principles (that is, proper accidents) must be caused by an external agent. The effect possesses this perfection in the manner of participation, and the perfection can be traced back to a cause that has this perfection in the manner of an essence. When the cause is essentially self-identical or wholly complete and perfect, we have reached the ultimate cause, and the answer to the question "Why?" or "What is the cause of?" (for example, "Why does God exist?" or "What is the cause of God's being?") becomes self-evident.

Let us turn now to Thomas' philosophical account of creation, which rests on the existence of a self-subsistent being, God. Given the metaphysical causal principle, it follows that all other beings exist through participation and thus must be caused by that which is being essentially. Interestingly, demonstrating the existence of self-subsistent being originates from contingent beings (thus, in Thomas' ontology, caused beings), as it must with Thomas' epistemology. Therefore, the argument is, in a sense, circular. (Though not viciously so; this would be the case if the truth of the premises depended upon the truth of the conclusion. The fact that contingent creatures exist is taken as evident.)[75] Thomas shows the existence of self-subsisting being by arguing from the existence of contingent beings. From the very fact of contingency, creatures are beings by participation (that is, they do not exist necessarily or are not essentially *esse*). Given the metaphysical causal principle, we next can argue that there must be something that is *esse* by its essence. Working in the other direction, we then can argue from the fact of self-subsisting being to all other beings as created effects of self-subsisting being. At any rate, Thomas assumes that he has shown the existence of God as self-subsisting being through his various cosmological arguments and their implications.

Thomas begins his treatise on creation in the *Summa Theologiae* by asking whether it is necessary that every being be created by God.[76] He answers:

1) It must be said that every being in any way existing is from God. For whatever is found in anything by participation must be caused in it by that to which it belongs essentially, as iron becomes heated by fire.
2) Now it has been shown above when treating of the divine simplicity that God is the essentially self-subsisting being; and also it was shown that subsisting being must be one; as, if whiteness were self-subsisting, it would be one, since whiteness is multiplied by its recipients.
3) Therefore, all beings apart from God are not their own being but are beings by participation.
4) Therefore, it must be that all things that are diversified by the diverse participation of being, so as to be more or less perfect, are caused by one First Being, who possesses being most perfectly.

Let us look at the details of Thomas' argument. In the first step, he simply states the causal principle that we looked at above. The argument then proceeds from an understanding of God as self-subsisting being to the conclusion that all other beings depend upon, and are created by, God. In the second step, Thomas states premises the truth of which he takes himself to have established elsewhere: God is essentially self-subsisting being, and subsisting being must be one.

Thomas develops his understanding of God as self-subsisting being at the beginning of the *Summa Theologiae*. We know God from creatures. In the strictest sense, we have no positive, univocal concept of God because, as material creatures, we are naturally suited to know only what exists in individual matter. The formula—self-subsisting being—is a way of summing up what we can say of God from creatures. God contains in himself all possible perfection of being. His essence is being itself, not as the common principle of things, but as subsisting. "Since therefore God is subsisting being itself," Thomas writes, "nothing of the perfection of being can be wanting to Him. Now all created perfections are included in the perfection of being; for things are perfect, precisely so far as they have being after some fashion."[77] Since God, as subsisting being, contains the whole perfection of being, subsisting being can only be one. There cannot be another self-subsisting being because there could be no distinction, no differentiation, no diverse perfection, from the original. They would necessarily be identical as containing the whole perfection of being.[78] Therefore, there is only one who is essentially being.

In step 3, Thomas maintains that it follows that any being apart from God must be a being by participation. Being is said of God *per essentiam*—God, in distinction from all else, *is* God's own being. Everything else is not being *per essentiam*. Anything other than God has in common that it *has* being. Being, then, must be predicated of everything other than God in the manner of participation. God alone is supremely simple. A creature that is not God, but God's effect, is a composite of essence and *esse*;[79] it cannot be essentially *esse*.

Given the premises, the conclusion of the argument for God's creation follows immediately. All beings that participate in being are caused by the one who is essentially being. As we will see, this argument forms the basis for Thomas' claim that creatures are good substantially and good by participation. He takes himself to have established that all beings other than God are beings by participation and thus are caused by God, who is essentially being. This analogical causation is called creation because God (being by his essence) creates the *esse* of creatures (beings by participation).[80]

By participating in God's being, Thomas argues, creatures can be said to imitate God. They reproduce, in their own way, the idea in the divine intellect and thereby imitate, in some way, the very nature of God. As beings by participation, creatures are not only fundamentally different from God but also completely dependent upon him. They derive their being from the first being; thus, their goodness comes from the first good. The goodness of creatures is modeled on divine goodness. Just as the being of creatures is received being, so the goodness of creatures is received goodness. Further, all creatures are good by virtue of the idea or exemplary form in the divine mind by which they come into being. Thus, they are good by participation in the same way that they are beings by participation, because this exemplary form is the mode in which they participate in being.

A brief exploration of Thomas' understanding of how creatures imitate God can lend clarity to his understanding of the goodness of creatures. God is the *efficient cause* of creatures because they are the effects of God's creative agency. God is the *exemplary cause* of creatures insofar as they receive a similitude of God, imitate God in some way, reflect the divine goodness. Since the divine essence contains all perfection in a simple unity, this essence is the sufficient exemplar of everything existing. But since it is infinite, it is not this universal essence of God that is itself the idea of each thing. Rather, the exemplary forms or ideas of creatures are the divine essence *as it is known by divine wisdom to be imitable by other things*. For example, Thomas maintains, "by conceiving His essence as imitable in respect of life and not of knowledge, it conceives the proper form of a plant: or again as imitable in respect of knowledge but not of intellect, it conceives the proper form of an animal, and so on."[81] The essence of a thing is simply the way that thing has being. Things are distinguished by species according to their characteristic mode of being. It is each type of thing's diverse relation to being, the way it imitates God's essence, rather than any formal hierarchy of essences as such, that distinguishes creatures. Since the idea of each creature is the way in which the divine essence is participated or imitated by that thing, then the distinction between essence and *esse* in creatures is already present in the notion of exemplary forms in the divine mind. In creatures, essence must be distinct from *esse* because the essence is determined by divine wisdom in its knowledge of the ways in which the divine *esse* can be participated.

Thomas uses this argument to demonstrate that creatures are both substantially good and good by participation. He maintains that "goodness is not taken as essential when a nature is considered absolutely but when it is taken in its act of existence."[82] Substantial or essential goodness is only found in a creature insofar as its nature or essence has *esse*. The *esse* of an essence is the foundation of its substantial goodness and the reason it is denominated substantially good. "Humanity, for instance," Thomas writes, "does not have the note of good or goodness except by its having existence."[83] Substantial goodness in creatures does not, and cannot, mean that they are good by virtue of their substance or essence. This is true only of God, whose essence is goodness itself. Creatures are good not by virtue of their essence but through participation. Their substantial goodness is the actuality of their essence or nature—their substantial existence. The *esse* of a creature's essence is its very being, the divine similitude that belongs to that creature as the actuality of its own nature. Because it is from this *esse* that a creature is denominated good, every creature is intrinsically (or, properly understood, substantially) good.

Still, the *esse* of creatures is received from God, whose essence and *esse* are one. Therefore, God, and God alone, has goodness solely by virtue of his own essence. "The nature or essence of any created thing is not its act of being but participates in being from another," Thomas states.[84] Creatures receive their *esse* from the one who is *ipsum esse subsistens*. Since goodness and being are convertible (in that both are actuality), then just as creatures receive their substantial act of being through participation, so they are good by virtue of participation. The substantial goodness of creatures is their received (and thus partial) substantial act of being.

With this formulation, Thomas believes that he has found a way to overcome the dilemma presented but not adequately solved by Boethius. This formulation accords a goodness to created substance that is more than a mere extrinsic relation to the first good but is nevertheless goodness by participation. By extending participation to include the *esse* of a substance, Thomas can maintain that creatures are substantially good by virtue of their own substantial being. The divine intellect forms the idea of each creature and, as effective cause, communicates this idea to creatures in the act of creation. This is the divine similitude belonging to each creature. Thomas summarizes, "Everything is called good from the divine goodness, as from the first exemplary, effective, and final principle of all goodness. Nevertheless, everything is called good by reason of the similitude of the divine goodness *belonging to it, which is formally its own goodness,* whereby it is denominated good. And so of all things there is one goodness, and yet many goodnesses."[85] Creatures are both good intrinsically and good by participation.

This analysis of the goodness of creatures in terms of their createdness, their participation in being and thus in goodness, does not alter the conclusions of the first section of this chapter—that the intrinsic goodness of creatures does not entail their moral worth. To say that creatures are intrinsically good means that God has communicated *esse* to them, that they are actual and have existence, and that they seek to preserve and augment their own being. This understanding of intrinsic goodness does not entail that creatures have moral worth because we have not yet clarified the criteria by which a creature is accorded such worth; we have only said that creatures are good by virtue of their own actuality, and that this actuality is communicated to them by the Creator. Whether or not this conclusion means that all creatures have moral worth ultimately depends on Thomas' teleology, on the relation of creatures to one another and to the universe.

This analysis of participation contextualizes Thomas' entire discussion of the goodness of creatures within a framework of complete dependency on, and fundamental differentiation from, the Creator. The language of participation, and Thomas' particular understanding of participation as including the communication of *esse* from the Creator to the creature, allows him to maintain that creatures are intrinsically denominated good *and* good by the first goodness. It provides the conceptual framework for articulating the relation between creature and Creator in a way that affirms both the real, intrinsic goodness of creatures and the absolute distinction between creature and Creator.

The discussion in this chapter of the ontological goodness of creatures has been a metaphysical one, not an ethical one. To this point, it merely leaves open the *possibility* that all creatures have moral worth. This is made clear when we consider that a thoroughgoing, mechanistic worldview (in which non-rational creatures are seen solely in mechanistic terms) positively precludes non-rational creatures from having moral worth. Thomas' understanding of the ontological goodness of creation does not, from the outset, preclude such a possibility. Indeed, it might seem that such intrinsic goodness would translate naturally into all creatures having some moral value as ends in themselves. To understand why this is not the case, I next consider Thomas' ontology in light of his teleology.

Chapter Two

The Moral Bifurcation of Creation

In this chapter, I argue that it is only in light of Thomas' teleology that the moral import of his ontology becomes clear. This moral import can be drawn out most directly through a consideration of the way creatures are ordered to one another and the way they contribute to the perfection of the universe. In order to clarify the broad outlines of Thomas' teleology, in the first section, I consider his account of the way all creatures are ordered to their final end—God. I then move to an examination of the relation of creatures to one another and to the whole. This ordering of creatures can be fruitfully examined through a consideration of God's providential care for creation, God's care for each creature according to its nature. And because only human beings are rationally free, or *causa sui,* only rational creatures are cared for for their own sakes. Non-rational creatures are "slaves" to be used as "instruments" by the free. When we look at the relation of the parts to the whole, it is important to consider the relation between the first and final perfection of the universe. Only human beings are suited for the final perfection; non-rational creatures cease to exist with the advent of this final perfection because they are no longer useful to human beings. I conclude that non-rational creatures are ordered to human beings in a strictly instrumental fashion, and that this ordering depends critically on Thomas' conception of the human soul. It is the rational freedom and immortality of the human soul that morally separate human beings from other material creatures.

In the second section, I demonstrate that this strict instrumental ordering is reflected in Thomas' moral theory. His understanding of natural law is built upon a conception of God's eternal law, which orders non-rational creatures to the rational in a strictly instrumental manner. His understanding of the virtue of justice, the relevant virtue for this discussion, is modeled on God's justice, which gives to each its due by this strict instrumental ordering. Because Thomas' moral theory is interwoven with his larger metaphysical project, the possibility of according moral worth to non-rational creatures is systemically excluded by this theory.

Teleology and the Moral Import of Thomas' Ontology

Thomas' teleology is a general teleology in the sense that all things, finally, have a single *telos*—God.[1] Not only is God the exemplary cause (or external formal cause) and efficient cause of all that exists, but he is also the final cause. An effective cause acts by its own form and so seeks to produce its likeness in its effects, to the extent possible. With God, being an efficient cause also entails being the final cause. As Thomas states, "All creatures are images of the first agent, namely, God: since the agent produces its like. Now the perfection of an image consists in representing the original by its likeness thereto: for this is why an image is made. Therefore all things are for the purpose of acquiring a divine similitude, as their last end."[2] All creatures are given a divine likeness in receiving substantial existence (as well as their appropriate essential perfections), and all creatures seek a divine likeness in actualizing the potentialities appropriate to their kind.

Thomas clarifies how all creatures seek God as their final end by considering what creatures seek when they act. As we saw in chapter 1, Thomas argues that all creatures act in order to preserve or acquire being. Because being is good, all creatures act for a good.[3] And insofar as all things seek perfection or goodness, they seek a divine likeness because God is self-subsisting being, pure perfection, goodness itself. What Thomas says in this regard when speaking of things devoid of knowledge applies to all creatures: "they seek a divine likeness, as well as their own perfection. Nor does it matter in which way we express it, the former or the latter. Because by tending to their own perfection, they tend to a good, since a thing is good forasmuch as it is perfect. And according as a thing tends to be good, it tends to a divine likeness: since a thing is like unto God forasmuch as it is good. . . . It is clear therefore that all things seek a divine likeness as their last end."[4] So God is the end of all creatures not in the sense of something produced by things nor in the sense that something is added to him by things, but only in the sense that things seek to attain God insofar as they seek their own perfection.[5] Indeed, all things seek to attain a divine likeness to the extent possible. They seek to actualize their potentialities so that they become not only substantially and relatively good but also accidentally and absolutely good. This is God's will in creating—that creation reflect, to the fullest extent, the divine goodness.

It is possible to discern the end of the whole and of the parts of the whole. Thomas does just this when he addresses the question of whether corporeal things are made on account of God's goodness.[6] He begins his response by rejecting the opinion of Origen, who maintained that corporeal creatures were not made according to God's original purpose but, rather, in punishment for the sin of spiritual creatures. Thomas maintains that the diversity of finite creatures, including material creatures, is necessary (and so part of the divine will) for the universe to attain most fully to the divine goodness. Thomas helpfully breaks down the various ways of considering the end of creatures and of the universe. He states: "[I]n the parts of the universe . . . every creature exists for its own proper act and perfection, and the less noble for the nobler, as those creatures that are less noble than man exist for the sake of man, whilst each and every creature exists for the perfection of the entire universe. Furthermore, the entire universe, with all its parts, is ordained towards God as its end, inasmuch as it imitates, as it were, and shows forth the Divine goodness, to the glory of God."[7] We explored above why and how it is that the universe finds its end in God. I want now to discuss the other parts of Thomas' analysis—namely, that each creature exists for (*est propter*) its own proper act and perfection, that the less noble exist for (*sunt propter*) the more noble, and that each and every creature exists for (*sunt propter*) the perfection of the universe.[8]

That each creature exists for its own perfection is basic to Thomas' general teleology and his account of goodness. As we have seen, it is on the basis of this claim that Thomas can demonstrate that God is the end of all things. All creatures seek God insofar as all seek their own perfection or goodness. It is also the way that Thomas, following Aristotle, defines goodness from its effects or in an a posteriori manner. And when Thomas says that each creature "exists for" its own perfection, it might be tempting to interpret this with some sort of morally normative force.[9] For example, one might argue: Insofar as creatures are given existence by God so that they might reach their own proper perfection, human beings ought to respect and seek to enhance the well-being of other creatures. To fail to do so would be to act immorally insofar as one fails to act in accord with the divine will, which wills for each creature to complete itself.

To interpret Thomas in this manner, however, would be a mistake. There is no such moral obligation because in stating that a creature exists for its own proper act and perfection, Thomas means that each creature seeks to preserve and augment its own being. Every creature strives to stay in existence and actualize the potentialities appropriate to its kind. This is simply to describe the end proper to each creature. In pursuing this end, each one develops relations with other creatures (and so the lower serves the higher, all serve the perfection of the universe, and each reflects a divine likeness), but the very fact that each creature preserves itself in existence and pursues the end proper to its kind is, in itself, morally neutral. It is only a statement about what every creature does by its very nature. That a creature seeks to preserve and augment its own being does not offer any indication of its moral worth. To be sure, it is an indication of its ontological goodness (only the good seek good), but I have already argued that bare ontological goodness does not of itself entail that a creature has moral worth. The fact that each and every creature exists for its own perfection does not result, for example, in any moral obligation for human beings similarly to seek the good of that creature. It is indeed God's will that each creature seek to actualize its own potentialities. This, however, says nothing about God's will for how *rational* creatures ought to act in relation to other creatures' pursuit of their own good.

It is the case that through actualizing potentialities, one creature becomes ordered to another. The ordering of creatures to one another is, according to Thomas, grounded in the differences between essential forms or between species. And it is in considering the ordering based on these differences that we can begin to draw out the moral import of Thomas' ontology. And, as we will see, far from supporting the notion that human beings have moral obligations to non-rational creatures, this ordering of the less perfect to the more perfect entails that other creatures are to be used as mere instruments for the human good.

Creatures are ordered to one another according to a scale of being and perfection. The distinction between creatures that is necessary for the perfection of the universe is not so much a division in quantity as a formal division. For Thomas, this entails a hierarchy of goodness and value because species are "like numbers" in the sense that they are distinguished from one another when the higher possesses all the essential perfections of the lower *plus* an essential perfection lacking in the lower.[10] Species are not simply different from one another but are hierarchically ranked according to the essential perfections possessed. This diversity and inequality of creatures is necessary for the perfection of the universe because "the good of order among diverse things is better than any one of those things that are ordered taken in itself: for it is formal in respect of each, as the perfection of the whole in respect of the parts."[11]

Thomas' hierarchy of perfection moves from primary matter to the elements to mixed bodies to creatures with vegetative souls to creatures with sensitive souls to creatures with intellectual souls.[12] This hierarchy is founded on the notion that every creature seeks to actualize itself and so strives to become as much as possible like the creature with an additional essential perfection. As noted, this hierarchy is not simply a static arrangement according to degrees of perfection (though it can be considered as such), but it is also more fundamentally a dynamic ordering of one kind of creature to another. Thomas concludes from this hierarchical ordering of creatures according to their forms that "the elements are for the sake of the mixed body, the mixed body for the sake of living things: and of these, plants are for the sake of animals, and animals for the sake of man. Therefore man is the end of all generation."[13]

While there are a number of arguments supporting the claim that the less perfect are ordered to the more perfect,[14] the conclusion is always that human beings are at the top of the chain of being of material things, and so other creatures are for the use of humans—just as, for instance, plants are for the use of animals. In theory, such instrumentality might be partial in the sense that a creature might be both instrumentally good for another and have moral worth of its own. For example, it is often the case in human affairs that one person is instrumentally good for another. The moral problem comes, in relations between humans, when this instrumental value is understood to be exhaustive. That Thomas understands the instrumentalization of other creatures to the human good to be exhaustive, rather than in addition to those creatures' moral worth, is clear. I will discuss this more fully below, but, for now, it is enough to note that Thomas argues that it is morally permissible "to make use of [animals], either by killing them or in any way whatsoever,"[15] and that cruelty to animals is forbidden only because it might lead to harm to a human being.[16]

The real crux of Thomas' understanding of the proper relation between human beings and other material creatures does not lie with his discussion of the empirical hierarchy he sees in the world around him. Rather, his view of this relation is most fundamentally shaped by his understanding of God's providential care for creation and his correlative conceptions of the human soul and the natures of non-rational creatures. I use the word "correlative" because Thomas' understanding of God's providence only makes sense in light of his conceptions of the human soul and the natures of non-rational creatures. God cares for creatures in the way he does— specifically, God orders non-rational creatures to human beings in a strictly instrumental fashion—because of the nature of the rational soul and other material creatures' lack of such a soul. In a sense, this is an obvious point— that God orders creatures to one another in accord with their (God-given) natures. To understand the natures of diverse creatures is, all implications taken into account (especially what final end is entailed by their diverse natures), to understand how God cares for such creatures. I am making this connection explicit because, in Part II, I argue that Thomas' conception of the human soul is philosophically untenable. Given this connection, the explicit critique of Thomas' conception is also an implicit critique of his understanding of divine providence. At any rate, the issue before us now is to grasp how Thomas understands the proper relation between non-rational creatures and human beings, and what his rationale is for so understanding this relation.

Whether we examine the way the parts are ordered to one another or the way the parts are ordered to the whole, the conclusion is that the ordering of non-rational creatures to the human being is strictly instrumental. Further, Thomas' most fundamental rationale for this ordering is that the human soul allows for the exercise of rational freedom and is immortal. I highlight freedom and immortality as the fundamental entailments of having a rational soul because of the prominence of these attributes in Thomas' work and because the dichotomies set up by these attributes (freedom/slavery, immortal/perishable) justify, in large measure, his strict instrumentalization of non-rational creatures. Absent these attributes and dichotomies, Thomas' other arguments for instrumentalizing non-rational creatures lose their force.[17] If all creatures possessed real freedom (though perhaps to differing degrees) and if all shared in the same *telos,* then the dichotomies noted vanish, and so likewise does Thomas' justification for morally bifurcating creation.

Returning to the discussion at hand, let us begin by examining the relation of parts to one another by turning to Thomas' discussion of divine providence. One of his most complete treatments of this issue occurs in chapter 112 of book IIIb of the *Summa contra Gentiles,* which is titled "That rational creatures are governed for their own sake, and other creatures, as directed to them." In this discussion, Thomas endeavors to demonstrate that the nature of material creatures is such that divine providence orders the lower to the higher in a strictly instrumental fashion.

As is typical in the *Summa contra Gentiles,* the question is arranged as a string of arguments designed to demonstrate Thomas' desired conclusion. At the end of each argument, he closes with a statement such as the following: "Accordingly intellectual creatures are ruled by God, as though He cared for them for their own sake, while other creatures are ruled as being directed to rational creatures."[18] There is little point in repeating this statement for each argument in Thomas' string of arguments. It is clear that creatures are ordered to one another instrumentally. And to make clear that this instrumentalization is strict (rather than being in addition to any possible moral worth), Thomas maintains that not only are non-rational creatures cared for by God for the sake of human beings, but also "they are cared for, *not for their own sake."*[19] At least as far as divine providence goes (which is to say at least as far as the true ordering of creatures goes), the lower are ordered to the higher in a strictly instrumental fashion. As Thomas puts it elsewhere, "According to the Divine ordinance the life of animals and plants is preserved not for themselves but for man."[20]

Lest one think that it is one thing for God to care for creatures for the sake of human beings and another for human beings themselves to treat other creatures as mere instruments, Thomas clarifies the issue. (Of course, the issue is fairly obvious on its face since God treats creatures according to their true natures.) Intellectual creatures, Thomas maintains, "are said to be provided for on their own account, and others on account of them, because the goods bestowed on them [intellectual creatures] by divine providence are not given them for another's profit: whereas those bestowed on others [non-rational creatures] are in the divine plan intended for the use of intellectual substances. . . . Hereby is refuted the error of those who said it is sinful for a man to kill dumb animals: for by divine providence they are intended for man's use in the natural order. *Hence it is no wrong for man to make use of them, either by killing or in any other way whatever.*[21] God intended that we use other creatures as instruments, and so there can be no moral problem in treating them as such. Indeed, as noted, Thomas makes it clear that the only reason for refraining from cruelty to animals is the effect that such cruelty might have on our relation to other human beings.[22]

God cares for creatures according to their natures, and so we can ask what it is about the nature of creatures that demands, so to speak, this instrumental ordering. In his first argument in question 112, Thomas states, "[T]he very condition of the rational creature, in that it has dominion over its actions, requires that the care of providence should be bestowed on it for its own sake: whereas the condition of other things that have not dominion over their actions show that they are cared for not for their own sake, but as being directed to other things"[23] (and, we might add, finally to human beings).[24] The conclusion is that non-rational creatures are ordered to human beings in a strictly instrumental fashion. The instrument is not required for its own sake, but for the sake of the principal agent, or, again, the divine governance makes provision for the free for their own sake, but for slaves that they might be useful to the free.

Because of its importance here and in subsequent chapters, I want to pause for a moment to consider Thomas' understanding of the freedom of creatures. The human being has rational freedom, or dominion over its own acts, and so is the cause of itself, *causa sui* (obviously, not in the sense that we are the first cause of our being but in the sense that we move ourselves to act). Because human beings have free will and so are self-caused, God cares for them for our own sakes. To fail to do so would be to do violence to human nature, to violate God's plan for the universe. Other creatures are not *causa sui*. Inanimate beings, which are moved only by others, have neither free movement nor free will. Non-rational animals have only free movement. As Thomas says, "Brute animals are moved by the impulse of a higher agent to something determined or according to mode of the particular form, the perception of which the sense appetite follows."[25] (In this conversation, it is animals that are most relevant because they are closest to human beings. If they lack moral worth, then the same must be true for creatures that are lower in the scale of perfection.) To be sure, Thomas does talk of the "conditional freedom" of animals, by which he means that they judge if they should or should not act. "But because their judgment is determined to a single course of action, their appetite and activity also are consequently determined to a single course."[26] They judge by natural instinct, as when a sheep fears and flees from a wolf, and so they act under necessity rather than free self-determination.

With human beings, our judgment is free, and so our activity is undetermined. Thomas maintains that "the whole formal character of freedom depends upon the manner of knowing."[27] Since the judgment of our reason is concerned with universals while movement and action are always about particulars, and "the universal contains many particulars potentially"[28] (that is, is indeterminate with respect to actual movement and activity), then "the judgment of the intellect is not determined to one thing only."[29] Human judgment, unlike the judgment of animals, is not determined by nature to one thing because human beings consciously relate to universals. We are capable not only of judging but also of judging about our judging, one might say, so we are not necessarily moved by things that present themselves to us or by passions that arise. Because of our capacity to relate consciously to universals, we can treat our own judgments as *possibilities,* and so are capable of judging these judgments. Since we have free judgment (and so free will), we are ourselves the cause of our own movement and activity. That which is free is its own cause.[30] Free will is the cause of its own movement because by free will a human being moves himself or herself to act.[31] Therefore, since divine providence cares for each according to its nature, human beings, as self-caused, are for their own sakes cared for, but other creatures, as slaves, are cared for not for their own sakes but for the sake of rational creatures.

In turning our attention now from the ordering of parts to one another to the ordering of the parts to the whole, we will see that the conclusion of strict instrumentality still holds. Here, divine providence and the immortality of the human soul are the primary rationale for this instrumentalization. One of the thorny issues raised by this strict instrumentalization of other creatures to the human good is that it seems to undermine Thomas' own argument against Origen that diversity itself is necessary for the universe most fully to reflect the divine goodness. After the discussion above, it would appear that all that is needed is whatever is required for the human good. There seems to be a tension between the two positions that Thomas seeks to hold simultaneously. First, he argues at length and in various places, primarily against Origen, that diversity itself is necessary for the perfection of the universe. Second, as we have seen, he argues that nonrational creatures are strictly instrumental to the human good.

Thomas himself seems to believe that these two positions—that other creatures are merely instrumental to the human good, and that all grades of creatures are necessary for the perfection of the universe—are compatible. For example, he states that "all the parts are directed to the perfection of the whole, in so far as one part serves another. . . . [T]hat other natures are on account of the intellectual is not contrary to their being for the perfection of the universe: for without the things required for the perfection of the intellectual substance, the universe would not be complete."[32] This might not seem to be problematic, but Thomas makes it clear that "one part serving another" is understood in a wholly instrumental way. As noted and quoted above, he argues that intellectual substances are provided for their own sake and for others on account of them. Once the ordering of material creatures to the human being is understood in this manner (that is, strictly instrumentally), then it is difficult to see how one can also maintain that all diverse "grades of goodness" are themselves necessary most fully to reflect the divine goodness.

Indeed, one could interpret all of Thomas' arguments concerning the need for diversity in creation as an elliptical way of saying that what is needed is whatever is necessary for the human good, and it turns out that the tremendous diversity of species that we find on earth is necessary for this good. This way of reading his arguments would, however, not only make them rather dubious but also drain them of their force, since it would entail that the diversity itself is not directly willed by God but only willed insofar as God wills what is necessary for the human good. But the whole point of these arguments is to demonstrate that the diversity itself is necessary for the perfection of the universe. This does not preclude the lower being ordered to the higher in an instrumental fashion, but it does seem to be in tension with any claim that such instrumentality is exhaustive. If the diversity is not per se necessary, then Thomas' position turns out to be not so different from that of Origen.

Some interpreters of Thomas have argued that there are two divergent organizing principles in his thought that generate divergent theories of the value of creatures. William French, for example, argues that there is a "dualist-anthropocentric principle" based on the ordering of creatures to one another that accords moral value solely to human beings.[33] It is this ordering and the resulting value theory that we examined above. But, French argues, there is a second principle, the "community of being principle," that "highlights the ontological continuity of being across the gradations and employs a model of a vast interrelated community of created being."[34] Instead of the linear means-end argument employed by the dualist-anthropocentric principle, the community-of-being principle employs "a spatial or mathematical model of the 'parts exist for the good of the whole' to establish that the greatest good short of God is the perfection and good of the universe."[35] Unfortunately, French cannot give us much detail on the axiology that results from this second principle and so has to resort to what he takes to be a similar axiology—the relation of the individual human being to the larger human community. The individual, while subordinate to the community, can never be a mere instrument in relation to it. I suggest that the reason he cannot give much detail on such a community-of-being axiology is not simply because it is not there in the work of Thomas, but also, more fundamentally, because it stands in contradiction to Thomas' own position, which, when all is said and done, is consistently anthropocentric in its axiology. In the end, whatever tensions there may be between the two principles articulated by French, where Thomas comes down axiologically is quite clear. To argue otherwise is not so much to interpret or develop Thomas' thought but to challenge it.

There are two basic problems with any claim that non-rational creatures have moral worth because they are necessary for the perfection of the universe, or because of the relation between parts and the whole. The first (which I will outline only briefly) is that Thomas' understanding of divine providence precludes the possibility that human beings could ever affect such perfection. Therefore, if one argues that human beings ought, for example, to preserve species[36] because they are necessary for the perfection of the universe, then for this precept to become operational implies a critique of Thomas' understanding of divine providence. That is, the only way this precept would ever need to be acted on is if God's providential care of the created order did not directly preserve species in existence. This is not Thomas' understanding of divine providence.

The second problem with the above claim is that it fails to take into account Thomas' understanding of the first and second perfections of the universe. When viewed in light of his discussion of the first and final perfection of the universe, it becomes clear that one cannot use Thomas' understanding of the relation of parts to the whole in order to support an axiology that accords moral worth to non-rational creatures. In its first perfection, or in its changeable state, all grades of material creatures are necessary for the perfection of the universe as well as for the human good.

However, the entire changeable universe is itself for the sake of the human good and passes away when the number of the elect has been realized. Since the whole is finally for the sake of the human being, then (since the parts are for the sake of the whole) so must the parts be for the sake of the human being.

Let us look in more detail at Thomas' position and consider these problems in turn. Thomas argues emphatically and often that all creatures exist for the good of the whole, for the perfection of the universe. And it is this perfection that God primarily wills in willing to create. Thomas argues that God created things in order to communicate God's goodness to them. Since no single finite creature can adequately represent the divine goodness, God "produced many and diverse creatures, that what was wanting to one in the representation of the divine goodness might be supplied by another. For goodness, which in God is simple and uniform, in creatures is manifold and divided and hence the whole universe together participates the divine goodness more perfectly, and represents it better than any single creature whatever."[37] In the next question, Thomas argues (against Origen) that the divine wisdom is the cause of the diversity of things for the sake of the perfection of the universe. This perfection requires diverse grades of goodness; any one grade is not sufficient.

The diversity of things that is necessary for the perfection of the universe refers primarily to species rather than to individuals. A key issue here for Thomas is that species, like the universe, are perpetual, while individuals (with the exception of intellectual substances) are subject to corruption.[38] Though the notion that species in this changeable universe are perpetual is not strictly the case for Thomas,[39] his point here is clear. It is the species of creatures that are primarily needed for the universe to be perfect because this perfection consists in the ordering of diverse "grades of goodness" (that is, species) to one another. Corruptible individuals are important only in the secondary sense that they are necessary for preserving the species in existence. Corruptible individuals are for the sake of their species. As Thomas puts it, "even though the corruption of a thing in the universe is not good for that thing, it is good for the perfection of the entire universe, because the continual generation and corruption of individuals makes it possible for the species to be perpetual; and it is in this that the perfection of the universe essentially consists."[40] So, even assuming that an axiology that accords moral worth to non-rational creatures could be developed out of this relation of creatures to the perfection of the universe (parts/whole), it would accord moral worth only to species. Or, to put the point another way, it would accord moral worth to individuals only insofar as they are necessary to preserve the species.[41]

A major problem, however, with such an axiology is that, precisely because they are necessary for the perfection of the universe, God directly preserves species in existence. As Thomas puts it, "Individuals . . . which undergo corruption, are not ordained as it were chiefly for the good of the universe, but in a secondary way, inasmuch as the good of the species is preserved through them. Whence, although God knows the total number of individuals, the number of oxen, flies and such like, is not pre-ordained by God *per se;* but divine providence produces just so many as are sufficient for the preservation of the species."[42] Since, first, species are necessary for the perfection of the universe, and second, it is this perfection that God primarily intends in creating, then God preserves species in existence by ensuring the ongoing existence of the requisite individuals.

Let me clarify Thomas' position briefly. In his discussion of divine ideas, he argues against the notion that the order in the universe was the accidental result of a succession of agents.[43] Instead, Thomas proposes, this order was intended by God and created immediately by God. The divine intellect conceived an idea or exemplary form for the order of the entire universe. This idea of the whole includes the ideas of the parts, or species. As we have seen, the proper idea of a thing is its exemplary form or its extrinsic formal cause. It is from the formal cause that a thing is designated as belonging to a certain species. These species are the necessary parts of the universe—the parts that, by their ordering to one another, constitute the perfection of the universe, which perfection is primarily intended by God. God is the cause of being because God is the cause of the species of things.

Since God wills that species be preserved in existence as necessary for the fulfillment of the divine will (that is, for the perfection of the universe), then for one to argue that human beings have a moral obligation (which becomes operational) to protect species is to offer an implied, and rather sweeping, critique of Thomas' understanding of divine providence. God infallibly carries out God's own will by God's own agency. And God maintains species in existence (for the duration of the universe in its changeable state) in order that God's primary objective in creating be fulfilled. To be sure, Thomas' position leaves him in a difficult state, since it has become clear that it is within the realm of human power to destroy entire species (whether understood in Thomas' sense or with modern biology) and to reduce dramatically the diversity of species on earth. But while this may call into question Thomas' understanding of divine providence, it cannot bolster any argument that he intends to (or can) attribute moral worth to other species.

Further, any such claim is undermined when we consider the second problem listed above. The entire discussion of the first problem takes place within a universe understood as changeable, as subject to time. But this changeable universe is itself for the sake of the universe in its final perfection, when all motion will cease. So the changeable universe can be considered as "ontologically instrumental" to the universe in its final, unchangeable state. Any interpretation of Thomas that accords moral worth to non-rational creatures because of the relation of parts to the whole fails to take into account this understanding of the first perfection and second perfection of the universe. It is precisely this understanding that bridges, though it may not fully resolve, the tension between Thomas' claim that all grades of goodness are necessary for the perfection of the universe and his claim that, in the end, all non-rational creatures are strictly instrumental to the human good.

Thomas maintains that the perfection of the universe is twofold. The first perfection is "the completeness of the universe at its first founding."[44] This first perfection concerns creatures in their created state in this world of time and movement. The second perfection, "which is the end of the whole universe, is the perfect beatitude of the saints at the consummation of the world."[45] In the second or final perfection, all movement and so all time cease. I want to explore Thomas' understanding of this final perfection in order to bring out its implications for the moral status of non-rational creatures.

One of Thomas' most complete treatments of this matter is in the fifth question of *On the Power of God*, where he discusses the general topic of God's preservation of things. In article five, Thomas asks whether the heavenly movement will cease at any time. This question is important for our discussion because, on Thomas' physics, the movement of heavenly bodies is the cause of generation of lower bodies. Thomas begins his answer by explaining that heavenly movement is not natural to the heavenly body in the same way an elemental body's movement is natural to the elemental body. This must be the case, he argues, because nature never tends to movement as such, but movement is always for the sake of some definite result. Because the movement of the heavenly bodies is circular, it does not result in their reaching a "whereabouts" to which they are inclined by nature. This circular movement is natural to heavenly bodies only in the sense that they have an innate aptitude for this kind of movement; they contain in themselves the passive principle of that movement. The active principle must be some separate substance, such as God or angels. There-fore, and this is Thomas' point, the permanence of the movement of heav-enly bodies cannot be argued on the basis of the nature of such bodies because they contain only an aptitude for such movement.

Thomas argues that we must look for the reason why the active prin-ciple causes the movement of the heavenly bodies. So he inquires into the end of their movement. If this end requires perpetual movement of heav-enly bodies, then such movement will continue without end. If this end re-quires that this movement should stop at some point, then the heavens will cease to be moved. Thomas maintains, "The movement of the heavens is for the completion of the number of the elect. For the rational soul is more excellent than any body whatsoever, even than the heavens: wherefore there is nothing unreasonable in supposing that the end of the heavenly movement is the multiplication of rational souls. . . . Therefore it is a defi-nite number of souls that is the end of the heavenly movement: and when this is reached the movement will cease."[46] We have now reached the rea-son for heavenly motion—*it is for the completion of the number of the elect.* Once this purpose has been accomplished, heavenly motion will cease. (Thomas takes this literally and maintains that the sun will reside perma-nently on one side of the earth.) There will be no more movement and no more time. Since heavenly movement is "the first principle of generation and corruption,"[47] and since "the heaven's movement gives life to all nature in its state of mutability,"[48] we can now ask what happens to plants and animals when the number of the elect is complete.

Thomas addresses this question in article nine. He states clearly that in the "renewal of the world no mixed body [that is, no mineral, plant, or animal] will remain except the human body."[49] Thomas supports this view by arguing on the basis of the four causes. He begins with the final one, which is the cause of the other three. The following helps to clarify the two points discussed above that seem to give rise to tension in his overall account:

The end of minerals, plants and animals is twofold. One is the completion of the universe, to which end all the parts of the universe are ordained: yet the aforesaid things are not ordained to this end as though
by their very nature and essentially they were required for the universe's
perfection, since they contain nothing that is not to be found in the
principal parts of the world (namely, the heavenly bodies and the elements) as their active and material principles. Consequently the things
in question are particular effects of those universal causes which are essential parts of the universe, so that they belong to the perfection of the
universe only in the point of their production by their causes, and this
is by movement. *Hence they belong to the perfection of the universe not
absolutely speaking but only as long as the latter is in motion.* Wherefore
as soon as movement in the universe ceases these things must cease
to exist.[50]

Viewed in light of the final perfection of the universe, it appears that
Thomas seriously qualifies his arguments on the need for diversity of species for the perfection of the universe. It turns out that mixed bodies are
not "by their very nature and essentially" required for the perfection of the
universe, but only provisionally needed for "as long as the [universe] is in
motion." With respect to plants and animals being necessary for the universe to most fully reflect the divine goodness, this is true apparently only
in this changeable state. Once the universe passes from its first to final
perfection, such creatures will no longer be necessary for this perfection,
which will require incorruptibility in all its members.

We saw above that the universe is in motion for the sake of human beings. When the requisite number of the elect is reached, there will no longer be any need for this motion, and so it will cease. With this cessation of
motion, the existence of all mixed bodies, with the exception of the human
body,[51] will also cease. By making, first, mixed bodies necessary only to the
perfection of the universe in its changeable state, and second, the universe
itself for the sake of the human good, Thomas can maintain both that all
species of creatures are necessary for the perfection of the universe (*in its
changeable state*) and that non-rational creatures are merely instrumental
to the human good.

Thomas further clarifies this issue in explicating the second end of
mixed bodies: "The other end is man, because as the Philosopher says
things that are imperfect in nature are ordained to those that are perfect, as

their end . . . : it follows that plants are for animals being prepared by nature to be the latter's food; and animals are for man, to whom they are necessary as food and for other purposes. Now this necessity lasts as long as man's animal life endures. But this life will cease in that final renewal of the universe, because the body will rise not natural but spiritual: hence animals and plants will also cease to exist then."[52] This puts the matter bluntly. Plants and animals are necessary for human beings as long as we have an "animal life." Once this animal life ceases in the final renewal of the universe, there is no reason for the continued existence of plants and animals. *This is a strikingly clear way of stating the solely instrumental value of plants and animals: their very existence ceases when they are no longer useful to human beings.*[53]

Thomas also discusses why mixed bodies will not exist after the end of the world in terms of formal and material causation as well as of efficient causation. He maintains that this is consistent with the matter and form of such bodies. They contain within themselves the principle of corruption (that is, matter) and are without a self-subsistent form to preserve them. Further, with respect to efficient or moving causation, "the very souls of plants and animals are wholly subject to the influence of the heavenly bodies."[54] When the heavenly movement ceases and when the number of the elect has been realized, such creatures cannot retain movement or life. This analysis is unsurprising since, given the purpose for which these creatures were made, the other causes must be consistent with the extinction of non-rational creatures when human beings no longer have need of them.

One might object that this analysis depends heavily on an obviously outdated and seriously flawed physics, so that if we excise this physics from the work of Thomas, the instrumentalization of non-rational creatures might similarly fall away. Such an objection is misguided because Thomas' analysis is itself guided by his understanding of the end of creatures. He explains how this end manifests itself in terms of the physics of his own day, but the end itself (that is, that non-rational creatures are for the sake of the perfection of the universe in its changeable state and are merely instrumental to the human good) does not depend crucially upon any particular physics but, rather, on a metaphysics. (It seems fair to say that even modern physicists would agree that the cessation of motion would result in the annihilation of material creatures.) The dichotomy between the changeable/unchangeable is at the heart of the matter. Another way to put it is to say that Thomas' analysis seeks to explain, in terms of the physics of his day, the twofold end of non-rational creatures. It is this two-fold end itself that is our concern here. And it is clear that the first end of mixed bodies (the universe in its changeable state) is subordinate to the second end of mixed bodies (the human good) because the whole universe in its changeable state is finally for the sake of human beings.

When discussed in terms of the relation of parts to the whole, it is the incorruptible soul that so distinguishes the human being from other material creatures that they become mere instruments for the good of human-kind. No other material creature is so suited. Any axiology that seeks to draw on Thomas to accord moral worth to non-rational creatures on the basis of their relation to the whole must, in the end, explain how these creatures can have such worth when the whole is itself finally for the sake of the human being.

I want now to demonstrate that the above analysis concerning the strict instrumentalization of non-rational creatures is augmented by a consideration of Thomas' moral theory. Through this discussion, I show that the moral worth of non-rational creatures is systematically excluded by Thomas' moral theory.

The Instrumentality of Non-rational Creatures in Thomas' Moral Theory

Thomas' moral theory is built upon a view of reality, and especially of divine providence, that dictates that non-rational creatures can have only instrumental value. Within this theory, direct moral concern for such creatures is positively or systematically excluded. The metaphysical underpinnings of Thomas' theory entail that non-rational creatures not have moral worth. This is reflected in his account of natural law and the virtues. This is so, finally, because first, Thomas' understanding of *natural law* depends upon his conception of the eternal law, which orders the lower creature to the higher in a strictly instrumental fashion; and second, his understanding of *human justice* (the virtue that relates us properly to others) is modeled on his conception of the divine justice, which orders the universe and the relations between creatures and according to which giving each creature its due means that non-rational creatures can only be instruments to the human good.

I do not mean to give an exhaustive account of Thomas' theory of natural law or theory of virtue. Clearly, any such undertaking would consume several volumes. My goal is more modest. I only intend to demonstrate that one of the primary conclusions reached earlier in this chapter, namely, that Thomas systematically excludes according any moral worth to non-rational creatures, is reflected in his moral theory. Any attempt to refute this conclusion must take into account the correspondence between this earlier analysis and the present one on Thomas' moral theory.

Let us begin by considering natural law. There are numerous theories of natural law, and there is little need for us to explore that wide diversity. Our interest is only in Thomas' understanding of natural law and its place in his moral theory. Unfortunately, even among interpreters of Thomas, there is little consensus on this understanding and the role it plays in our moral life. Therefore, any reading of Thomas on this issue is one among many. Below I shall sketch what I take to be the most plausible reading of Thomas on natural law and base my conclusions thereon. However, though the argument might take a different form, I believe it likely that the same conclusions would be reached on any reading of Thomas' understanding of natural law that has an adequate basis in his texts.

In brief, I agree in large measure with Vernon Bourke,[55] who argues that Thomas' understanding of natural law "stresses the rational discernment of norms of human conduct, working from man's ordinary experiences in a world environment of many different kinds of things."[56] What is central here is the stress upon "right reason" and an objective order, including the moral order, that reason can discern. Law is a function of reasoning. On this reading, the precepts of natural law are neither deduced, in some quasi-logical manner, from the first principle of practical reason (which we will look at below), nor are these precepts regarded as innate in the sense that they are naturally ingrained in our minds.

To be sure, there *are* precepts of natural law, and they must be in accord with, or be specifications of, the first principle of practical reason. But this is not because they need to be directly deduced from that principle. Rather, it is because that principle articulates in the most general form what any human action ought to pursue—the good as perfective of the human being. A precept governing the pursuit of any particular good must be a specification of this general principle. But the specific precepts are learned through reason discerning the proper relations between and among creatures and actions. What is good or what is evil is not simply a set of precepts written on our hearts in the manner of a scroll that can be read to tell us what is good and what is evil. Rather, the precepts of natural law are written in our hearts in the sense that we can use our reason to discern what is truly desirable and perfective, and insofar as reason can, in some measure, discern what is truly perfective and how God orders our natures and the universe. Though the tendencies of our nature are innate, knowledge of how we are to rectify these tendencies so that they may accord with the human good depends upon our use of reason.

This understanding of natural law moves it away from an emphasis on fixed precepts and toward an emphasis on the use of reason in discerning what is truly good. This accords well, I think, with Thomas' continuous emphasis on virtuous action as action in accord with right reason and on sinful action as against right reason. Right reason discerns the moral order, and, insofar as it correctly articulates more or less general principles on the basis of this order, it formulates the precepts of natural law.[57]

This understanding of natural law best accords with Thomas' later works and frees natural law theory from the rigidity and implausibility of holding that we are born with innate moral precepts that guide our actions. It also relegates Thomas' theory of natural law to a subordinate place in his moral theory, with the priority given to right reason about things to be done. What this reading does hold fast to is the notion that there is a rational ordering to the universe that our reason can, fallibly and fragmentarily, discern. (In other words, we have real insight into what is truly good for, or perfective of, human beings.) It is this relationship between reason (and so natural law) and the eternal law that is crucial for our present purpose. And it is because this relationship is relatively uncontroversial that the conclusions reached in this section are likely to apply to any interpretation of Thomas' understanding of natural law that has an adequate grounding in the texts.

Turning to the content of natural law, Thomas frequently compares the first principles of the speculative intellect to the first principles of the practical intellect, namely, the precepts of natural law. "The precepts of the natural law are to the practical reason, what the first principles of demonstrations are to the speculative reason; because both are self-evident principles."[58] Being is the first thing that falls under apprehension because whenever we know a thing, we know it as a being, whatever else it might be. On this apprehension of being is founded the first indemonstrable principle of the speculative intellect: "the same thing cannot be affirmed and denied at the same time."[59] All the other principles of the speculative intellect must be in accord with this first one. And just as "*being* is the first thing that falls under apprehension simply, so *good* is the first thing that falls under the apprehension of the practical reason, which is directed to action."[60] Any agent acts for an end that it takes to be good, to be perfective of the agent, to complete the agent in some way. The good is not simply that which is the object of pursuit but is also that which is taken to be somehow perfective and so is pursued. The first principle of the practical intellect, founded on the notion of the good as that which all things seek, is that "good is to be done and pursued, and evil is to be avoided."[61]

Thomas makes the transition from "the good as that which all things seek" to "good is to be done and pursued, and evil is to be avoided." Whatever is done is done under the formality of the good, as that which is taken to be perfective of the agent. I do not take Thomas here to be making a merely tautologous remark that all agents are to pursue what, in fact, they do pursue. If that was the case, there would be little point in articulating the principle. The good to be done concerns not merely what is taken to be desirable but also that which is truly desirable or that which truly perfects the agent. All other precepts of natural law are in accord with, and particularize, this first precept. But they cannot simply be derived from it because it does not indicate what is good or perfective of human beings. Reasoning based on the actual conditions in the world is necessary to make this determination.

It is because good has the note of an end that those things to which human beings are naturally inclined, reason apprehends as good; so "according to the order of natural inclinations, is the order of the precepts of the natural law."[62] Thomas goes on to argue that human beings have inclinations, and so goods, first, that we share with all substances (for example, to preserve ourselves in being); second, that are general to all animals (for example, to educate our offspring); and third, that are particular to human beings (for example, to seek truth and live together in society). All of these goods, to be perfective or truly good, must be pursued according to reason. The outcome of the reasoning process, articulated in terms of the precepts of natural law, guides the pursuit of any and all goods in order to relate them to the pursuit of the general or comprehensive human good. The goods we pursue must be so ordered that the pursuit of any one of them does not interfere with those others that constitute human perfection.[63] It is the goods appropriate to human life and the order among them that are formulated in the precepts of natural law.

On account of their relation to reason, the precepts of natural law distinguish what is good from what is evil, what is perfective from what is destructive. This can be seen in two complementary ways. First, "all acts of virtue [considered under the aspect of the virtuous] are prescribed by the natural law."[64] And second, "every sin is evil through being prohibited since it is contrary to natural law, precisely because it is inordinate."[65] Both of these are true because "to the natural law belongs everything to which a man is inclined according to his nature. . . . [And] since the rational soul is the proper form of man, there is in every man a natural inclination to act according to reason."[66] To act according to reason, or according to the precepts of natural law, is to act virtuously, and to act against these precepts is to sin. Natural law prescribes virtuous acts and proscribes sinful ones.

Turning to the topic at hand, we will see that (considered without reference to the effects of the actions on other *humans*) there are neither virtuous acts nor sinful acts in our relations with non-rational creatures. That is to say, these interactions are beyond the pale of moral consideration. Or, in other words, non-rational creatures have no moral worth. Natural law does not directly regulate human interaction with non-rational creatures because these creatures are not morally relevant. This can be seen, for example, in Thomas' equation of the first precept of natural law ("good is to be done and pursued, and evil is to be avoided") with the principles, "Thou shalt love the Lord thy God" and "Thou shalt love thy neighbor as thyself."[67] Short of stretching the term "neighbor" past its breaking point, I see no plausible way that any precept that demands direct moral consideration of non-rational creatures can be a specification of these latter principles.

I want to return to the notion that natural law prescribes what is virtuous and proscribes what is sinful. Below I will demonstrate that Thomas' theory of virtue systematically excludes the possibility of considering non-rational creatures to be the direct object of any virtuous action. Let me consider now his account of sin in order to show that there is no sin that is directly relevant to our interactions with non-rational creatures. Thomas argues that sin is fittingly divided threefold into sin against God, sin against oneself, and sin against one's neighbor.[68] Note that this division includes no category for sin against non-rational creatures. Indeed, in a quote we shall have occasion to look at again, Thomas holds that "there is no sin in using a thing for the purpose for which it is. Now the order of things is such that the imperfect are for the perfect . . . wherefore it is lawful . . . to take life . . . from animals for the use of men. In fact this is in keeping with the commandment of God Himself."[69] And, as Thomas puts it elsewhere, "it is no wrong for man to make use of [animals], either by killing or in any other way whatever."[70] So there is no room in Thomas' schema for sin against non-rational creatures; they are beyond the moral pale. No precept of natural law can be invoked that would imply that any direct moral consideration is due to such creatures.

Still, one might argue, perhaps such exclusion is accidental rather than systematic. Perhaps there is nothing inherent in Thomas' understanding of reality that prevents natural law from being developed in a direction that does accord such moral worth to non-rational creatures. Such a view, however, is mistaken. Thomas maintains that "the natural law is the rational creatures' participation of the eternal law"[71] and that the eternal law is "the whole community of the universe [as] governed by Divine Reason."[72] Recall that it is the divine reason which orders the less perfect to the more perfect in a strictly instrumental fashion, as is reflected in the quotations in the previous paragraph and as has been argued in the previous section of this chapter. Therefore, since natural law is based in the eternal law and the eternal law establishes the order among creatures, then to argue that it is possible for natural law to be developed in a fashion that accords moral worth to non-rational creatures is fundamentally to challenge Thomas' conception of the eternal law and, finally, his understanding of the last end of the human being. (According such moral worth is not transparently consistent with Thomas' understanding of the last ends of non-rational and rational creatures.) It is this crucial link between the precepts of natural law discerned by reason and the objective moral order as a manifestation of the eternal law that positively precludes any possibility of according moral worth to non-rational creatures. To challenge this conclusion, to maintain that Thomas' understanding of natural law can accommodate the moral worth of non-rational creatures, is to challenge the very core of his conception of reality—his understanding of God's nature, God's relation to and providential care of the world, and the final end of the human race.

Let us turn now to a consideration of Thomas' virtue theory in order to demonstrate that this theory also leaves no room for according moral worth to non-rational creatures. We saw above that the precepts of natural law prescribe all acts of virtue. Thomas maintains that the principles of natural law are "seeds of the moral virtues."[73] By this he means that the proper ends of human action, in their most general form, are given with human nature, given with our appetite as directed by reason. The role of the virtues is to habituate us so that we incline to these ends as by second nature. As Thomas says, "The end concerns the moral virtues, not as though they appointed the end, but because they tend to the end which is appointed by natural reason."[74] He directly connects this understanding of natural reason to natural law: "natural reason known by the name *synderesis* appoints the end to moral virtues."[75] Natural reason "appoints" the end in the sense that it discerns those ends that are truly perfective of the human being (not, obviously, in the sense that it determines those ends).

Because human beings are rational creatures, we are not determined to any one action but inclined indifferently to many. We can consciously entertain universals and so can choose among possible courses of action with awareness. It is this rational freedom that makes us moral (as opposed to non-moral) creatures with the capacity to choose between good and evil. On Thomas' ontology, this rational freedom, as noted, is one way of articulating the ontological divide that separates human beings from non-rational creation. But in human beings this indeterminacy is also a kind of incompleteness or imperfection. The powers of the soul that are rational, either essentially or by participation, require habituation in order to be disposed to a certain kind of act. As Thomas says, "The rational powers, which are proper to man, are not determinate to one particular action, but are inclined indifferently to many: and they are determinate to acts by means of habits."[76]

For the moral life, the point is that we are disposed to use our freedom well by good habits that perfect the powers of the soul by disposing them to act in accord with reason. A good habit is a virtue, or "a certain perfection of a power."[77] The virtues so shape the character of a person that she spontaneously desires and seeks, as by a second nature, the good life, the life that is truly perfective. That is to say, a virtuous person is disposed to seek those ends which reason discerns as appropriate to our nature, to pursue those ends that accord with the precepts of natural law. A virtuous person does not always need to think explicitly about whether a given action is in accord with the human good because she is naturally disposed to seek that good.

On Thomas' account, there are two principles of movement in human beings: the intellect and the appetite.[78] Those virtues that perfect the intellect are called intellectual virtues, and those that perfect the appetite are called moral virtues. Given the focus of this work, it is the moral virtues that are of primary interest to us. And it is justice in particular that is most relevant to our discussion.[79]

Justice, the virtue of the rational appetite, concerns the right ordering not of our passions but of our operations. As such, it is the virtue of the will and concerns the relation of the individual to the larger community. "The other [moral] virtues are commendable in respect of the sole good of the virtuous person himself, whereas justice is praiseworthy in respect of the virtuous person being well disposed towards another, so that justice is somewhat the good of another person."[80] (As we will see, Thomas' phrase "good of another *person*" is significant.)[81] Let us turn then to an exploration of Thomas' understanding of justice, the virtue that perfects the will. Unlike the passions, the will is naturally directed to the individual's own good (or what the individual takes to be her own good). Therefore, again unlike the passions, no virtue is necessary to direct the will to the individual's own good. But the virtue of justice is necessary to direct the will to the pursuit of the good of others.[82]

Let us go next to Thomas' understanding of particular justice.[83] "It is proper to justice, as compared with the other virtues, to direct man in his relations with others: because it denotes a kind of equality, as its very name implies; indeed we are wont to say that things are adjusted when they are made equal, for equality is in reference of one thing to some other."[84] The notion of equality is the bedrock and foundation of Thomas' understanding of justice. He states in numerous places that "justice is a kind of equality."[85] Or, again, "it belongs to justice to establish equality in our relations with others,"[86] "equality is the general form of justice,"[87] and "the essential character of justice consists in rendering to another his due according to equality."[88] He argues that "right" is the object of justice and that the just or right is making equal. It is because justice denotes a kind of equality that it must be concerned with relations between individuals, since equality implies the relation of one thing to another.[89] But understanding justice in terms of equality also has the effect of eliminating the possibility that justice extends to non-rational creatures, since, as we have seen, such creatures are not ontologically equal with human beings.

Time and again, Thomas makes it clear that he takes it for granted that, properly speaking, justice is strictly between human beings. Indeed, he states this as something assumed and obvious, without need for argument. For example, he maintains, "[J]ustice is of one *man* to another."[90] Or, again, "justice is concerned about external things, not by making them, which pertain to art, but by using them in our dealing with other *men*,"[91] and "the matter of justice is an external operation in so far as either it or the thing we use by it is made proportionate to some other *person* to whom we are related by justice."[92] I take it as clear that, for Thomas, justice in its proper sense is restricted to relations between humans. Further, justice is the virtue that is most directly relevant to the present conversation.[93] It is the only virtue that might find a place for the direct moral consideration of non-rational creatures. So the conclusion that I seek to demonstrate—that Thomas' virtue theory excludes direct moral consideration of non-rational creatures—does not seem in need of much demonstration after all. It follows more or less obviously from the following facts: first, justice is the only virtue that might bring our relation with non-rational creatures into the realm of morality; and second, Thomas restricts the realm of justice to relations between human beings. If concern for non-rational creatures does not fall under the ambit of justice, then it does not fall under the ambit of any of the virtues.

This analysis, so far as it goes, seems correct. But the interesting issue is not whether Thomas' account of the virtues excludes direct moral consideration of non-rational creatures. It seems clear that it does. Rather, the interesting issue is whether this exclusion is systematic, whether it is deeply rooted in Thomas' understanding of reality. This would be so, for example, if Thomas' account of justice could not be used constructively today in a way that accords direct moral worth to other creatures without simultaneously offering a deep critique of his larger metaphysical project. We can now state more precisely the task set for the remainder of this section. I will demonstrate that Thomas' understanding of justice systematically excludes the possibility of according moral worth to non-rational creatures.

Justice, as we have noted, is concerned with our life together. It is the virtue by which a certain equality is established and preserved between human beings. The notion of equality of justice is closely linked with the Aristotelian understanding of justice as "rendering each his due." Thomas articulates the relation as follows: "a person establishes the equality of justice by doing good, i.e., by rendering to another his due,"[94] or, again, "the essential character of justice consists in rendering to another his due according to equality."[95] To "render each his due" means to establish or to preserve the equality of justice.

There are two species of particular justice, distributive and commutative; the equality of justice means something different for each type. "Distributive justice . . . distributes common goods proportionally,"[96] while "commutative justice . . . is concerned about the mutual dealings between two persons."[97] Distributive justice directs the order of the whole to the part, or the order that belongs to the community in relation to each individual. Commutative justice directs the order of one part to another, or of one individual to another.[98] Let me begin with commutative justice because demonstrating that it cannot concern our relations to non-rational creatures is a relatively trivial matter. Commutative justice concerns the dealings between two individual persons. "In commutations something is paid to an individual on account of something of his that has been received, as may be seen chiefly in selling and buying."[99] Here the equality of justice is according to an arithmetical mean. "It is necessary to equalize a thing with a thing, so that the one person should pay back to the other just so much as he has become richer out of that which belonged to the other."[100] So, for example, a person should sell a thing for its actual worth or pay the wages of a laborer in accord with the value of the services received. One renders another his due in the precise sense that the value of that which is given is equivalent to the value of that which is received. There is an equality of the thing done and the thing received. Cheating, stealing, fraud, and murder would all be examples of (communative) injustice because they involve the failure to render another his due.

Given the nature of the transactions involved, only two rational agents can engage in commutation. Commutative justice cannot be relevant to our dealings with non-rational creatures because the point is to respect the (ontological) equality of the parties involved. What would it mean to render a deer its due for the value of its meat? Thomas addresses this issue explicitly when he considers the vices or sins opposed to commutative justice. He begins his consideration of murder with the question "whether it is unlawful to kill any living thing." He maintains, in a quote we looked at earlier, that "there is no sin in using a thing for the purpose for which it is. Now the order of things is such that the imperfect are for the perfect."[101] He concludes that "it is lawful [and so in accord with commutative justice] both to take life from plants for the use of animals, and from animals for the use of men. In fact this is in keeping with the commandment of God himself."[102] We see now that this discussion takes place under the rubric of justice and, in particular, commutative justice. Through this discussion, Thomas makes it clear that a non-rational creature cannot be the object of an act of (commutative) justice because such creatures lack the requisite ontological equality. They are ordered to the more perfect in a strictly instrumental manner.[103]

Distributive justice differs from general or legal justice insofar as legal justice directs the individual to the common good, while distributive justice directs the common good to the individual.[104] "In distributive justice something is given to a private individual, in so far as what belongs to the whole is due to the part, and in a quantity that is proportionate to the importance of the position of that part in respect of the whole."[105] So the greater the importance of the position occupied by a person, the more she is due of the common goods.

Thomas makes it clear that there must be some cause that renders a person worthy of the thing conferred. It is not simply preference for one person over another. In fact, there is only one vice or sin opposed to distributive justice, which sin Thomas calls "respect of persons." This sin occurs "if, in conferring something on someone, you consider in him not the fact that what you give him is proportionate or due to him, but the fact that he is this particular man (e.g., Peter or Martin)."[106] When this happens, "then there is respect of the person, since you give him something not for some cause that renders him worthy of it, but simply because he is this person."[107] Equality is achieved in distributive justice when that which is received from the common goods by two different persons accords with the respective positions of these persons in the community.[108] "Distributive justice considers the equality, not between the thing received and the thing done, but between the thing received by one person and the thing received by another according to the respective conditions of those persons."[109] Instead of an arithmetical mean, there is a geometric proportion.

Distributive justice might seem like a promising place to look for a way to incorporate direct concern for non-rational creatures into Thomas' moral theory. Perhaps there could be some sort of proportion between human beings and non-rational creatures (or perhaps some types of non-rational creatures). Maintaining the equality of proportion would then entail that at least some of the common goods are due to non-rational creatures as a matter of (distributive) justice. However, there is no justification for maintaining that there can be any proportionality between rational and non-rational creatures. Indeed, Thomas' ontology militates against such proportionality. Whatever the similarity between human beings and other material creatures, the immaterial subsistent soul of the human so separates the human from these creatures that such proportionality is not possible. There is simply no proportion between material and immaterial entities; that is, there is no measure according to which these two types of entity can be compared. To be sure, one might argue that the comparison is between non-rational creatures and human beings (that is, the body and the soul) and not simply between material and immaterial entities. Unfortunately, this approach will not help. The problem persists of somehow comparing a being without a subsistent soul to a being with a subsistent soul, when the natures of such souls are not comparable on the basis of any common metric.

This same point can be put more simply if we consider that Thomas' understanding of distributive justice is strongly influenced by the Greek understanding of order in human society. Distributive justice ensures peace and stability by adjusting what is due to any individual according to the station occupied by that person, with meeting the basic needs of everyone overriding any demand for unequal distribution. This is a thoroughly sociological understanding of distributive justice. Human beings with differing social status are due differing proportions of the common good, but the goal is thereby to maintain a kind of equality of proportionality that is conducive to the well-being and stability of the entire society. It is difficult to see how such a notion could be extended to include non-rational creatures because such creatures are not part of the human society with which distributive justice is concerned. Thomas does not even consider the possibility of any sin against distributive justice that involves our relations with non-rational creatures.

Still, in a discussion of virtues annexed to justice, Thomas does consider what he takes to be inherently unequal relations, those of human beings to God and of children to parents. Perhaps here we can find some sort of analog for a discussion of how distributive justice, or rather a virtue "annexed" to it, might apply to our relations to non-rational creatures. Virtues annexed to a principal virtue "have something in common with the principal virtue"[110] and "in some respect they fall short of that virtue."[111] Thomas argues that since the essential nature of justice is to render each person her due according to equality, a virtue directed to another may fall short of the perfection of justice by "first, falling short of the aspect of equality; secondly, by falling short of the aspect of due."[112] With respect to our relation to God, religion—which consists in worshiping a superior nature—is annexed to justice because we are not able to render to God equal due or as much as we owe him. With respect to the relation of children to their parents, piety—which consists of service and deference—is annexed to justice because it is impossible for a child to make an equal return of what she owes her parents. The key point here is that the lower has additional moral obligations to the higher. As Thomas states elsewhere, "The mean of justice is the equality that is established between those between whom justice is. . . . But in certain cases perfect equality cannot be established, on account of the excellence of one, as between father and son, God and man . . . wherefore in such cases, he that falls short of the other must do whatever he can."[113] Therefore, no virtue annexed to justice can be relevant to our relations with non-rational creatures since this would mean that lower creatures have obligations to human beings—not vice versa.

I take these arguments to demonstrate that Thomas' conception of justice does not, and cannot, offer any justification for according moral worth to non-rational creatures. Though there may be numerous ways to demonstrate that justice cannot entail any moral obligations of human beings toward non-rational creatures, in the end it is the fact that human justice is modeled on divine justice that underlies these various demonstrations. It is because Thomas' account of human justice takes place within, as it were, the larger framework of divine justice that moral consideration of non-rational creatures is positively excluded from human justice.[114] I want to close this portion of our discussion with an examination of the relation between divine and human justice. In *Disputed Questions on Truth*, Thomas asks, "[D]oes justice as found among created things depend simply upon the divine will?"[115] Though his concern is to refute the notion that justice among created things depends merely on the *arbitrary* will of God, this question also allows for the fruitful exploration of the relation of divine justice to human justice.

In answering the question posed, Thomas draws on Anselm and Aristotle to explain that justice is a certain "correctness" or "equation." Therefore, "the essential character of justice must depend first of all upon that in which there is first found the character of a rule according to which the equality and correctness of justice is established in things."[116] There must be some rule, some standard, according to which each thing receives its due proportion in its own nature, in its relation to other things, and in its relation to its cause. The will does not have the character of such a rule because it is directed by reason. But in God the will and the intellect are really the same so that the measure or correctness of the will is really the will itself. "Consequently the first thing upon which the essential character of *all* justice depends is the wisdom of the divine intellect, which constitutes things in their due proportion both to one another and to their cause. In this proportion the essential character of created justice consists."[117] Justice then cannot be said to proceed simply from the will of God because this would suggest that "the divine will does not proceed according to the order of wisdom, and that is blasphemous."[118] For Thomas, divine simplicity has the important consequence of rendering rational the order in the universe.

As he makes clear in his reply to an objection, he seeks to protect the notion of a free creation. The creation of things, the "establishing the natures themselves,"[119] is not a matter of justice but is purely voluntary and "depends simply on the divine will."[120] Still, he explains that God provides each thing "with whatever belongs to its nature."[121] In this operation, there is the character of something due, so it is a matter of justice. "It is due every natural being that it have the things which its nature calls for both in essentials and in accidentals. But what is due depends upon the divine wisdom inasmuch as the natural being should be such as to imitate the idea of it which is in the divine mind."[122] It is in this way that the first rule of justice is in the divine wisdom. The divine will, proceeding according to the divine wisdom, establishes the nature of things as well as the nature of the relations between things. This establishment of created natures in their relations to each other, according to the divine ideas, is the divine justice.

Thomas, in the next article, argues that "everyone is obliged to conform his will to God's."[123] As he goes on to explain, "[E]very good will is . . . good by reason of its being conformed to the divine good will. Accordingly, since everyone is obliged to have a good will, he is likewise obliged to have a will conformed to the divine will."[124] One's will is conformed to the divine will when she wills what God wants her to will. This conformation of the human to the divine can be put in terms of justice, since (human) justice is the virtue of the (human) will. A will that is habituated well (that is, is just) is disposed to follow the divine will. Or, to say the same thing, human justice is modeled on divine justice.[125]

Divine justice establishes the natures of created things in their relations to one another. So we might ask: In what manner does divine justice establish the relation between human beings and non-rational creatures? This is a question we have, in fact, already addressed earlier in this chapter, though our focus there was not on divine and human justice. Still, what we said there is relevant to our present conversation. In his discussion on divine providence, Thomas explains the manner in which God cares for rational and non-rational creatures. It is a simple matter to translate Thomas' discussion of *divine providence* into an understanding of *divine justice* because God's continuing care of creatures accords with the divine wisdom from which proceeds the divine will. That is, God's will in creating the natures of creatures in their relation to one another (a matter of divine justice) is in accord with God's will in caring for these creatures in their relation with one another (a matter of divine providence).

As noted in our earlier discussion, because of the rational soul of the human being, and the freedom and immortality that this rationality entails, only rational creatures are cared for for their own sakes. Non-rational creatures "are cared for, not for their own sake, but as being directed to other things."[126] Specifically, "intellectual creatures are ruled by God, as though He cared for them for their own sake, while other creatures are ruled as being directed to rational creatures."[127] This providential care for creatures reflects the ordering of the universe, and the ordering of the universe reflects the will of God and the divine justice. As Thomas says, "the order of the universe, which is seen both in effects of nature and in effects of will, shows forth the justice of God."[128] And he puts in terms of divine justice what was discussed above in terms of providence. "It is . . . due to a created thing that it should possess what is ordered to it; thus it is due to man to have hands, and that other animals should serve him. Thus . . . God exercises justice, when He gives to each thing what is due to it by its nature and condition."[129] So it is clear that the divine ordering of the universe, the divine justice, dictates that non-rational creatures are ordered to human beings in a strictly instrumental fashion. Non-rational creatures are cared for (and indeed were created) not for their own sakes but for the sake of humankind.

Human justice is modeled on divine justice, and the human will is to conform to the divine will. In the present context, this means that human justice cannot include within its ambit our relations to non-rational creatures. Interestingly, then, precisely because divine justice includes the ordering of all creatures to one another (and orders them as it does), human justice can only include the ordering of relations between human beings. Excluding our relations to other creatures is one important way in which human justice is modeled on divine justice. This is the basic systematic reason that Thomas' moral theory positively excludes the possibility of according moral worth to non-rational creatures. The underlying metaphysics and the divine ordering of the universe simply do not allow for that possibility.

There is one other issue worth mentioning before closing this chapter. Thomas argues explicitly that a non-rational creature cannot be the object of the supernatural virtue of the will—namely, charity, which is a kind of friendship. He gives three reasons, and all of these reasons depend critically on a human being's possession of a rational soul (and a non-rational creature's lack thereof). First, a non-rational creature "is not competent, properly speaking, to possess good"[130] because it does not have the free will that would enable it consciously to choose the good. Second, non-rational creatures "have no fellowship in human life [because this life is] regulated by reason. Hence friendship with irrational creatures is impossible."[131] Third, "charity is based on the fellowship of everlasting happiness, to which the irrational creature cannot attain."[132] Unsurprisingly, Thomas adds: "Nevertheless we can love irrational creatures out of charity, if we regard them as the good things that we desire for others, in so far, to wit, as we wish for their preservation, to God's honor and man's use; thus too does God love them out of charity."[133] At any rate, I merely mention his systematic, reasoned exclusion of non-rational creatures from the ambit of charity because he addresses it so clearly and concisely, and because it reinforces the conclusion reached above. Thomas' moral theory systematically excludes the possibility of according moral worth to non-rational creatures.

In this chapter, I have argued that Thomas' moral separation of human beings from non-rational creatures fundamentally reflects his freedom/slavery and imperishable/perishable dichotomies. What needs to be challenged in the writings of Thomas is his ontological divide between human beings and non-rational creatures. In Part II, I demonstrate that Thomas' conception of the human soul is philosophically untenable. If this internal critique is successful, then Thomas' primary rationale for the strict instrumentalization of non-rational creatures falls away, and so we have good reason to look for an alternative. In Part III, I offer such an alternative conception of human beings and creatures more generally that finds the freedom/slavery dichotomy untenable. On this alternative conception, all creatures enjoy some degree of freedom, so there is ontological continuity rather than an ontological divide. This alternative conception agrees in significant respects with Thomas' understanding of the nature of human freedom. But it diverges sharply from Thomas by maintaining that the freedom of other creatures differs only in degree and not in kind from human freedom. Although I will say a few words on the topic, I do not take a position on whether human beings (and perhaps other creatures) enjoy renewed life after this world passes away. My argument is that Thomas' articulation of the renewal of the world, which articulation results in a moral bifurcation of creation, is unsuccessful. The asymmetry of the *exitus/reditus* so prominent in Thomas' account might vanish if all creatures were understood to truly come from, and then return to, God.

PART II

The Human Soul

Analysis and Critique

This part is organized into two chapters. In Chapter 3, I intend to present Thomas' conception of the human soul by first introducing his general conception of the human soul, as a form and an entity. I next focus on Thomas' theory of cognition and explain, on the basis of this theory, how we gain knowledge of the human soul. My goals in this chapter are both to unfold the contours of Thomas' understanding of the human soul and to establish that the reception of a form in a knower, which gives rise to the existence of knowledge, is as much an ontological concern as the reception of a form in matter, which gives rise to the existence of a composite.

This discussion provides the analysis necessary to look further into Thomas' arguments for the subsistence of the human soul in chapter 4. There, I critically examine Thomas' arguments that the soul is an entity, a subsistent form. I then offer a critique of his conception of the human soul. Thomas' demonstrations are unsuccessful, I maintain, because he attempts to infer from the representative qualities of our thoughts to their ontological qualities without any suitable middle term. I conclude this chapter with some remarks on why I believe that this flaw is systemic rather than accidental.

Chapter Three

Thomas' Conception of the Human Soul

The thirteenth century was, doctrinally speaking, a time of roiling controversy. Much of this controversy was precipitated by the flood of Aristotelian writings that engulfed the intellectual centers of the Latin West beginning in the twelfth century. These writings, with their unsparing criticism of some major tenets of Platonism, broke in on an age whose Christian doctrines, developed by Saint Augustine and his followers, owed more to Plato than to any other non-Christian thinker.[1] Further, Aristotle's writing came accompanied by commentaries, especially those of the Arabian philosophers Avicenna and Averroës, which emphasized a number of positions at odds with Christian teaching.

Despite condemnations of Aristotle and prohibitions against the use of his work by local church authorities and the papacy, the study of his thought, often as interpreted through his commentators, spread through many of the institutions of learning. At the University of Paris, nearly all of his works were mandatory reading in the faculty of arts.[2] This led to sharp clashes that pitted those who took their philosophical bearings from Plato against those who sided with Aristotle. Some of the deepest disagreements between Platonists and Aristotelians centered on the nature of the human being.

The Platonic conception of the soul, which seemed to fit so well into the Christian scheme of things, came under strong criticism, especially in the work of Thomas. This happened as the full implications of the underlying

Platonic metaphysics became clear through a careful and detailed examination of the criticisms to which Aristotle had subjected his teacher. The Christian followers of Plato took safeguarding the immortality of the soul as their central concern. They did this by adopting a basically Platonic position that the soul is a complete substance and therefore independent of the body and not doomed to finally perish with it. The problem with this conception for Christians became how to explain the substantial or real unity of the soul and the body. For Plato, according to Thomas, the soul uses a body in the way a sailor sails a ship. There was no substantial unity.

Thomas argues that this conception is philosophically untenable for a number of reasons. For example, if the soul is only joined to the body as its motor, then the body does not receive its specific character from the soul. Therefore, the body would have the same species with or without the soul. This, Thomas argues, is clearly false since with the separation of the body and soul (that is, with death), the body no longer possesses an operation that is specifically human.[3] Further, Christianity demands a substantial union between soul and body. Any accidental unity of the two would pose serious theological problems, such as explaining why God, in creating the human being, saddled the soul with a body that was in no way essential to its own operation.

To be sure, Christian Platonists left nothing to be desired in their insistence upon the unity of the human as a composite of body and soul. While they formulated various ways to account for that unity, they steadfastly refused to allow that being the form of the body is essential to the soul. That is, they refused to countenance Aristotle's argument that the soul is the form of the body. To do this would be to endanger the immortality of the soul since as a form of a material thing (united *essentially* with matter), the soul would, seemingly, perish when the unity between body and soul was dissolved with the corruption of the body. Since it is as a form of the body that the soul is essentially or substantially united with it, this refusal was criticized as making true unity between body and soul impossible. This, then, is the way the problem of the soul presented itself to Thomas: the soul is either a purely material form or a complete substance.[4] If the soul is a purely material form (that is, the substantial form of matter), then the unity of the human being is safeguarded but at the cost of the immortality of the soul. If the soul is a complete substance, then it is immortal, but the unity of the human being is shattered.

Given this context, Thomas' opening question in his disputation, *Questions on the Soul,* was almost certain to have generated considerable interest. This question, "Whether the soul can be both an entity and a form,"[5] cut to the heart of the controversy. Thomas uses this controversy not only as the occasion to argue for a positive answer to this question but also to argue that in a deep sense the full *substantiality* of the soul *requires* the body. He sees no difficulty in holding both that the soul is subsistent (and so immortal) *and* that the soul is the substantial form of the body that confers existence upon the composite (thereby assuring the real or substantial unity of the human being).[6] Whether or not the form of material substance is more than a form of material substance depends on what *kind* of form it is and not on *whether* it is the form of a composite.[7] That is, so Thomas maintains, there is no difficulty in holding that the human soul has existence per se and confers that existence on the composite as the substantial form of the body. It is an imperfection of forms of other material substances that they cannot exist apart from the matter they inform. They do not possess the added perfection of subsistence, but this added perfection is no obstacle to also being the form of a material substance. The real difficulty arises for Thomas in seeking to show why the human soul requires this union with the body.

In what follows, I take Thomas' opening question of his *Questions on the Soul* as my starting point and draw on his more general account of metaphysics in order to flesh out and clarify his position. I focus my attention especially on Thomas' attempt to demonstrate that the human soul is an entity because it is this understanding of the soul that to a large extent justifies, in Thomas' view, the moral bifurcation between human beings and non-rational creatures discussed in Part I. One of the central points that I will argue in the latter portions of this chapter is that the reception of a form (in a knower) that causes knowledge is as much an ontological matter as the reception of a form (in matter) that causes the existence of a composite.

The Soul as Entity and Form

Thomas argues in the opening question of his *Questions on the Soul* that the soul is both a form and an entity. A form, specifically a substantial form, is that by which something exists and exists as the determinate kind of thing that it is. An entity is an individual in the category of substance, a first substance.

Let us now consider Thomas' understanding of the soul as a form. Thomas defines the soul, with Aristotle, as "the first principle of life of those things which live: for we call living things 'animate' [that is, having a soul], and those things which have no life, 'inanimate.'"[8] This understanding of the soul means that all living bodies have souls. In his refutation of the notion that the soul is itself a body, Thomas does not begin with an understanding of the soul that already entails immateriality. Rather, he argues to this as a conclusion. He maintains that though not every principle of vital action is a soul (for example, an eye, which is a principle of vision, is not a soul), the *first* principle of life is the soul. Something corporeal can be a principle of life, but nothing corporeal can be the first principle of life because to be a principle of life does not belong to a body as such. If it did, Thomas argues, then every body would be a principle of life or a living thing. That any body is actually a living being, it owes to some principle that is called its act, and this is the soul.[9] The soul is what distinguishes living from non-living, animate from inanimate.

This is essentially a regress argument that maintains that all of the vital functions of living creatures cannot be traced to physical agents. It is not yet an argument for any kind of spirituality. In fact, at the end of his argument, Thomas compares the soul to heat—in much the same way as the soul is the first principle of life and the act of a body, so heat is the principle of "calefaction" (or heating) and an act of a body.[10] There is, of course, the difference that the soul actualizes a body simply (that is, it makes it live), while heat actualizes a body in a particular way (that is, it makes it hotter). Still, Thomas' aim here is to compare them on the point of immateriality. And this comparison makes it apparent that Thomas' claim that the soul is not a body is a rather modest one. It is not, and is not meant to be, a refutation of materialism since many materialists can allow the properties of matter, and not only matter itself, into their ontology.[11] And to this point no stronger claim has been made regarding the soul than that it is not itself a body. That is, the soul is immaterial in the weak sense that it cannot be reduced to a merely physical agent. To put the point another way, no claim has yet been made about the subsistence or substantiality of any soul. Once this claim is made, then a decisive break has been effected with any kind of materialism.

Thomas has maintained that it is by the soul that the living body lives. In numerous places, he uses this as the beginning of his argument that the soul is the form of the body. The next step in the argument is the claim that the act by which living things live is the act by which they exist. Or, as Thomas puts it, "to live is the 'to be' of living things."[12] That is, a cat or a person only exists as an entity with its own essential operation when it is alive. The soul is the act by which a living body exists. If a human being dies, then her body is no longer a human body, except in an equivocal sense. The dead body no longer has an *operation* that is specifically human. The human body, then, in the strict sense, no longer exists because that person whose body it was no longer exists as embodied.

As noted in the discussion of substantial form, it is the form by which a substance has existence. Therefore, the conclusion that the soul is the substantial form of the body is inescapable. As Thomas summarizes, "A soul is said to be the form of its body insofar as it is the cause of life, just as form is the principle of existing."[13] Thus, the human soul is that by which a human body actually exists as a *human* body. And since to confer existence is characteristic of a form, the human soul is the substantial form of the human body. Thomas argues, in sum, that since the function of the soul is the same as the function of a substantial form (that is, to confer existence), then the soul must be the substantial form of a living body. Body and soul are substantially united or comprise one substance because they share in one act of existence.[14] But now the problem arises: If the soul is one in existence with the body, does it not perish when the body perishes? Clearly, Thomas must address the problem of the immortality of the soul. Let us turn our attention, then, to his understanding of the soul as an entity.

Thomas does not believe that the very fact that the human soul is the form of the body need be an impediment to the soul also being immortal. In numerous places, such as question fourteen in *Questions on the Soul*, he addresses this issue. In this question, as is typical, a number of objections are posed which argue that the soul cannot be immortal if it is the form of a material body. The objectors maintain that the form of a material thing only exists in that in which it is the form.[15] A form of a material thing is said "to be" only in the sense that *by it something else exists* but not in the sense that it has independent existence or subsists. It is abstract rather than concrete. Further, if the soul is by its essence the form of the body, then it must be corruptible according to its essence. Finally, if the body and the soul are substantially united or constitute a single existent—the human being— then when the body is corrupted, the soul must be corrupted. This summarizes the central arguments against the notion that a conception of the soul as the substantial form of the body (understood in an Aristotelian sense) can provide the resources necessary to validate the claim that the soul is immortal. If the soul is the form of the body, then the soul perishes when the body is corrupted.

In his response to these objections, Thomas maintains that there are two kinds of forms of material things: those whose existence depends upon the substance of which they are the form, and those whose existence is independent of the substance of which they are the form. That is, he argues that there is nothing about being a form of a material thing that, in itself, prevents such a form from being a subsistent form. As Thomas puts it, "Although a soul and its body unite to achieve a single act of existence of a human being, still that act of existence accrues to the body from the soul, so that a human soul communicates to its body the soul's own existence by which it subsists. . . . Consequently, when its body is taken away, a soul continues to exist."[16] So, Thomas holds, there is no problem with maintaining that the human soul can both subsist *and* confer existence on the composite. The human soul is the only subsistent form of a material substance. By one and the same act of existence the human soul subsists *and* the composite subsists by the human soul.

This is only to say that there is no logical problem in claiming that a subsistent form can be the form of a material substance. Whether or not Thomas is correct on this point, he has not yet demonstrated that the human soul is such a form. In the next chapter, I consider some of Thomas' most prominent arguments that the human soul is indeed a subsistent form. But before turning to that discussion there is some preliminary work to be done. In the next section, I lay out Thomas' theory of cognition with its embedded theory of intentionality. This discussion provides the framework for an analysis in chapter 4 of Thomas' most prominent arguments for the immaterial subsistence, and so immortality, of the human soul. My primary aim in this discussion is to demonstrate that the reception of a form in a cognitive being, by which cognition occurs, is no less an ontological reality than the reception of a form in matter, by which a composite comes to exist.

The Theory of Cognition

Thomas adopts Aristotle's principle: "Everything which is received in a thing is received in it according to the mode of the recipient,"[17] and not according to the mode of the giver. He repeats this principle in numerous places for numerous purposes.[18] I am concerned here with its use in his theory of cognition. By maintaining that a thing is in the knower according to the mode of the knower, Thomas is able to make a general distinction between cognitive beings (or "cognizers") and non-cognitive beings (or "non-cognizers"). Further, with cognitive beings, this principle underlies Thomas' theory of intentionality.

Thomas' distinction between cognitive beings and non-cognitive beings rests on the manner in which each is suited to receive forms. "[C]ognitive (*cognoscentia*) beings are distinguished from non-cognitive (*non cognoscentia*) beings in that the latter possess only their own form; whereas the intelligent being is naturally adapted to have also the form of some other thing; for the idea of the thing known is in the knower."[19] Since change is the result of the reception of form, it can also be said that cognizers are distinguished from non-cognizers by the kind of change they are in potency to undergo. The only kind of change that non-cognizers are in potency to undergo is what Thomas terms "material or natural change." Knowing subjects, or cognizers, are in potency to undergo "spiritual or intentional change" as well. Thomas clarifies this distinction in a discussion of the senses: "I mean by 'material change' what happens when a quality is received by a subject according to the material mode of the subject's own existence, as e.g. when anything is cooled, or heated, or moved about in space; whereas by a 'spiritual change' I mean, here, what happens when the likeness of an object is received in the sense-organ, or in the medium between object and organ, as a form causing knowledge, and not merely as a form in matter."[20] We can add here that "spiritual change" is also what happens when the likeness of an object is received in the *intellect,* as a form causing intellectual knowledge.

Although material change and spiritual change differ in important respects (which we will examine below), they are similar in one fundamental way: they are both ontological realities. Both involve the reception of a form that brings about change. My particular concern in this section is to demonstrate that the "intelligible species," which is the form by which human beings actually understand, is an ontological reality rather than, say, a merely representative reality (like concepts). To put the matter a different way, the form by which a cognizer is informed and gains knowledge is as much an ontological issue as the form by which matter is informed to bring about a composite. Much of what follows is meant to clarify and support this contention.

I want now to look more closely at Thomas' distinction between material change and spiritual change as well as the closely related distinction between natural existence and intentional existence. Let us begin with the latter. Natural existence is the existence had by things that can be known,[21] by both substances and accidents. Intentional existence is the existence had by things as cognized or represented by the knower, that is, as known. The concept or "word" in our intellect has intentional existence, while the intellect itself has natural existence. The color on the wall has natural existence, while to the eye it has only intentional existence.[22] Since material or natural change is change that does not bring about cognition, such change can only result in something with natural (or extracognitive) existence, either a material substance or an accident inhering in such a substance. Since spiritual or intentional change is change that brings about knowledge, spiritual change can only result in something with intentional (or cognitive) existence.

Thomas maintains, "[T]hings that are not receptive of forms save materially, have no power of knowledge whatever—such as plants."[23] If natural change were sufficient for sensory knowledge, then all natural bodies would feel it when they undergo alteration. (See ibid., Ia, 78, 3.) For instance, a vegetable brought in from the garden and placed in the freezer would not only get cold but would also feel cold. It might seem that "material change" is change that occurs when a form is received in such a manner that it contracts matter. But we must be careful here because the sense organs, as material, can only undergo change that contracts or informs matter, and yet they are capable of sense knowledge.[24]

It is also tempting to say that "material change" is change that occurs when a form is received in such a manner that the patient becomes literally like the agent. And this may be a valid way of understanding material change (and so distinguishing it from spiritual change) when both the patient and the agent are material creatures that do not differ generically. For example, a rock heated by fire becomes hot in the same specific way that fire is hot. Still, this will not do as a general formulation of the distinction. For example, if the agent is an immaterial entity and the patient is a material one, then the patient cannot become literally like the agent, and yet material change is still possible. Or if the agent, say, the sun, confers its generic, but not its specific, likeness to earthly creatures, then material change takes place without the patient becoming specifically like the sun. The most we can say in the general case (that is, as applicable to the interactions between a material creature and any other entity) is that "material change" affects the natural or material mode of existence of the creature undergoing change and does not bring about knowledge. So material change is "material" in the sense that it brings about modification of matter and does not bring about knowledge.

Spiritual change in the most general case is "immaterial" only in the sense that it is different from the change that occurs when matter is informed to bring about something with natural existence, and such spiritual change does bring about knowledge. Spiritual change, as noted, always results in something with intentional existence. We can say the same in terms of the immateriality of intentional existence. The point is nicely summarized by Yves Simon: "When we say that the form of the being [which is] known exists immaterially in the one knowing, it is necessary to understand that the former maintains a relation with the latter which is of another kind than the relation the form of a composite maintains with its matter; and such a state of affairs would be possible only on the supposition of emancipation from matter purely with respect to the conditions which matter imposes on form when form is educed from matter in order to establish a natural existent. That is what is signified by the term 'immaterial existence,' and nothing else besides."[25] That is to say, the intentional existence of a form in the senses or intellect is "immaterial" only in the way that it has a relation of a different order to the cognizer than the form of a composite has to its matter. The composite of a form with its matter establishes something with natural existence. An intentionally existing form, upon informing the sense organs or the intellect, establishes no such natural existent but only brings about knowledge. It is this difference, and this difference only, that qualifies all intentional existence as "immaterial." Still, as noted, in one important respect the relation of the cognizer to a form that brings about knowledge is like the relation of matter to the form that brings about the existence of a composite. In both cases the relation and the change that occurs are ontological realities.[26]

Let us now consider the human intellect. The human being is a material entity capable of intellectual knowledge. In the case of human knowing, the natural mode of existence of the thing (naturally) known is material, while the intentional existence of that thing in the intellect is immaterial. When Thomas inquires into the nature of the intellectual powers of the soul, he begins with the evident fact that human beings have the capacity to understand universals. And since we do not always actually understand, he argues that the human intellect is "in potentiality with regard to things intelligible, and is at first 'like a clean tablet on which nothing is written.'"[27] The human intellect is passive insofar as it moves from potentiality to actuality, from potentially understanding to actually understanding. And, "wherever something is sometimes in potency, sometimes in act, it is necessary that there be a principle through which that thing is in potency. . . . [S]ince a human being is sometimes understanding in act and is sometimes only in potency to understand, . . . there is in a human being an intellective principle which is in potency to intelligible things."[28] Thomas follows Aristotle in calling this intellective principle the "possible intellect." In a manner analogous to the way in which sense powers are in potency to sensible objects, the possible intellect is a power of the soul, which is in potency to intelligible objects.

It is by the possible intellect that we understand. But because the possible intellect is a potentiality, we cannot know it directly. We cannot know the soul through its essence. "The human intellect is only a potentiality in the genus of intelligible beings. . . . Hence it has in itself the power to understand, but not to be understood, except as it is made actual."[29] Since "in this life our intellect has material and sensible things for its proper natural object . . . it understands itself according as it is made actual by the species abstracted from sensible things."[30] The intellect, then, knows itself through its act. To demonstrate that the soul is indeed a substance in its own right, Thomas then argues, as he must, from the act of the intellect. And since we know this act from its object, Thomas argues from the object of the intellect to the act of the intellect, from the act of the intellect to the nature of the powers of the intellect and then to the nature of the intellect itself. This point will be important in our discussion of Thomas' arguments for the immaterial subsistence of the human soul.

In numerous places, Thomas compares the potency of the possible intellect to the potency of prime matter. He says that "the possible intellect in the order of intelligibles is like prime matter in the order of sensibles."[31] Prime matter and the possible intellect prior to the reception of form are similar in that they are both in potency to the reception of suitable forms. "[A] soul does not possess intelligible perfection in its own nature but is in potency to intelligible objects, just as prime matter is in potency to sensible forms."[32] However, they differ in the mode in which they receive the forms. "[P]rime matter receives form by contracting it to the individual being. But an intelligible form is in the intellect without any such contraction."[33] Thus far, the distinction between prime matter and the possible intellect is one between forms received in a natural mode and forms received in an intentional mode. But this explication would not yet pick out the possible intellect alone because it also picks out the sense faculties. So, Thomas goes on to say that "the intellect understands the intelligible chiefly according to a common and universal nature, and so the intelligible form is in the intellect according to its universality."[34] Insofar as prime matter receives form individually (or as producing something that exists individually) and intellect receives form universally (or as producing something that signifies universally), they are, in that sense, opposites. Still, they are similar in the respect that they are both in potency to receive (appropriate) forms, and the reception of such forms brings about change that is an ontological reality.

As a preliminary to a consideration of Thomas' understanding of the active aspect of the intellect, let us turn to his understanding of universals. Following Aristotle, Thomas rejects Plato's doctrine of the forms in which universals have separate existence. Thomas maintains that universals do not have extracognitive existence. They exist only in the intellect and are instantiated in particular things. So there is no "horse as such" or "universal horse" that exists extracognitively. On the contrary, there are only particular horses. But since these creatures share certain features that define what it means to be a horse, we can consider these common essential features in isolation from any particular horse and thereby cognize the idea of "horse." Once we have this idea, we are able to identify the particular object in front of us as a horse. The same is true of anything that we can bring to language (that is, any universal).

The features picked out by a universal have existence only in some particular thing; it is only by knowing the essence or nature of a particular thing that we can know it as just this one type of thing. "Universals as such exist only in the soul; but the natures themselves, which are conceivable universally, exist in things."[35] Since the universal does not exist extracognitively and since the intellect requires the intelligible species (by which the universal is produced) in order to be reduced from potency to actuality, or to actually understand, it is necessary for the intellect itself to create the intelligible species by which we understand. In saying this, there is a danger of reifying the intelligible species, of seeing it as a static "thing" rather than a state in a dynamic process. Although nothing that follows need imply this reification, it is a continuous concern because of the nature of our analysis (especially in chapter 4, where we will further discuss the nature of the intelligible species). So it might be helpful to highlight at the outset that the intelligible species, analogously to the sensible species, is a state or property of the intellect that enables the intellect to produce an act with suitable intentional content.[36]

In order to account for the creation of the universal by the intellect, Thomas posits an active power that he calls the "agent intellect" or "active intellect."[37] Since universals do not exist outside the mind, there must be some power to "make the objects that are intelligible in potency to be actually intelligible, by abstracting the species of things from matter and from individuating conditions; and this power is called the agent intellect."[38] Thus, the agent intellect is a power that actively abstracts the intelligible species. This abstractive process is a stripping away of all that individuates in order to cognize the essential characteristics of a thing, in order to cognize universals, and in order to cognize a thing as a species, in the logical sense, rather than as an individual. The intelligible species moves the intellect to actual understanding. "[A]nd since this intelligible object does not pre-exist in reality, it must be produced by the agent intellect."[39]

In our intellect, then, there is both an active and a passive potency: first, the agent intellect, whose object is moved by the agent intellect so that it becomes actually intelligible; and second, the possible intellect, whose object moves the possible intellect so that it actually understands.[40] The agent intellect makes the "phantasm" (that is, the sensitive likeness of a thing, with all its particularity) in the imagination, which is intelligible in potency, to be intelligible in act by extracting the likeness of the essence of the thing from material conditions. It is by the light of the agent intellect that things are rendered actually intelligible. By being actually intelligible, they are made to be homogeneous with the possible intellect and so capable of acting on the possible intellect.[41] The intelligible species abstracted by the agent intellect is, as Thomas says, a likeness that represents the thing reflected in the phantasm only as to its specific conditions. That is, it is stripped of matter and the conditions of matter. The agent intellect causes the possible intellect to take on the formal characteristics of the object and so to come to be in a certain state, which state results in an appropriate intelligible content.

The intelligible species is a likeness of the object. As Thomas says, "as the sense is directly informed by the likeness of its proper object, so is the intellect by the likeness of the essence of a thing."[42] Since it is the likeness of the object or, more specifically, the likeness of the essence of the object (that is, as stripped of materiality and the conditions of matter) that becomes the form of the intellect, the intellect in act *is* the intelligible in act. The two are formally identical. The intellect in act is informed by the form of the object, but this form is the intelligible in act that was abstracted from the phantasm by the agent intellect and exists only in an intentional manner.[43] The act of understanding is the operation that is consequent on the received form that causes the intellect to be in act. "The act of understanding is brought about by the union of the object understood with the one who understands it, as an effect which differs from both."[44]

The act of understanding and the intelligible species are related in the way that proper operation is related to the form by which it operates. "To understand is not an act passing to anything extrinsic; for it remains in the operator as his own act and perfection; as existence is the perfection of the one existing: *just as existence follows on the form, so in like manner to understand follows on the intelligible species*."[45] The act of understanding is a perfect act, or an imminent act, insofar as it remains in the operator and perfects him. An imperfect act, say, building a house, is one that passes out of the operator and perfects an external object. Therefore, Thomas compares the act of understanding to existence insofar as both follow on an appropriate form and perfect the one informed. The informing of the possible intellect by the intelligible species is an ontological change, which issues in the act of understanding.

Just as an extracognitive being receives its species from the form whereby it has existence, so, too, the intellectual act receives its species from the intelligible species by which the intellect is in act.[46] "Since form is the principle of action, a thing must be related to the form which is the principle of an action, as it is to that action."[47] The act of understanding is an ontological reality that is constituted determinately by its form, just as the thing known is constituted determinately by its form.[48] When informed by a given intelligible species, the intellect can know only that of which the species is a likeness. "The intelligible species represents one thing in such a way as not to represent another. Hence when we understand what man is, we do not forthwith understand other things which belong to him."[49] It seems fair to say, then, that the intelligible species gives the intellect (or, better, gives thought) its shape or character insofar as this intelligible species is the principle that makes thought to be determined or confined to those intelligible objects of which the intelligible species is the likeness. Indeed, the intelligible species is the form or character of the intellect in act.

It is because of the identity between knower and known that Thomas can infer from the nature of the intelligible species to the nature of the intellect. The possible intellect cannot be known as it is in potentiality because a thing can be known only insofar as it is in act. "Hence the form is the principle whereby we know the thing which is made actual thereby, and in like manner the cognitive power is made actually cognizant by some species. Accordingly our intellect does not know itself except by the species whereby it is made actual in intelligible being."[50] So the possible intellect is "knowable in the same way as other things, namely, by species derived from phantasms, as by their proper forms."[51] If we come to know the form of a thing, then we know that thing's nature because a thing receives its nature or species from its form. So if we can learn the nature of the intelligible species, which is the form of the intellect in act, then we will come thereby to an understanding of the intellect itself. Thomas summarizes the point nicely: "The soul is not known through a species abstracted from sensible beings, as though that species were understood to be a likeness of the soul. Rather, *from a study of the nature of the species abstracted from sensible things we discover the nature of the soul in which such a species is received, just as matter is known from form.*"[52] This sentence bears repeating. If we come to know *the nature of the species* abstracted, then we come to know the nature of the soul in which this species is received, just as matter is known by its form. So coming to know the nature of the intelligible species is crucial to coming to know the nature of the soul. And, in the next chapter, I argue that an articulation of this nature is the crux of Thomas' most prominent arguments for the soul's subsistence.

Once informed by the intelligible species, the possible intellect becomes the intellect in act. It is the intellect in act that actually understands, and the term of the act of understanding is the "inner word." This inner word is either a simple concept or a proposition. A simple concept, our focal concern, is a universal that represents the nature or quiddity of the object.[53] The inner word differs from the intelligible species as term differs from principle.[54] The intellect, then, is not only informed by the intelligible species in the way the exterior senses are informed by sensible species, but the intellect also forms for itself a mental word, which is a universal or a proposition. The intelligible species is a likeness of the external object, which is abstracted from the phantasm by the agent intellect and then effects an ontological modification of the possible intellect, an "intentional change." This intentional change is the informing of the intellect by the intelligible form. The intelligible species, then, in thus informing the intellect, is the form or the shape that thought takes on. The intelligible species effects or, more precisely, *is* an ontological modification of the possible intellect and so, as noted, concerns the intrinsic features of thought. Through its activity, the intellect forms the universal, and the universal *represents* extramental objects.[55]

We can now see more clearly how it is that the good of the soul *requires* the body. Both the sensory and intellectual levels of cognition are necessary for intellectual understanding. Unlike Plato, Thomas holds with Aristotle that the human soul does not possess innate intelligible species. Rather, it is like a blank slate with nothing yet written on it. The soul must acquire the intelligible species by which it understands, and it can only acquire them through the sense organs. Therefore, it cannot, of itself, accomplish its own essential operation, which is to understand.[56] The soul must be united to the body for its own good.[57]

Since Thomas argues that the soul cannot perform its own essential operation, to understand, without the body, it is not complete in species but rather itself completes the human species. It is a part of the species.[58] Only as united with the body can the soul be part of a complete substance or an entity in the full sense, as both subsistent and complete in species. A thing is placed in a species according to its substantial form, but it is complete in species only if it can perform its own essential operation, and to do so, human beings need both the sensitive and intellectual cognitive powers. And to the question of whether the soul is an entity, Thomas answers that the soul is an entity in a qualified sense; it is an entity insofar as it is subsistent but not insofar as it is not a complete species. Thomas' arguments for the soul's subsistence, then, are only that the soul has its own existence and not that it is complete in species.

Thomas summarizes much of the discussion in this chapter as follows:

Now the one who understands may have a relation to four things in understanding: namely to the thing understood, to the intelligible species whereby his intelligence is made actual, to his act of understanding, and to his intellectual concept. This concept differs from the three others. It differs from the thing understood, for the latter is sometimes outside the intellect, whereas the intellectual concept is only in the intellect. Moreover the intellectual concept is ordered to the thing understood as its end, inasmuch as the intellect forms its concept thereof that it may know the thing understood. It differs from the intelligible species, because the latter which makes the intellect actual is considered as the *principle of the intellect's act,* since every agent acts forasmuch as it is actual: and it is made actual by a form, which is necessary as a principle of action. And it differs from the act of the intellect, because it is considered as the *term of the action,* and as something effected thereby. For the intellect by its action forms a definition of the thing, or even an affirmative or negative proposition.[59]

Thomas distinguishes the external object understood from the intelligible species, the act of understanding, and the universal. It is the relation between these latter three that is of primary interest for our discussion. Summarily, the intelligible species is the principle or source of the act of understanding, and the universal or the concept is the term of this act. And, as we have seen, the intelligible species actualizes the possible intellect and gives the intellectual activity its intrinsic character or shape insofar as it becomes the form of the intellect. Such a species is the state or character of the intellect in act; it ontologically modifies the possible intellect, thus causing the possible intellect to become the intellect in act. And the intellect in act produces the inner word in which we understand the world.

With this understanding of the basic contours of Thomas' conception of the human soul and theory of cognition, we are ready to turn to his arguments for the immaterial subsistence of the human soul. In what follows, I focus on what the intellect in act forms in its first operation—the inner word as a universal. It is from the nature of this inner word, as universal, that Thomas infers the nature of the human soul. The universal, simply put, is the term we apply to what can be predicated of more than one thing.[60] In my discussion, I am reserving the term "intelligible species" for the form by which the possible intellect is actualized. And, unless the context makes clear another use, I am reserving the term "universal" for that which is the object of the intellectual knowledge, for that which is produced by the first operation of the intellect in act—the "inner word" as the nature of a thing.[61]

Chapter Four

The Soul as an Entity

A Critical Assessment

Thomas offers a number of different types of arguments for the subsistence of the human soul. In this chapter, I examine his most prominent ones and maintain that they do not succeed in demonstrating that the human soul is subsistent because they depend upon an inference between representative immateriality and ontological immateriality without any suitable middle term.

Thomas' two most prominent arguments for the soul's subsistence concern the soul's knowledge of universals and the soul's potential knowledge of all things.[1] These are not truly independent arguments, but rather the second type depends critically on the first.[2] That is, it is not the extent or breadth of knowledge that is crucial to demonstrating the soul's subsistence. After all, the senses potentially have the same breadth. What is crucial is the type of knowledge that the soul is capable of attaining—a knowledge of the nature of things, of universals.

After demonstrating the dependence of the second type on the first, I hold that Thomas' argument for the soul's subsistence that infers from our knowledge of universals is fatally flawed. He directly infers from representative immateriality to ontological immateriality, from the way our thoughts represent to their intrinsic nature. But this is like arguing that because I am thinking about the incredible speed of a rocket, my thought is itself incredibly fast. Insofar as my analysis can be sustained, Thomas' most prominent arguments for the soul's subsistence fail.

I conclude this chapter with a sketch of the systemic nature of this failure. I maintain that Thomas presupposes the legitimacy of the distinction between material and immaterial entities, or, what comes to the same thing, he presupposes the existence of immaterial entities (such as angels and God). On this presupposition, a suitable middle term can be offered for the inference between representative and ontological immateriality, namely, that immaterial entities could only know in an immaterial manner. And since such entities are intellectual creatures, immaterial knowing must be intellectual or of universals. That means that creatures that are solely material know only in a material or sensitive manner, and so only know singulars. But Thomas' presupposition of the legitimacy of the distinction between material and immaterial entities is not justified because the distinction itself can only be maintained by relying upon arguments that are viciously circular. Or so I shall argue.

Returning, then, to Thomas' claim that the soul is both a form and an entity, we focus on his demonstration that the soul is an entity. It is on this claim (with its attendant understanding of the renewal of the earth at the end of time) that the moral separation between human beings and non-rational creatures depends. So to challenge this claim successfully is simultaneously to challenge the primary basis for Thomas' moral bifurcation.

To claim that the soul is an entity is to claim, minimally, that the soul subsists. (As noted, this is not to claim that the soul is complete in species. Rather, the soul is, according to Thomas, a subsistent form that itself completes the human species when united with a body.) But if the soul subsists, then it can only subsist as a form since Thomas has already argued that the soul is the form of the body. So Thomas' demonstration that the soul is an entity is reduced to a demonstration that the soul is subsistent. A subsistent form is incorruptible because it does not contain within itself any matter, which, because it is in potency to contrary substantial forms, is the principle of corruption.

A Critical Analysis of Thomas' Argument for the Soul's Subsistence

Let us start with Thomas' argument for the soul's subsistence that is framed in terms of the soul's potential knowledge of all things. A clear example of this type of argument occurs in question fourteen of *Questions on the Soul:*

To understand . . . is not an act that is completed through a bodily organ. For it is impossible that there should be found a bodily organ which is capable of receiving all sensible natures, especially because a recipient must be free of the nature received, just as the pupil of the eye lacks color. Now every bodily organ has a sensible nature. On the other hand, the intellect by which we understand is capable of knowing all sensible natures. Hence it is impossible that the intellect's operation, which is to understand, be carried out through anything that is corporeal. Hence it is clear that the intellect has an essential operation in which its body does not share. Now each thing operates in accordance with what it is. For things which exist through themselves operate through themselves, whereas things which do not have existence through themselves do not have an operation through themselves; for heat does not through itself produce warmth, but something which is hot does. Accordingly, there-fore, it is clear that the intellective principle by which a human being understands possesses an existence that transcends its body and is not dependent upon its body.[3]

Before looking at the core of this argument, let us consider its ending. The close of this argument is an essential, though often implicit, part of nearly all of Thomas' arguments for the incorruptibility of the soul. *The in-tellect has an essential operation, to understand, in which the body does not share.* What comes before this point varies, depending on the type of argu-ment employed. But if Thomas can successfully get to this point, then the argument is over. If he can show, in some manner, that the intellect's oper-ation (that is, understanding) is one in which the body cannot share (as he attempts to do, for example, by showing that the intellect's operation in-cludes the possibility of knowing all sensible natures, or that, in the under-standing, contraries can be simultaneously entertained, or that understand-ing involves the reception of immaterial intelligible species), then he has shown that the intellect must have an operation of its own. In Thomas' ontology, there are no "free-floating" acts (with the possible exception of God). All acts are acts of something. So to say that the intellect has its own operation is to say that it is "a something" capable of operating. And since this something operates independently of the body, it must have existence independent of the body. Thus, it must be a subsistent form.

Now let us turn to the core of this particular argument. For the intellect to be in potency to all sensible natures means that it is capable of receiving the intelligible form of any sensible thing intentionally. Such reception of the form results in a formal identity between the intellect and the thing, so that "the intellect in act is the intelligible in act." In order for the intellect to be capable of "becoming" the nature of any sensible thing, it must not first be that thing. That is, in order for something to be in potency to something else, it must not first be that thing. If it was that thing, then it could not also be in potency to that thing. So if the intellect is in potency to *all* sensible natures, then it must not itself be *any* of them. It follows that since the intellect's operation of understanding, with its potency to all sensible natures, cannot be carried out by any bodily organ, it must have an operation of its own and hence be a subsistent form.

This argument, however, has two related flaws (or, perhaps, one flaw looked at from two different perspectives).[4] First, the interior senses of imagination, memory, and the cogitative power are in potency to have a kind of knowledge of all sensible natures, and yet they are material.[5] The common sense distinguishes between the sensory inputs of the proper senses—sight, taste, smell, hearing, and touch—and leads to an awareness of how these particulars are related to the sensed object. And the cogitative sense even has the capacity to make particular judgments regarding the objects sensed. So the breadth of possible knowledge (that is, the fact that it is of *all* sensibles) cannot distinguish the intellect from the interior sensitive powers. Second, on the one hand, the argument depends on the difference between intentional and natural existence insofar as things that exist in the intellect do not cause the intellect to become literally like the external things; that is, they exist intentionally in the intellect and naturally in the sensible thing. But, on the other hand, the argument also depends upon a conflation of intentional and natural existence insofar as it depends upon a confusion between kinds of potency. To argue that the intellect cannot be a sensible nature in order to be in potency to knowledge of all sensible natures presupposes that the kind of potency under discussion is potency to material change in the technical sense discussed earlier. As we see in the case of the interior senses, it is possible to be in potency to (some aspect of) all sensible natures and still be a sensitive power if the kind of potency under discussion is to intentional change. Since the argument applies equally to the interior senses which are material (and hence corruptible) and to the intellect, it fails to show that the intellect is incorruptible.

The argument can be provisionally salvaged by shifting the emphasis from the breadth of the intellect's potency to precisely what it is that the intellect is in potency to receive. The intellect is in potency to receive all sensible *natures*. This is the distinguishing mark of the intellect; it is capable of consciously relating to universals. And, on Thomas' ontology, this clearly distinguishes it from the sensitive powers. The argument now needs to demonstrate why being in potency to receive the natures of things makes the intellect incorruptible. Such incorruptibility follows on the fact that only a subsistent form, as an immaterial entity, could entertain universals or know the natures of things because this requires an immaterial act. The argument, then, becomes a form of the argument from universals rather than an independent argument for the incorruptibility of the soul. Therefore, this argument finally depends for its success on the argument from universals.

It is to that position that we now turn. The argument for the soul's subsistence, which begins from our evident knowledge of universals, occurs in numerous places in Thomas' writings and takes different forms. These arguments share a starting point in the soul's knowledge of universals and, of course, in the conclusion that the soul is a subsistent form. I examine two versions below in order to clarify the flaw that cripples the argument. Let us begin with a clear example that occurs in question fourteen of Thomas' *Questions on the Soul:* "An intellective principle of this kind is not composed of matter and form, because species are received in it in a wholly immaterial way. This is made clear from the fact that the intellect is concerned with universals, which are considered in abstraction from matter and from material conditions. Therefore one can conclude that the intellective principle by which a human being understands is a form that possesses existence. Hence it necessarily follows that it is incorruptible."[6]

From the fact that the intellect knows universals, Thomas maintains that the species by which the intellect knows must be received in a wholly immaterial way. From the fact that the intelligible species are received in a wholly immaterial way, he concludes that the soul is a subsistent form, an immaterial entity. An unstated premise of this argument is the Aristotelian principle, "Everything is received in another according to the mode of the recipient." If the species are received in an immaterial way, then the recipient itself must be immaterial. In some variants of this argument Thomas is explicit in his use of this principle.[7]

I argue that this type of argument has the fatal flaw of inferring from the representative qualities of our thoughts to the intrinsic qualities of our thoughts without any suitable middle term.[8] It assumes that the intrinsic character of our thoughts must literally resemble what they are about. This argument from universals infers from the content of our intellect (the intellect knows universals) to the intrinsic features of our intellect (the intellect is a subsistent form). While it is absurd to hold that because an intellect has the thought, "the North Pole is cold," the intellect itself must be cold, something like this is, in fact, going on here.

Thomas criticizes the Platonists and the materialists for their adherence to a literal understanding of the principle, "Like is known by like." For example, against the materialists, he argues that the logical implication of their theory of cognition is that in order to know a rock, we must have rocks in our heads. But here Thomas himself falls into a similar trap. He (implicitly) uses the "like is known by like" principle not to maintain that the soul and objects in the world must be literally alike, so one can infer from the nature of the one to the nature of the other. Rather, he presumes a literal similarity between the representative and intrinsic qualities of our thoughts, and so infers from the representative to the intrinsic.

Universals are representative. And whatever properties they have do not seem to translate easily into inferences about the intrinsic qualities of the intellect entertaining them. The immateriality of universals merely concerns the way universals represent (that is, they can refer to more than one existing thing and so cannot be particulars in which matter is the principle of individuation). It is clearly of a different order than, or categorically different from, the ontological, entitative immateriality of immaterial entities. When Thomas argues from the immateriality of universals to the immateriality of thought, and so of the intellect, he is inferring from one kind of immateriality to another. Such an inference requires a suitable middle term—a suitable argument—that Thomas does not, and perhaps cannot, supply. To be more precise, it is from the nature of the intelligible species, the form of the intellect in act, that Thomas infers the nature of the intellect. Intelligible species are the form of the intellect in act, and so are an ontological reality. It is the inference from the nature of the universal to the nature of the intelligible species (either implicitly or explicitly) that is the locus of Thomas' error.

In order to make my case, I want first to clarify precisely what is being maintained in this argument for the immateriality and subsistence of the human soul. I then focus on the locus of the problem in Thomas' argument. The argument above can be reordered in terms of this progression:

1) The intellect is concerned with universals, which are considered in abstraction from matter and material conditions.
2) Species are received in it (that is, the intellect) in a wholly immaterial way.
3) An intellective principle of this kind is not composed of matter and form.
4) The intellective principle by which a human being understands is a form that possesses existence.
5) It necessarily follows that it is incorruptible.

Let us start with the object of the intellect. This argument states that "the intellect is concerned with universals (*intellectus est universalium*), which are considered in abstraction from matter and material conditions." This translation is, like the Latin, rather vague. The intellect "is concerned with" or "has to do with" or "pertains to" universals. Obviously, this is true for Thomas. But what precisely does it mean? The most obvious interpretation is that the intellect knows universals, as Thomas argues repeatedly. But the passage might also be interpreted to refer to the intelligible species by which the soul knows. These, let us recall, are likenesses only of the specific nature of a thing, and so are also universals.[9] Indeed, because Thomas believes that these intelligible species and universals must be of the same nature, the context often does not clarify which is under discussion. Nevertheless, he clearly holds that the universal *in which* we know the world and with which the sciences are concerned must be distinguished from the intelligible species *by which* the intellect produces the universal and which are not directly known (though they can be made the object of reflection, as is evidenced by this discussion).[10] Therefore, it seems likely that the universal referred to in this argument is the universal as the inner word. The starting point of the argument, then, would be uncontroversial. It would simply be saying that our intellect entertains, or is consciously related to, universals.

If the intelligible species is being referred to, and we do not know this directly, then to begin by positing the nature of this species as universal and immaterial seems to skip a step. That is, we first need to argue to the nature of the intelligible species itself. To be sure, Thomas believes that the intelligible species and the universal that we know must be of the same nature. But I will argue below that this belief is unwarranted. If we assume that he is beginning by positing the nature of the intelligible species and that my argument is successful, then Thomas' argument for the subsistence of the human soul collapses at the outset. Again, on these assumptions, we have no reason to accept this premise that intelligible species either are abstracted from matter and material conditions or are wholly immaterial. Further, to begin by positing the nature of the intelligible species is to begin with a marked deck since the intelligible species is the form or state of the intellect in act. If we already know the nature of the intelligible species, then we already know the form of the intellect in act; and so we already know the nature of the intellect, since we know the nature of a thing by its form. But if we interpret Thomas to mean that the intellect forms and entertains universals in which it understands things in the world, then these problems drop away and the starting point is no longer problematic.[11] So I will proceed with the understanding that the intellect is concerned with the universals in which we know the world, the universals formed by the first operation of the intellect.

The next step in the argument is to move from object to act. Thomas maintains that from the fact that the intellect knows universals, "species are received in it in a wholly immaterial way." Again, the term "species" has some ambiguity; it might refer to the inner word or the intelligible species. Because Thomas speaks of the species being received (*recipiuntur*), however, it seems safe to say that he refers here to the intelligible species by which the possible intellect is actualized. This seems all the more likely because it is by the reception of form that change occurs in the recipient, and it is the intelligible species—the "agent object"—that brings about intentional change in the possible intellect by informing it. Further, since Thomas must argue from object to act, this can be seen in a double sense if "species" is taken as intelligible species because this species is the form, or act, of the possible intellect, and the reception of this species is an operation or act (in the sense of undergoing) as well. At any rate, it seems necessary to take the term as intelligible species in order to reach the conclusion that Thomas seeks, since the nature of the possible intellect is known by its form, which is the intelligible species.

Thomas' argument that "species are received in [the intellect] in a wholly immaterial way" refers to the actualization of the possible intellect by the intelligible species. This act is an undergoing. The possible intellect is moved by the "agent object" that is the intelligible species. Once actualized, the intellect is in act, and its act is the act of understanding by which it forms the universal. So the intelligible species is the principle of the act of understanding, and the universal is the term of this act.

The act of understanding is a perfect act insofar as it remains in the agent as a perfection and does not pass into something external. "[I]n the action which remains in the agent, such as to understand and to will, . . . the form by which the agent becomes actual causes necessity in the action itself, since for its being nothing extrinsic is required as term of the action. Because when the sense is made actual by the sensible species, it is necessary for it to perceive, and in like manner, when the intellect is made actual by the intelligible species."[12] So when the intellect is made actual by the intelligible species, it is necessary that it understand. The form of the intellect in act and the act of understanding are always conjoined insofar as the action of the intellect necessarily follows upon this form. Not only does the act of understanding follow necessarily from the intelligible species, but it also takes its general classification or characteristics from these species.[13] Only a wholly immaterial species could bring about a wholly immaterial act—an act that is nót the act of any body. Again, only a wholly immaterial species could be received in a wholly immaterial mode. The nature of the act and the nature of the intelligible species that brings about the act must be relevantly similar. So this step in the argument depends upon the intelligible species (by which the possible intellect is actualized) being wholly immaterial or of the same nature as the act of receiving.

In this argument, however, Thomas does not clarify *how* we gain knowledge of the nature of the intelligible species or the mode of reception of this form. If this species can be shown to be wholly immaterial, then (since it is the form of the intellect in act) it is possible to account for the wholly immaterial act of reception—which act, Thomas maintains in the second step of his argument, is necessary to account for the production of the universal. But how are we to gain knowledge of the nature of the intelligible species? After all, Thomas is very clear that it is not the first and proper object of the intellect in act; it is that by which, and not that which, we understand. We only know it by a secondary act of reflection. We reason from the nature of the object to the nature of the act. The proper object of the intellect in act is the universal. So I now want to turn to Thomas' argument of what general characteristics the intelligible species must have in order to produce a universal.

Thomas makes this argument in his discussion of the union of the body and the soul in the *Summa Theologiae*.[14] Here, he maintains that the intellect is multiplied according to the number of bodies. One of the objectors argues that if every human being has his or her own intellect and a thing is received according to the condition of the receiver, then the species of things would be received individually. However, this is contrary to the nature of the intellect that knows universals.[15] Thomas' response is to argue that the issue here is not the *individuality* of the intellect or the species but rather the *immateriality* of the intellect or the species. Such individuality does not exclude knowledge of universals. Rather, he continues, it is "the materiality of the knower, and of the species whereby it knows, [that] impedes the knowledge of the universal."[16] The remainder of his argument is concerned solely with the immateriality of the intelligible species, which is also our concern here. And he argues for this immateriality from the fact that we know universals. The immateriality of the species, and the fact that it produces universals, is sufficient to deduce the immateriality of the intellect.

Let us, then, turn to the rest of Thomas' argument. He continues with the principle that is central to deducing the character of the intelligible species from the character of universals: "For as every action is according to the mode of the form by which the agent acts, as heating is according to the mode of the heat; *so knowledge is according to the mode of the species by which the knower knows*."[17] Thomas then applies this principle by comparing the knowledge produced by sensible forms with that produced by intelligible forms. And from the nature of the knowledge produced, we know the nature of the forms that are the principles of the act of cognition: "Now it is clear that common nature becomes distinct and multiplied by reason of the individuating principles which come from the matter. Therefore if the form, which is the means of knowledge, is material—that is, not abstracted from material conditions—its likeness to the nature of a species or genus will be according to the distinction and multiplication of that nature by means of individuating principles; so that knowledge of the nature of a thing in general will be impossible. But if the species be abstracted from the conditions of individual matter, there will be a likeness of the nature without that which make it distinct and multiplied; thus there will be knowledge of the universal."[18] Thomas has now argued from the nature of the universal to the nature of the intelligible species, which species is a likeness of an object. The intelligible species is "wholly immaterial" insofar as it is the likeness only of the nature of a material thing, without those things that make it distinct and particular. And it is only because it is such a likeness that it is capable of being the principle of an act that produces universals. That is, only because the intelligible species is wholly immaterial is it able to inform the intellect so that the intellect produces a universal that represents things in a wholly immaterial manner.

Once we have arrived at the nature of the intelligible species, it is straightforward to argue for the immateriality of the intellect as an entity. The nature of the species and the nature of the intellect that receives it become complementary notions. This can be shown in a number of ways. For example, in the above argument for the soul's subsistence, Thomas maintains that the species must be received in the intellect in a wholly immaterial way. This reception produces a wholly immaterial change. Further, a wholly immaterial form can produce such a change because only such a species can affect an immaterial entity,[19] and only an immaterial entity can undergo wholly immaterial change. The argument would then be seen to move from the nature of universals (object) to the nature of intelligible species (act),[20] and from the nature of the act to the nature of the intellect itself. So, Thomas can maintain that "an intellective principle of this kind is not composed of matter and form" but is a pure form without admixture of matter. And, since it is by the form that a thing has existence and the human intellect is pure form, then "the intellective principle by which a human being understands is a form that possesses existence." It then follows that "it is incorruptible" because matter is the principle of corruption insofar as it is in potential to contrary substantial forms.

Thomas summarizes the matter when speaking of the way that philosophers have usually argued for the immateriality of the human soul:

> Our mind cannot so understand itself that it immediately apprehends itself. Rather, it comes to knowledge of itself through apprehension of other things, just as the nature of first matter is known from its receptivity for forms of a certain kind. This becomes apparent when we look at the manner in which philosophers have investigated the nature of the soul. *For, from the fact that the human soul knows the universal natures of things, they have perceived that the species by which we understand is immaterial. Otherwise, it would be individuated and so would not lead to knowledge of the universal.* From the immateriality of the species by which we understand, philosophers have understood that the intellect is a thing independent of matter.[21]

Note that the knowledge of the nature of the intelligible species is inferred from the knowledge of the nature of the universal. This accords with Thomas' own method in his most prominent arguments for the subsistence of the human soul.

I want to turn back now to Thomas' inference from the nature of the universal to the nature of the intelligible species. With this step, he is attempting to argue from representative immateriality to ontological immateriality. He maintains that the only kind of form that is capable of producing a universal which represents immaterially is a form that itself exists immaterially—that is, a form abstracted from matter and material conditions. This latter form is the intelligible species that is the form of the intellect in act. And, recall, it is because this intelligible species is the likeness(es) of some determinate object(s) that the intellect is able to form the universals appropriate to the object(s). The intelligible species intrinsically shapes the character of the thought or, more accurately, is itself the intrinsic character of the thought. The intelligible species is *produced* in order to perform this function. When the intellect is in act, the intelligible species characterizes the intrinsic features of our thought, much as a naturally existing form characterizes the intrinsic features of the thing it informs. But then to argue from the immateriality of universals to the immateriality of the intelligible species is to infer from the way our thoughts *represent* to the *intrinsic* qualities of our thoughts. As noted earlier, this is akin to arguing that because I am thinking of the redness of my wife's car, my thought itself is red. Thomas confuses the way our thoughts represent with the way they exist, and so he commits something like a category mistake in inferring from one kind of immateriality to another.

Thomas himself distinguishes between the mode in which the intelligible species exists and the way it represents. In another context, he rejects the notion that wholly immaterial species can only represent immaterially. Let us look at Thomas' argument, as well as an interpretation of it, as an entry into a consideration of a series of possible objections against my argument. When arguing that angels and God know singulars, Thomas maintains that the way a form exists and the way it represents can be *different*. That is, the intelligible species exists immaterially in an angel or God, but it can represent a material thing.[22] So Thomas does, in some contexts, distinguish between the way a form represents and the way it exists in the knower. They need not be the same. An immaterial intelligible species can produce knowledge of a singular material thing. So why is it that with the human intellect, the mode of existence and the mode of representation must coincide?

Thomas maintains that the reason why the intelligible species of angels and God can represent individual material things is that these species are the causes of, rather than being abstracted from, these material things. Because human beings must abstract the intelligible species from the phantasms of individual material things, they must be abstracted as universal, and so wholly immaterial, forms. This, then, seems to be a promising route to argue for the immateriality of the intelligible species independently of the nature of the universal. It can, seemingly, be argued for on the basis of Thomas' general metaphysics and its attendant account of human knowing. If this can be done successfully, we may have the needed bridge between the representative immateriality of the universal and the ontological immateriality of the intelligible species. Or, perhaps, we simply have an alternative route to the nature of the intelligible species that does not depend upon arguing from the nature of the universal.

Let us see how such an argument might unfold. Matter cannot act. Form acts. Therefore, only forms can act on the cognitive organs. Forms, however, do not convey information about particulars, since things are particularized by matter. Therefore, the intelligible species by which we understand, being a form, can only give rise to universal knowledge. However, it is because they must be stripped of matter in order to act, to be the agent object of the possible intellect, that these intelligible species are wholly immaterial. We can then go on to argue for the immateriality of the intellect from the nature of these species. Since we did not have recourse to the representative immateriality of the universal in our own argument, then the critique articulated above is irrelevant. On this reading, Thomas does not, or at least need not, argue from the immateriality of universal to the immateriality of the intelligible species. Rather, it is because matter cannot act that the intelligible species by which the intellect is in act must be immaterial.

Let us recall that "an intellective principle of this kind is not composed of matter and form, because species are received in it in a wholly immaterial way. This is made clear from the fact that the intellect is concerned with universals, which are considered in abstraction from matter and from material conditions."[23] With regard to the nature of the intelligible species, this argument might be interpreted as follows: The intellect is pure form because the species by which it knows are wholly immaterial, since they are received immaterially. Now, the fact that the intellect is concerned with universals is simply an indication that the intelligible species are wholly immaterial. This fact itself is argued independently from Thomas' general metaphysics.

There are, however, several problems with this interpretation. First, Thomas' argument clearly does take the immateriality of the universals as its starting point and so as *evidence* for the immateriality of the act of the intellect. Second, the notion that forms do not convey information about particulars is called into question when we consider the fact that the senses know particulars by way of form. Independent of an argument from the nature of the universal, it is only with the *presupposition* of an immaterial, subsistent intellect that the intelligible forms become wholly immaterial. This is so because only such forms, devoid of matter and the conditions of matter, can act on an immaterial entity. Obviously, however, we cannot presuppose that the intellect is an immaterial entity since that is what we are trying to argue for. This interpretation also falls prey to the fallacy of moving between the ontological and the representative levels of immateriality without any middle term. This time it is in the other direction. This interpretation is committed to the presupposition that wholly immaterial forms can only represent immaterially or as universals. One still needs to know why this is so.[24]

Still, one might argue that we obviously do know universals and, on Thomas' theory of cognition, human knowledge is derived from particular material things; so, given these two premises, the intelligible species by which we know must be wholly immaterial. That is, in order to have universal knowledge derived from particular things, we must abstract from materiality, which is the principle of individuation. Insofar, this seems right. And, the argument concludes, to do so requires that the form or the shape or the character (that is, the intelligible species) of the thought itself must be immaterial. It is not clear how this conclusion follows. Why could a wholly material thought process not represent things in the world in terms of universals, namely, as immaterial? This is not to say that this is, in fact, the case, but it is to say that Thomas seems simply to assume, and not argue, that this cannot be the case. That is, he assumes that the intrinsic character of thought must literally resemble the representative qualities of thought. This assumption is troubling for many of the same reasons that Thomas himself found troubling the Platonists and the materialists' use of the principle, "Like is known by like."

There are further objections to my argument. First, perhaps the argument for the immateriality of the soul has been misconstrued above. Thomas, it might be said, is arguing directly from the object to the nature of the operation or activity of understanding, and so the nature of the intelligible species can be left out of the discussion, at least initially. Again, and this is the second counterargument, perhaps this argument can be understood to infer directly from the nature of the universal to the nature of the intellect without recourse to either the nature of the act of understanding or the nature of the intelligible species. Third, Thomas maintains that the principle and the term of an action must be of the same nature, so that the intelligible species and the universal must be of the same nature. Therefore, one can infer from the nature of one to the nature of the other. And fourth, if the apprehending in question is material, then only singulars can be represented. Since the intellect knows universals, intellectual apprehension must be wholly immaterial.

Let us examine these propositions in more detail. First, perhaps the nature of the intelligible species is not needed for Thomas' argument, or perhaps this nature can be deduced from the nature of the activity. The argument would then proceed from the nature of a universal representing the world in an immaterial manner to the immateriality of the activity and then on to the immateriality of the intellect as an entity. This latter inference is reasoned on the basis of the fact that only an immaterial entity could have an immaterial act, where this simply means an act that is executed independently of any body. With regard to the first inference, one might argue from the fact that Thomas maintains that the act receives its species (or specification) from its object.[25] And if the object of an act is a universal, then this object is immaterial. Therefore, the act itself must be immaterial. There are some tricky issues here, including what is the object of the act of understanding (the universal or the intelligible species) and what it means to claim both that the act receives its species from its principle and from its object. But however the details of this inference are worked out, it runs into the same problem as the inference from the nature of the universal to the nature of the intelligible species. Let us recall that the act of understanding is an ontological reality constituted determinately by its form, just as the thing known is constituted determinately by its form. The problem is precisely how to get from representative immateriality to ontological immateriality. Leaving out the nature of the intelligible species does not resolve this problem but leaves it precisely as it was. Why does the representative immateriality of our thoughts entail that our thinking is itself immaterial? If I am thinking of an orange basketball, am I then thinking orangely?

Second, perhaps we can leave out arguing from the universal to either the act of understanding or the intelligible species. Then the debate would be construed as going from the nature of the universal to the nature of the intellect, with the step, "species are received in it in a wholly immaterial way," referring to the nature of the intellect. That is, the intellect must be such that it can receive a form in a wholly immaterial way, and only an immaterial entity can do this. The problem is that if we want to know *why* the form must be received in an immaterial way, then we are back to arguing from the universal to the act of understanding or the immaterial species. Further, if Thomas were to argue directly from the immateriality of the universal as representative to the immateriality of the intellect as an entity, there again seems to be the blatant fallacy in going from one kind of immateriality (representative) to another (ontological) without any suitable middle term. Why would ontological or entitative immateriality follow on merely representative immateriality? Why does the fact that the intellect represents things in an immaterial fashion, or as stripped of particularity, imply that the intellect that entertains these universals is immaterial as an entity? The kinds of immateriality under discussion are of two different orders, and so one wants to know *why* one kind (immateriality of universal as representative) has any implications for the other (immateriality of intellect as an entity). At any rate, interpreting Thomas' argument in this manner (as arguing directly from the nature of the universal to the nature of the intellect) seems wrongheaded. Thomas says time and again that knowledge of the nature of the intellect is gained only by moving from object to act, from act to powers, and from powers to essence.

Third, one might argue, as Thomas does, that the term of an act must be proportioned to its principle, as heat is to something hot. Therefore, the intelligible species must be immaterial since the universal is immaterial. This analogy, however, does not work because whereas the agent and the patient are hot in the same way in the first example, the immateriality of the intelligible species and of the universal are of different orders. Therefore, the comparison fails. It sidesteps the issue by asserting without argument that the universal and the intelligible species are relevantly similar.

Fourth, one way of asking for the middle term that sustains the move from representative immateriality to ontological immateriality is to ask, as I did above, "Why could a wholly material thought process not represent things in the world in terms of universals, namely, as immaterial?" Thomas, or an advocate for him, might respond that this could not be the case because when apprehending is material, the representation is singular.[26] The argument might go something like this:

1) If the apprehending is material, then the intentional content is singular.
2) The intentional content of intellectual apprehending is universal, not singular.
3) Therefore, intellectual apprehending must not be material.

The first premise, then, might be considered the middle term that is generally suppressed in Thomas' formulations. That is, material apprehension can only bring about representation of singulars. Then, since the intellect knows only universals, intellectual apprehension must be wholly immaterial. The problem is that this first premise begs the question. Although sensitive apprehension may be material, this premise requires that a material apprehension be sensitive. Only with this requirement does it follow, given Thomas' account of sensitive apprehension, that the intentional content of the apprehension must be singular. This argument simply repeats the same fallacy of moving between the properties of the ontological and the representative without any suitable justification. It leaves the original question unanswered since we want to know why material apprehension can only represent things materially or as singulars. This argument, however, may offer us some insight into why Thomas commits the fallacy of moving so fluidly between the representative and ontological levels of immateriality, and I shall return to it in my concluding remarks.

Before closing this section, I want to look at another version of Thomas' argument from universals as well as an argument based on the intellect's capacity to know contraries. Examining these arguments allows us to explore further the fallacy articulated above and the way it pervades many of Thomas' central arguments for the soul's subsistence. Let us consider the following version of his argument from universals:

Whatever is received into something is received according to the condition of the recipient. Now a thing is known in as far as its form is in the knower. But the intellectual soul knows a thing in its nature absolutely: for instance, it knows a stone absolutely as a stone; and therefore the form of a stone absolutely, as to its proper formal idea, is in the intellectual soul. Therefore the intellectual soul itself is an absolute form, and not something composed of matter and form. For if the intellectual soul were composed of matter and form, the forms of things would be received into it as individuals, and so it would only know the individual: just as it happens with the sensitive powers which receive forms in a corporeal organ; since matter is the principle by which forms are individualized.[27]

Let us lay out the steps in this argument:

1) Whatever is received into something is received according to the condition of the recipient.
2) A thing is known in as far as its form is in the knower.
3) The intellectual soul knows a thing in its nature absolutely.
4) Therefore, the form of a stone absolutely, as to its proper formal idea, is in the intellectual soul.
5) Therefore, the intellectual soul itself is an absolute form, and not something composed of matter and form.

Two crucial premises for this argument are: step 1, "whatever is received into something is received according to the condition of the recipient"; and step 2, "a thing is known in as far as its form is in the knower." Thomas goes on to argue in step 3 that "the intellectual soul knows a thing in its nature absolutely." As the next sentence in his argument makes clear, he simply means here that the intellectual soul knows universals, that is, it knows a stone as a stone. In step 4, "therefore the form of a stone absolutely, as to its proper formal idea, is in the intellectual soul." From steps 1 and 4,[28] Thomas concludes that "therefore the intellectual soul itself is an absolute form, and not something composed of matter and form" (step 5). That is, a form is received into the human intellect "absolutely" or, one might say, wholly immaterially (and wholly immaterial or universal knowledge is produced). Therefore, given that "whatever is received into something is received according to the condition of the recipient" (step 1), the human soul itself must be an absolute form. Only such a form is capable of receiving another form absolutely.

Although Thomas does not do so here, it is an easy move from step 5 to the conclusion that the human soul is incorruptible. For example, he could argue that an absolute form, or a form capable of receiving another form in such a manner that knowledge of universals is produced, has an operation in which the body does not share. Whatever has its own operation has its own existence. Therefore, the human soul is a form that possesses existence. And since matter is the principle of corruption, the human soul, which is without such matter, must be incorruptible.

The key, in my judgment, is step 4: "therefore the form of a stone absolutely, as to its proper formal idea, is in the intellectual soul." The form referred to here is the intelligible species. This is apparent both from the fact that step 2 must be referring to the intelligible species since it is by this form that the intellect is in act, and from the fact that Thomas goes on to compare the form received in the intellect with the sensible species received in the senses. (Note that it can only be the sensible species because the senses do not form any other conception. There is no "agent sense.") The only appropriate form to compare to the sensible species is the intelligible species.[29] That there must be a form in the intellect in order for knowledge to occur follows from Thomas' general theory of cognition that the cognizer in act is the cognized in act. But to know what kind of cognizer it is, one must know what kind of form it receives. This form becomes the form of the cognitive faculty; and so, in knowing the nature of the form, one knows the nature of the cognizer.

Step 4 claims that this intelligible species is an absolute form, a pure form, which means that it is without any admixture of materiality or material conditions. It is a purely immaterial form, a purely formal one. A form of this kind characterizes the intellect in act and becomes the form or shape of our thought. But how does Thomas reason to this conclusion? From the fact that we know universals, and universals, are themselves absolute forms or are purely immaterial. As step 3 says, "the intellectual soul knows a thing in its nature absolutely: for instance, it knows a stone absolutely as a stone." But this is the fallacy that has been pointed out above. Thomas infers from the fact that what we think is an immaterial representation of things to the conclusion that our thinking is itself immaterial. Where is the middle term that justifies Thomas' inference from the content of our thought to the intrinsic nature of our thought (and so of the intellect itself)?

Perhaps one might object that the first step, "whatever is received into something is received according to the condition of the recipient," could be interpreted to provide this middle term. I have interpreted it to mean that since the intelligible species is wholly immaterial and we know universals, then the recipient of the intelligible species must itself be wholly immaterial. But perhaps it could also be understood to mean that since the intelligible species represents the thing known in a wholly immaterial fashion (that is, in terms of universals), then the recipient of the intelligible species must itself be wholly immaterial. If this were the case, then there would be no need to bridge the gap between the intelligible species and the universal. They would both represent universally. But the problem then becomes, Why do we need the additional operation of forming the inner word? More fundamentally, this interpretation again simply begs the question. If the intelligible species represents things immaterially but is itself material, then the conclusion that the intellect is immaterial does not follow since an immaterial entity cannot be affected by a form of matter or an individual form. If the intelligible species represents things immaterially and is itself immaterial, then the conclusion that the intellect is immaterial does indeed follow. But we are still left with our question: What is the relation between the representational immateriality and the intrinsic immateriality? That is, our original problem is left untouched. The nature of the soul, in this case, would not be argued to but simply posited.

I want now to demonstrate that this problem is present in another prominent type of argument for the incorruptibility of the human soul. Thomas' argument for the incorruptibility of the soul on the basis of its capacity to receive contrary forms as not subject to contrariety, or as not mutually incompatible, is found in numerous places in his works. Let us consider the following version of this type of argument: "Granted even that the soul is composed of matter and form, as some pretend, we should nevertheless have to maintain that it is incorruptible. For corruption is found only where there is contrariety; since generation and corruption are from contraries and into contraries. Wherefore the heavenly bodies, since they have no matter subject to contrariety, are incorruptible. Now there can be no contrariety in the intellectual soul; for it receives according to the manner of its existence, and those things which it receives are without contrariety; for the notions even of contraries are not themselves contrary, since contraries belong to the same knowledge. Therefore it is impossible for the intellectual soul to be corruptible."[30]

This argument depends upon Thomas' understanding of corruption and generation being brought about by the reception of contrary forms. To be contraries, forms must be *capable of existing* in the same subject but must not be *able to exist together* in that thing. Something is corrupted (and something else generated) by the reception of a different substantial form. Since it is by the substantial form that something is and is what it is, then to receive a different substantial form naturally entails that one thing is corrupted and another thing is generated. (Something is corrupted in a relative manner, or changed relatively, by the reception of an accidental form.) In order to receive a contrary form, a being must be in potency to contraries. Since it is matter that is in potency to diverse substantial forms, Thomas argues that it is matter that is the principle of corruption. Heavenly bodies, which are material, are incorruptible because they are not composed of elements; and the matter they do possess, unlike the matter of earthly bodies, is in potency to only one form.[31] So heavenly bodies are not in potency to contraries because of the special matter of which they are composed.

Unlike heavenly bodies, the intellect is in potency to that which are contraries in themselves. However, it is in potency to them in such a manner that they are not contraries in the intellect. Whatever exists in the intellect exists intentionally and so in a manner that does not contract matter so that it becomes like the naturally existing form of the agent. (We cannot here argue in terms of the immateriality of the intellect as an entity since that is what we are trying to demonstrate.) Contraries corrupt precisely because they contract matter in a way that is incompatible with the continued existence of the original substance. Such forms are not contraries when existing intentionally. As Thomas says, "the notions even of contraries are not themselves contrary, since contraries belong to the same knowledge."[32] That is, the notions or concepts of contraries are not contrary to one another. In fact, one contrary can become a fruitful source for the knowledge of its contrary, which I take is what Thomas has in mind in another rendition of this argument: "one contrary is the intelligible ratio of the other, since one is understood through the other."[33] The idea that one contrary is the basis for knowing the other is founded on the notion that "of two contraries one is always a lack or privation of the other."[34] The mind knows the contrary that is a privation by knowing the contrary that is the perfection, so it knows evil by good, black by white, cold by hot. The notion that one contrary is known in terms of the other serves to emphasize that, in the intellect, those things which are contraries in their natural existence are so far from contraries in their intentional, intelligible existence that one is even known in terms of the other.

Seemingly, this argument for the soul's subsistence trades on the fact that forms can have different types of existence—intentional and natural—and that intentionally existing forms cannot be contrary in the natural sense, which contrariety causes corruption. But the problem is that the senses are composed of matter and form and yet, like the intellect, receive contraries intentionally. While the sense of touch may not be able to experience, say, hot and cold at the same time in the same place, this is because natural change accompanies the intentional change for this sense. In the case of sight, however, contraries are received without any material change, so sight sees contraries, say, white and black, simultaneously. Likewise, hearing can presumably listen to at least some contraries simultaneously.

Yet the senses, as composites of matter and form, are corruptible. Insofar as the senses are corruptible, they are in potential to contrary forms *as contrary*. And it seems apparent that the senses are, in fact, corruptible. For example, a person may lose the sense of sight by exposure to a light of too great an intensity. So the contrary forms that are not contrary in the senses—that is, those that they receive intentionally—must be limited, and the senses must be in potency to receive contrary forms naturally as well. Thomas' point, then, seems to be that the intellect is not in potency to receive any forms naturally and so cannot be corrupted. Insofar as contraries are rendered intelligible, they are no longer contraries capable of corrupting. Thus understood, the argument is not only about receiving forms in an intentional manner but also about the extent of this reception. The intellect, but not the senses, is in potency to receive any and all forms of material things in a purely intentional manner.

The problem with this argument is that this conclusion does not follow directly from the premise that natural contraries are not contraries in the understanding. Thomas maintains that "there can be no contrariety in the intellectual soul; for it receives according to the manner of its existence, and those things which it receives are without contrariety; for the notions even of contraries are not themselves contrary, since contraries belong to the same knowledge. Therefore it is impossible for the intellectual soul to be corruptible."[35] But this is to skip between the representative and the ontological with no suitable middle term. That is, to argue that all contrariety is far removed from the *nature* of the intellect because of the way contraries are *understood* is, at least on the face of it, to infer from the representative to the ontological without any argument as to why they should be literally the same. Why should the fact that our intellect represents one contrary in terms of another imply that the nature of the intellect itself is such that it is "far removed" from all contrariety?

In this case, the problem involved in inferring directly from the representative to the ontological can best be seen through considering the fact that the restriction to forms that are known (or knowable) seems a priori to rule out the possibility of there being any form contrary to the form of the intellect. This would be akin to saying that if we restrict our consideration of forms to those that the eyes can see, then there are no contraries to the sense of sight. Thomas' response would be, of course, that limiting forms to what can be known is no restriction at all since the intellect is in potential to be *all* material things, insofar as it is assimilated to their natures. Restricting the sense of sight to what can be seen would be a severe restriction on the forms to which sight is in potency since, as material organs, the eyes are also in potency to receive forms naturally.

Still, it is not the forms that inform the possible intellect so that it becomes the intellect in act that are in question here. Of interest in the discussion of the incorruptibility of the intellect are the forms that might be contrary to the form that is the intellect. These are not forms that would themselves be understood since they would cause the destruction of the intellect. That is, the issue is not whether or not contraries are contrary *in* the intellect. Rather, the issue is whether there is some form that is contrary *to* the intellect. To put it another way, we cannot, without begging the question, presuppose that the intellect is not in potency to receive forms naturally. One might reply that the forms of material things cannot act directly on what is immaterial, so that indeed the only forms that are under discussion are those that do, or can, inform the possible intellect. The response to this objection is that the immateriality of the intellect must be demonstrated and so cannot be assumed.

If Thomas could use this argument in such a way as to demonstrate the soul's immateriality, then indeed it would be justified to say that the soul is in potency only to intentional forms. Perhaps the argument can be so understood. One might argue something like the following: The intellect is in potency to all contraries and so not destroyed by any of them *if* we understand the intellect in such a way that it is in potency to becoming all things (insofar as it is assimilated to the form of the thing, and so becomes formally identical with the thing). This concerns the intellect's capacity consciously to relate to universals because the object of the intellect is the nature of a thing known. Thomas would then have open to him the route of going from the nature of the universal to the nature of the intellect. The problem is that to construe the argument in this way is to reduce it (like the argument from the soul's potency to all material natures) to an argument from the soul's capacity to know universals. As we saw, that argument also infers from the representative to the ontological with no suitable middle term.[36]

Both the universal and the intelligible species are intentional forms insofar as they only have mental existence and do not contract matter. But Thomas' theory of intentionality fails properly to distinguish between a form's representative nature and its ontological nature, or the way a form represents and the way it exists. Thomas argues that because a universal represents in an immaterial fashion, the form by which a universal is produced must exist in an immaterial fashion. Insofar as he seeks to argue from the immateriality of the universal to the immateriality of the act or the intelligible species, and hence to the immateriality of the intellect as an entity, his argument fails. It seeks to infer one kind of immateriality (ontological or entitative) from another (representative) that is clearly of a different order. Thomas does not, and perhaps cannot, justify this move. With this failure of Thomas' most prominent arguments for the soul's subsistence, a significant barrier to the direct moral consideration of non-rational creatures falls away.

Material and Immaterial Entities

In this section, I sketch a position intended to demonstrate that the flaw in Thomas' arguments is systemic rather than accidental. That is, I do not believe that one can successfully find, or finally even provide, a middle term for Thomas.

If the existence of immaterial entities that are intellectual is *presupposed*, or, similarly, if the validity of the distinction between material and immaterial entities is presupposed, then this presupposition can serve to legitimate the move between representative and ontological immateriality. I suggest that Thomas takes it as more or less apparent that wholly material apprehension can only represent singulars or be sensitive because he presupposes the existence of immaterial entities that are intellectual. If there are such entities, then intellectual apprehension (that is, apprehension of universals) must be wholly immaterial, and vice versa. Wholly material apprehension, then, can only be sensitive (and so of singulars). My primary argument in the remainder of this section is that Thomas' presupposition is unwarranted.

There is an ontological (and epistemological) gulf in Thomas' metaphysics between material and immaterial entities. Our knowledge begins with material things, from which we form the phantasms that are the basis of intellectual knowledge. We naturally know only the natures of material things and anything we can reason to from these. Therefore, Thomas argues that we cannot directly know the essences of immaterial entities. "Both [the active and the possible] intellects, according to the present state of life, extend to material things only, which are made actually intelligible by the active intellect, and are received in the passive intellect. Hence in the present state of life we cannot understand separate immaterial substances in themselves."[37]

Still, despite our need to begin with material things, Thomas argues that we can know that immaterial entities exist. He maintains that created immaterial entities exist on the basis of his understanding of the divine will in creating the universe and the goodness of creation. As Thomas says, "What is principally intended by God in creatures is good, and this consists in assimilation to God Himself. And the perfect assimilation of an effect to a cause is accomplished when the effect imitates the cause according to that whereby the cause produces the effect; as heat makes heat. Now, God produces the creature by His intellect and will. Hence the perfection of the universe requires that there should be intellectual creatures."[38] He goes on to argue that such creatures must be immaterial because intelligence is not the action of any body.

As noted, even if we can know that such creatures exist, we cannot directly know the essences of such creatures. But, Thomas argues, "[W]e cannot know *that* a thing is without knowing in some way *what* it is, either perfectly or at least confusedly."[39] So, given that there are created intellectual substances, from the standpoint of logic that considers concepts in themselves, we can know that they belong to the same logical genus as other creatures insofar as their essence differs from their existence. That is, we can know that they belong to the logical genus of substance because

they are created, even if we cannot directly know their particular properties. But because they are incorruptible, or because they are immaterial,
from the standpoint of natural philosophy or metaphysics (which considers things as they exist in reality), created intellectual substances must belong to a different genus than corruptible and material substances, from
which they differ essentially.[40] As Thomas puts it, "Created immaterial substances, . . . even though from the viewpoint of logic they share the same
remote genus of substance with sensible substances, from the viewpoint of
physics they do not belong to the same genus, as neither do heavenly and
terrestrial bodies. For the corruptible and the incorruptible do not belong
to the same genus."[41] With regard to the extracognitive reality of a naturally
existing thing, material and immaterial substances do not belong in the
same genus.

This leaves the intellectual soul in a peculiar position. It is the form of a
body, and it is capable of intellectual knowledge. Insofar as it has the power
to represent things in the world in terms of universals, it shares a cognitive
power with immaterial substances or angels. And insofar as it shares a cognitive power (an essential attribute) with immaterial substances, it must itself be, in some sense, an immaterial substance. From the standpoint of the
actual existence of things, there is no genus that includes both material and
immaterial substances because they differ essentially.[42] Therefore, any substance that shares the essential attribute of understanding with immaterial
substances must itself be in the same genus. (The fact that the intellectual
soul is also the form of the body simply means that it gains its intellectual
knowledge through the senses, whereas other intellectual substances are
not subject to this limitation.) As an immaterial entity, the intellectual apprehending of the human soul must be wholly immaterial. So, if we assume the existence of immaterial entities, then the gap between representative and ontological immateriality is bridged.

Thomas' discussion of the need for immaterial, intellectual creatures for
the perfection of the universe, however, has little force against an argument
that questions the very *possibility* of the existence of forms without matter,
or the validity of the distinction between material and immaterial entities.
To one questioning whether it is possible to make sense of the notion of
subsistent forms, or the distinction between material and immaterial entities, the reply that they are necessary for the perfection of the universe
evades the question.[43] The question itself can be seen as an implied critique

of this understanding of the perfection of the universe. If the very notion of subsistent form is problematic, then far from an argument for the existence of such creatures based on the value of creation, the problematic nature of this notion of subsistent form calls into question the cogency of this understanding of value in creation. But one might well question the cogency of the distinction between material and immaterial entities (or the possible existence of immaterial entities) because, for instance, it implies or presupposes the cogency of the claim that there can be material and immaterial creatures in metaphysically differing meanings of the word "creature." Since there is no more general category in which these metaphysically diverse "creatures" can be placed, how can they be compared? Or, perhaps more to the point, how can both be the object of thought? Or, again, is not the distinction meaningless since there is no category, no basis in reality, that the distinction itself can be made? I take the fact that Thomas never felt the need to offer a sustained argument for the existence of created immaterial entities as an indication that he never doubted the existence of immaterial entities that are intellectual. In essence, he takes it as a given that such creatures exist, and so he takes it for granted that the distinction between material and immaterial entities—entities that differ metaphysically—is legitimate. But he has provided little basis for crediting this distinction, and there are good reasons to question it.

In turn, this fundamental distinction in Thomas' metaphysics between material and immaterial entities serves to legitimate the move from representative to ontological immateriality, but only on the assumption that immaterial entities exist. Or, to say the same thing, this move between representative and ontological immateriality is legitimated only on the assumption that the distinction between material and immaterial entities itself is valid. If Thomas can demonstrate that the human soul is an immaterial entity, then he will have redeemed the distinction that divides his metaphysics into material and immaterial entities. But this demonstration itself depends, I have argued, finally on the assumption that this distinction is valid, or that immaterial entities that are intellectual actually exist. That is, Thomas needs to demonstrate that the intellectual soul is an immaterial entity in order to establish the validity of his distinction between material and immaterial entities. And he needs to assume the validity of this distinction in order to demonstrate that the intellectual soul is an immaterial entity.

An immediate objection to the above position is that Thomas' arguments for the existence of God offer an independent source for establishing the legitimacy of the distinction between material and immaterial entities. Insofar as these arguments are successful, then Thomas has demonstrated the validity of the distinction between material and immaterial entities since, on his metaphysics, God can only be wholly immaterial. Then his demonstration that the human soul is an immaterial entity would be likewise successful. But the problem is that these arguments for God's existence must also assume, and thus cannot demonstrate, the possibility of immaterial subsistence. An extended consideration of why I believe this to be the case would take us too far afield, so the brief discussion of Thomas' theistic proofs that follows should be viewed only as the barest outline of the argument needed to sustain my point.[44]

Thomas maintains that we can speak positively and univocally of God's essence only with the gift of faith. For example, only by faith do we know that God is Triune or omnipotent.[45] With natural reason, Thomas argues that we can speak of God's essence either negatively or analogically. We cannot know God as God is in God's self because of our mode of knowing. Still, through the use of reason, God's *existence* can be demonstrated from God's effects that are known to us. Thomas offers five arguments, proceeding from things that are evident to our senses—motion, the nature of efficient causation, contingency, the gradation of things in the world, and the design or governance of the world—to the conclusion that God exists. Thomas then goes on to assert that God is *ipsum esse subsistens* and so wholly immaterial. For example, in the proof that starts from motion and argues to God as the Unmoved Mover, Thomas maintains that because there is motion (understood as the reduction of potency to act) in the world, there must be a first being that is completely actual without any potentiality. This is so because, in the reduction of potency to act, actuality is absolutely prior to potency since something potential is reduced to actuality only by something actual. Therefore, the first mover must be completely actual, and hence immaterial, simple, and so forth.

Let us look more closely at Thomas' explanation of how humans can know God through reason. This account is essential because only in this way can we know what Thomas means when he calls God the First *Cause* or the Unmoved *Mover*. While Thomas' discussion of analogicals in his *Summa Theologiae* mentions such predicates as "wise" and "good," analogical predication must also extend to the predicates used in the proofs because these are positive predicates of God known through reason.[46] If the predicates in the proofs are not analogical, then the only other options on Thomas' account are that they are sheerly negative or based on faith. In his *Summa contra Gentiles*, he says explicitly that they are based on reason and not faith.[47] And if they are sheerly negative, then that would be to say that he has not, in fact, proven anything. Therefore, these predicates must be analogical.

Now, let us turn to Thomas' account of analogical predication. We can gain knowledge of God through creatures, but (setting aside the way of negation) whatever is said of God and creatures is said according to the relation of a creature to God as its principle and cause, wherein all perfections of things preexist. For Thomas, to say "God is wise" does not mean that "God is the cause of wisdom in things." Rather, these names, applied to God essentially and preeminently,[48] signify not only that God is the cause of wisdom and of goodness but, more important, that these attributes exist in God in a more excellent way. The perfections flow from God to creatures. If we say "Socrates is wise," we mean that Socrates has that property which in God is called wisdom. So with respect to what the terms signify, God is the primary analog and creatures are the secondary analog. But we do not know perfections as they exist in God because we do not know the divine essence. So, given our mode of knowing, we first know the meaning of terms from creatures. Therefore, with respect to what the terms mean, or how we use them, creatures are the prime analogs and God is the secondary analog. Ontologically (in reality) the terms apply first to God, but epistemically (in our mode of knowing) the terms apply first to creatures.

Given this disjunction between what and how the terms signify, and since we cannot know that being which is the prime analog with respect to what the terms signify, we can ask, How does Thomas know that there is *any* being to which the perfections of creatures apply most eminently? How does he know that his entire theory of analogy is not simply empty without any prime analog with respect to what the terms signify, or any secondary analog with respect to how the terms signify? Thomas would almost surely answer that the proofs for God's existence have settled this question. The proofs demonstrate the existence of one who is completely actual, the Unmoved Mover. His theory of analogical predication of God, then, presupposes the success of the proofs.

In looking again at the proofs, I use the proof from motion as an example. Here, Thomas proceeds negatively to the conclusion that the existence of motion in the world (which is evident to our senses) means that there must be an Unmoved Mover, who is without potentiality. But if the proof is actually to prove the existence of a Mover, then it cannot be sheerly negative. "Unmoved Mover" must itself include an analogical predicate because "Mover" is a positive predicate; there is some Mover that moves and yet is itself unmoved. So the proofs seem to presuppose that we can use terms analogically to refer to God. But now we have a vicious circle. The proofs presuppose that we can speak analogically about God, and to speak analogically about God presupposes that we can prove that God exists.

Analogical predication fails to yield any positive information about God because it is built on a metaphysics that posits two fundamentally different kinds of entities, to which predicates cannot be applied univocally. One kind of entity is *actus purus* or *ipsum esse,* and the other kind is a composite of act and potentiality or being by participation. That these are fundamentally different is confirmed when Thomas asserts that "being" in application to God and creatures is itself an analogical term.[49] If this fundamental divide can be sustained, then, a fortiori, the divide between immaterial and material entities is also sustained. But this fundamental divide cannot be sustained because Thomas cannot identify the relation between the two kinds of entities except by speaking analogically, and analogical speaking assumes that the relation between the primary and secondary analogs is independently understood. The possibility of understanding the relation independently of analogy is excluded because "being" in application to God and to creatures is itself analogical; that is, the two kinds of entities are fundamentally or metaphysically different. The point is that *some* positive univocal predication of God must be possible in order for *any* meaningful predication to be possible.

If the proofs for the existence of God fail (because they presuppose that we can speak analogically of God, but to speak analogically of God presupposes the success of the proofs), then using them to demonstrate the validity of the distinction between material and immaterial entities also fails. If this distinction cannot be validated, then the move between representative and ontological immateriality cannot be legitimated. Therefore, Thomas' most prominent demonstrations that the human soul is a subsistent form fail because they rely on this move between different levels of immateriality.

Thomas attempts to forge an anthropology that integrates both Aristotelian and Platonic elements in an effort to validate what he takes to be central Christian claims about the human being: namely, that we are a real
union of body and soul and that our soul is immortal. I have argued that
he fails to show the compatibility of these two strands. The soul, as the
form of the body, needs the body to fulfill its own proper function, which
is to understand. It understands by abstracting phantasms from material
things. Because it is the form of the body (and so needs the body in order
to fulfill its own proper function), Thomas cannot demonstrate that it is an
immaterial entity (and so immortal). That is, because the soul only knows
directly the natures of material things, Thomas cannot finally demonstrate
that the soul knows that it is itself an immaterial entity. The epistemology
that follows on the soul being the form of the body precludes an argument
demonstrating that the soul is an immaterial entity. Insofar, this claim becomes a mere assertion. Thomas' attempt to jump the chasm by moving
directly between the representative and the ontological fails. With that failure, his conception of the human being is shown to be philosophically untenable. And since this anthropology is untenable, its attendant vision of
the end times is called into question. With this critique, Thomas' fundamental moral divide between human beings and non-rational creatures
can no longer be legitimated.

Because of the problems entailed by Thomas' anthropology, and especially by the divide between material and immaterial entities, in the next
part of the book I seek to develop a more adequate and robust anthropology, one that draws on a metaphysics that finds such a divide untenable.
Thomas uses the human capacity consciously to relate to universals to
argue for both the utterly unique (among material creatures) *telos* of the
human being and the freedom/slavery dichotomy between human beings
and other creatures. The alternative anthropology that I propose in chapter 5 eschews these conclusions because the neoclassical metaphysics on
which it is based holds that all creatures are related to universals and so are
in some measure free and that all creatures truly share a common *telos*. As
we shall see, with this anthropology the chasm between human beings and
the rest of material creation falls away, and all creatures have some degree
of moral worth.

PART III

The Unity and Moral Worth of All Creation

In this third part of the book, I present a viable alternative to Thomas' understanding of creation and the place of human beings therein. My goal in chapter 5 is to present an alternative conception of the human being, and of creatures generally, that avoids the problems in Thomas' account and accords all creatures some measure of moral worth. This alternative conception of creatures is informed by an alternative metaphysics, developed primarily by Alfred North Whitehead some six centuries after Thomas, which finds untenable any ontological divide between human beings and other creatures. To do this, I present the outline of a value hierarchy as well as show how an alternative understanding of God and God's relation to the world is central to this value theory.[1]

In chapter 6, I summarize some of the central insights of this value theory for an ecological ethic. I also demonstrate that this value theory yields rich fruit for those concerned with the current ecological state of the created world (as well as the long-term trends that seem to ensure its continual, and indeed accelerating, ecological decline). This value theory offers a justifiable rationale for why it is our moral obligation to protect the well-being of other life and ecosystems. In this chapter, I enter the contemporary conversation in ecological ethics in order to demonstrate that this value theory is more robust and philosophically sound than two of the current leading theories of the intrinsic value of non-human creatures and ecosystems, those articulated by Holmes Rolston III and J. Baird Callicott.

Chapter Five

An Alternative Metaphysics

To clarify the parameters of what I will be addressing in this chapter, let us consider the following series of conditionals that act as a bridge from the previous chapters to the present one. If one seeks to develop an ecological ethic that accords moral worth to non-rational creatures (for example, because such an ethic reflects the reality of creaturely existence), then Thomas' project is not viable as a constructive alternative today. That is, Thomas' understandings of the human soul and of divine providence systematically exclude the possibility of according moral worth to non-rational creatures. If one seeks to develop a Christian theological ethic, and if one believes that Christianity itself demands an ethic in which all of God's creatures are accorded moral worth, then Thomas' project is not viable as a constructive alternative. And if the critique of Thomas' understanding of the human soul detailed above is convincing, then the viability of using his work constructively is undercut since his understanding of the human soul justifies, in large measure, his strict instrumentalization of other creatures to the human good.

I believe that all creatures do, in fact, have some degree of moral worth and that in Christianity, God is properly understood to love and to care for each and every creature for itself.[1] I find the resources of the neoclassical metaphysical tradition helpful to articulate and defend the convictions that all creatures have moral worth and that God is truly affected by—indeed, truly loves and cares for—the world.

Let me turn now to a more detailed discussion of the overlap and divergence between Thomas and Whitehead. Under the influence of the philosophical critique of the possibility of engaging in the enterprise of metaphysics as well as the massive modern technological success built upon the ever-expanding ability of the natural sciences to explain (in terms of efficient causation) the world around us, a modern consensus has developed that rejects the notion of final causation as a factor in the causing of things. The work of both Thomas and Whitehead stands in sharp contrast to this consensus. They share the belief that all things have a final cause or are determined in some respect by a purpose, end, or *telos*.

However, the difference between these thinkers in understanding how things are determined by their final cause is crucial to the current discussion. For Thomas, non-rational creatures must be moved to their *telos* by another—and finally a rational—being. Only rational creatures are self-caused, or *causa sui*, because only they can consciously entertain universals and so can consciously entertain and choose among alternative possibilities for the future. While this does not necessitate the strict instrumentalization of non-rational creatures, it does lend itself to such instrumentalization. And when this understanding of how a creature is moved to its final cause is coupled with Thomas' understanding of the rational soul as uniquely suited for the final perfection of the universe, such instrumentalization becomes all but inevitable. This instrumentalization is of a piece with Thomas' understanding of divine providence in which non-rational creatures are thought to be cared for not for their own sakes but for the sake of rational creatures. Indeed, the very purpose of the existence of non-rational creatures is to serve the human good.

For Whitehead, *every* creature is self-caused, or *causa sui*. Every creature moves itself to its own *telos*. And every creature is in some measure free and creative. The difference between human beings and other creatures is a matter of degree rather than of kind. Though so far as we know, only human beings are capable of being consciously aware of our relation to universals or possibilities, on this metaphysics, *all* creatures do, in fact, relate to universals or possibilities. With this assertion, a decisive break is made with any metaphysics that posits an ontological divide between human beings and the rest of creation. Not only are the grounds for morally segregating human beings from other creatures undermined, but also positive grounds (that is, creaturely creativity) are given for understanding all creatures to have value in and for themselves, for according moral worth to all creatures.[2]

The decisiveness of the break between these two thinkers is put into still sharper relief when we consider not only *how* creatures reach their *telos*, but also the *nature* of that *telos*. For Thomas, this *telos* is the actualizing of potentialities inherent in a given nature. In actualizing its potentialities, a creature becomes properly related to other creatures, enhances the perfection of the universe so that it reflects the divine goodness to the extent possible, and becomes more like God, who is pure actuality. It is in this sense (a creature becoming more like God and contributing to the perfection of the whole) that God is the *telos* of the universe. No creature could actually contribute to the divine reality itself because the divine reality is wholly perfect and contains all the possible perfections of being. God is *ipsum esse subsistens, actus purus*. Further, there is a duality of the final ends of creatures in Thomas' account insofar as, among material creatures (or, more precisely, among "mixed bodies"), only human beings enjoy the final and unchangeable perfection of the universe, when all changeable things will pass away.

For Whitehead, the *telos* of creatures is to maximize creativity or, what comes to the same thing, to realize beauty both for their own subjective enjoyment and for the relevant future. Creatures thereby contribute to God's experience, which encompasses and includes all creaturely experience. Like Thomas, every creature is to actualize its potentialities to the extent possible. Unlike Thomas, in so doing, every creature makes a real contribution to the divine life. All creatures already share in the same *telos*, though each contributes to it according to its own capacities. There can be no ultimate duality of final ends. All creatures contribute here and now to God's experience, and it is this divine experience that finally secures creaturely value.

I want now to submit a brief roadmap of this chapter. In the first section, my goals are to introduce some basic concepts from Whitehead's metaphysics, offer an initial characterization of what he takes to be the metaphysically fundamental units of reality, and provide the rationale for why this metaphysic is attractive as an alternative to Thomas for building an ecological ethic. After introducing Whitehead's project, I show that there is only one generic kind of final real thing in his metaphysic. There can be no ontological divide between human beings and other creatures. All metaphysically fundamental entities, all true individuals, are "subjects" and as such have intrinsic value. Subjectivity characterizes all levels of reality, and so the world cannot be divided into subjects and objects, slaves and free, principals and instruments.

In the second and third sections, I lay the groundwork for an ecological ethic by developing a value hierarchy and then showing how God's relation to creatures ultimately secures the value and meaning of the world. I conclude by summarizing the basic issues that are central for building the foundation of an ecological ethic.

Reality as Unitary and Suffused with Value

Let me turn now to a cursory exploration of Whitehead's metaphysics. He contends, "[T]he final problem is to conceive a complete fact. We can only form such a conception in terms of fundamental notions concerning the nature of reality."[3] A "complete fact" is whatever it is that exists in the complete sense. It is the logical or linguistic equivalent of the ontological "final real things," the building blocks of which the universe is composed. Whitehead conceives of final real things, the ultimate ontological unit of existence, atomistically; they are the microscopic building blocks of reality. His favored terms for these final real things are "actual entities" or "actual occasions."[4] Descartes, Whitehead explains, uses the term "*res vera*" in the same sense that Whitehead uses the term "actual." As Whitehead says, "It means 'existence' in the fullest sense of the term, beyond which there is no other."[5] Thomas uses the term "substance" or "first substance" to designate this reality. And just as accidents exist only in a dependent sense in Thomas' metaphysics, so, too, in Whitehead's, do things (such as thoughts, universals) other than actual entities exist in a dependent sense. "Actual occasions," he states, "form the ground from which all other types of existence are derivative and abstracted."[6]

Final real things are concrete in the sense that all other things that are real must either be composites of them, constituents of them, or abstractions from them.[7] And since *anything* at all must either be a composite of, a constituent of, or be abstracted from that which exists in a complete sense, the metaphysical problem is the attempt to determine the nature of the complete fact. To identify the nature of an actual entity is to identify those characteristics that apply to all actual entities and so to have developed a metaphysical scheme. Since all metaphysical characteristics are exemplified by all possible or actual existents, then the presence of any one characteristic implies the presence of all the others. Put another way, since metaphysical characteristics are all necessary or completely universal, the formulation of any one of them implies the formulation of all the others.[8] That is to say, we could formulate an entire metaphysical scheme by working out all the implications of any statement that truly designates a metaphysical characteristic.[9] Whitehead calls the requirement of mutual implication "coherence," which, for him, "means that the fundamental ideas, in terms of which the scheme is developed, presuppose each other so that in isolation they are meaningless."[10] A coherent metaphysical scheme is one in which the fundamental ideas or ultimate notions employed are mutually implicative. Since metaphysical characteristics must be mutually implicative, then an exemplification of one must be an exemplification of all. These metaphysical characteristics identify different aspects, or different ways of considering, the one thing that exemplifies them.

In the present context, the most important point in this brief characterization of Whitehead's metaphysical project is this: There can only be one generic kind of actual entity. All actual entities, as the final real things of which the universe is composed, exemplify metaphysical characteristics. Since to exemplify one is to exemplify them all, then these actual entities must have the same generic nature. As Whitehead summarizes, "'Actual entities'—also termed 'actual occasions'—are the final real things of which the world is made up. There is no going behind actual entities to find anything more real. They differ among themselves: God is an actual entity, and so is the most trivial puff of existence in far-off empty space. But, though there are gradations of importance, and diversities of function, yet *in the principles which actuality exemplifies, all are on the same level*."[11] All actual entities exemplify the same metaphysical characteristics.[12] This is what it means to say that all actual entities have the same generic nature. All creatures, and even God, belong to the same genus insofar as all actual entities exhibit the same metaphysical characteristics.[13]

If a coherent metaphysical scheme is one in which the principles in terms of which the metaphysics is developed presuppose one another, then incoherence is "the arbitrary disconnection of first principles."[14] For Whitehead, any ontological divide between human beings and the rest of creation is untenable because it is finally incoherent. Thomas' metaphysics has two generic kinds of final real things—material entities, and immaterial entities—and so is dualistic. His distinction between material and immaterial substances indicates that the metaphysical term "substance" finally has no univocal meaning or has two meanings. In his discussion of Descartes' dualism, Whitehead speaks in terms that apply equally to the dualism of Thomas, "Neither type requires the other type for the completion of its essence."[15] This ontological divide renders the metaphysical scheme incoherent. Material and immaterial substances differ generically and do not presuppose one another. Since there is no more basic category in terms of which such entities can be conceptualized, they both cannot truly be the object of thought. One type must merely be the sheer negation of the other, and sheer existential negation cannot be the object of thought because there would be no object for the thought to be about. Whitehead's reasoned rejection of such a divide means that his own metaphysical system preserves the ontological continuity between human beings and other creatures.

Let us now consider Whitehead's understanding of these final real things. Recall that, for Thomas, species are like numbers in the sense that if one considers a given species, then by adding an essential attribute one changes the species under consideration. The essential attributes of any member of any given species must be unchanging. The primary substance that is the actual, existing member of a given species may also undergo accidents that modify the substance, but these do not enter into the definition of the thing. These primary substances are, for Thomas, the ultimate ontological units of existence. They are unchanging in their essential natures. It is this notion that is fundamentally challenged by Whitehead's metaphysics.[16] Rather than presupposing an enduring subject that encounters a datum or directs an operation, Whitehead "presupposes a datum which is met with feelings, and progressively attains the unity of a subject."[17] The datum is felt and directed toward an organism not yet fully concrete that will be the outcome of integrating the datum. It is this process of meeting the datum and integrating it into one final "satisfaction" that is the actual entity. It is this droplet of experience that is really real. "The actualities of the Universe are processes of experience, each process an individual fact."[18] As Charles Hartshorne states, "a particular person or thing, enduring and changing through time, is really a kind of low-level universal, compared to the momentary states or events in which alone the individual is fully concrete and actual."[19] This momentary event is the actual entity that Whitehead takes to be metaphysically fundamental. Actual entities, in Whitehead's metaphysics, essentially reverse the substance paradigm;

instead of an enduring subject that encounters data, there is a process of meeting and integrating the data. It is this process that is metaphysically fundamental. In what follows, I will address this general idea from a couple of different angles.

Whitehead seeks the most concrete entities conceivable because only these can form the building blocks of the universe. He concludes that these building blocks, these final real things, can only be momentary experiences. "The final facts are, all alike, actual entities; and these actual entities are drops of experience, complex and interdependent."[20] If you consider a moment of experience in your own life, you encounter an actual entity. It is complex and interdependent because it is influenced by all the moments or drops of experience that precede it, and it anticipates its influence on the moments that come after it. Roughly, actual entities in the process of becoming are the present drops of experience of every entity in the universe.

Actual entities are drops of experience that perish upon achieving complete determination, upon unifying the data into one felt content. This determination is the aim or final cause of the actual entity. The process is directed toward the organism as superject. This process is the becoming of an actual entity.[21] The key point here is that the "being" of an actual entity is its "becoming."[22] This becoming exists in the full sense and is the central concern of metaphysics. Whitehead summarizes his view: "The ancient doctrine that 'no one crosses the same river twice' is extended. No thinker thinks twice; and, to put the matter more generally, no subject experiences twice."[23] No subject/superject could ever experience twice because it is itself a moment of experience. The subject might be seen as the actual entity in the process of becoming. The superject is what that subject aims to become. But to put it this way is artificially to separate the subject and superject. The subject is the particular droplet of experience that it is because of what it inherits from the past *and* because of what it aims to become (the superject).[24] Substance metaphysics, by concentrating attention on the outcome of the process, does not have the resources to analyze the process itself and so cannot truly penetrate to the nature of things, or, finally, cannot truly explain such things as causation, inferences from the past, or change.

Having gained some initial flavor for what Whitehead seeks to convey when he uses the term "actual entity," I want to turn to his more detailed

analysis of these final real things. As we will see, a primary aim of Whitehead's metaphysical scheme is to overcome duality so that reality at its very
core is characterized by valuation.

Whitehead maintains, "The first analysis of an actual entity, into its most
concrete elements, discloses it to be a concrescence of prehensions, which
have originated in its process of becoming. All further analysis is an analysis of prehensions."[25] An actual entity is a "concrescence" of "prehensions"—
hardly a transparent statement. Webster's dictionary defines concrescence
as "a growing together."[26] Whitehead uses the term to describe how a drop
of experience coalesces into being, how "becoming" hardens into "being,"
how the many become one.[27] "'Concrescence,'" he states, "is the name for
the process in which the universe of many things acquires an individual
unity in a determinate relegation of each item of the 'many' to its subordi-
nation in the constitution of the novel 'one.'"[28] The many things in the universe of an actual entity are united into a complex unity in the concrescence
of that entity. When we speak of an instance of concrescence, we are speaking of an actual entity. They are one and the same. An instance of concrescence *is* an actual entity.[29]

If an actual entity is the "growing together" of "prehensions," what are
"prehensions"? Webster's dictionary defines prehension as "the act of taking hold, seizing, or grasping." An actual entity, then, is a growing together
of the acts of taking hold. What these acts of taking hold indeed take hold
of, in the first instance, are past actual entities, which are the data for the
novel concrescence. Whitehead calls past actual entities, the "actual world"
of the concrescing actuality. So the data for any instance of concrescence
are the actual world of that actual entity. There are both positive prehensions, termed "feelings," and negative prehensions, which are said to "elimi-
nate from feeling." If data are positively prehended or felt, they pass "from
the objectivity of the data to the subjectivity of the actual entity in question."[30] They are included as a positive contribution to the subject's own
real internal constitution. And if data are negatively prehended or elimi-
nated from feeling, they are excluded from contributing to the subject's
own real internal constitution.[31]

It is not only important whether data are negatively or positively prehended, but it is also important how they are negatively or positively
prehended. The "subjective form" of the data is a way of expressing the
point that there is no such thing as bare data. They are is always prehended
with some subjective form, or "feeling-tone." Whitehead holds that "there

are many species of subjective forms, such as emotions, valuations, purposes, adversions, aversions, consciousness, etc."[32] Both negative and positive prehensions affect the subjective form of the datum. It is difficult to overstress the centrality of this notion of the subjective form in this metaphysics.

One of the most significant, misleading, and pervasive errors in philosophical thought is, Whitehead holds, the notion that "the primary activity in the act of experience is the bare subjective entertainment of datum, devoid of any subjective form of reception."[33] According to this notion, the qualities given in the sense experience of a human are bare data—green, sweet, pain—which, in themselves, are simply given, value-neutral, without emotional tone. To be sure, proponents of this view understand that these qualities are often connected with values and emotional tones, but such a connection is understood to be a subsequent, subjective response to what was initially entertained without response. There is, on this understanding, a difference in kind between first, the qualities given in sense experience; and second, emotional tone. Much of Whitehead's work is dedicated to the refutation of this view, and his own metaphysics is developed as an alternative that purports to make better sense of the full range of human experience as well as to accord better with contemporary science.[34]

Primitive feelings have both an object and an emotional tone. Indeed, it is because of this dual aspect of the word "feeling" that Whitehead finds it a helpful synonym for positive prehension. As he says, "the word 'feeling' has the merit of preserving this double significance of subjective form and of the apprehension of an object."[35] Whitehead argues that his analysis of feelings is consistent with the best evidence of psychology and science. He "attributes 'feeling' throughout the actual world, [and] bases this doctrine upon the directly observed fact that 'feeling' survives as a known element constitutive of the 'formal' existence of such actual entities as we can best observe."[36] Those observable entities, say, an atom or the dominant entity in an animal or plant cell, all respond to their environment. This indicates that they feel the environment in the sense that they take in its content both as objective datum and in a certain way.

Let us now consider Whitehead's characterization of actual entities or concrescing actualities as "subjects of experience."[37] As we will see, this understanding is integral to Whitehead's attempt to overcome the duality between subject and object insofar as every actual entity has *both* subjective and objective poles. His argument that all actual entities are subjects of experience begins with a discussion of the "subjectivist principle" accepted by Descartes and David Hume as well as by most subsequent philosophers. The subjectivist principle is that "the datum in the act of experience can be adequately analyzed purely in terms of universals."[38] It is often coupled with Descartes' "subjectivist turn," which is the claim that "those substances which are the subjects enjoying conscious experiences provide the primary data for philosophy, namely, themselves as in the enjoyment of such experience."[39] So the primary data for philosophy are the subject enjoying conscious experiences, and the data of these experiences can be adequately analyzed purely in terms of universals.[40]

Whitehead argues that the subjectivist principle, rigorously adhered to, leads to "solipsism of the present moment." And it is only by the introduction of covert inconsistencies that philosophers adhering to this principle have avoided this conclusion. Indeed, this is a conclusion to be avoided because it so clearly and obviously collides with common sense, which is inflexibly objectivist. Nevertheless, the subjectivist principle as articulated above cannot avoid such a conclusion. If the bare entertaining of universals is taken as our most basic experience, then there is no escape from solipsism. The qualities that we perceive do not, of themselves, tell us that there are any other substances in the world. If they are taken as the ultimate data of experience, then all we have is the subject alone with her perceptions.[41] Further, since universals do not refer to the past or future, this solipsism is of the present moment.

Although the subjectivist principle presupposes the substance philosophy rejected by Whitehead, the subjectivist turn articulated by Descartes[42] is one that Whitehead calls the greatest philosophical discovery since the age of Plato and Aristotle.[43] He makes a form of this principle basic to his own metaphysics. As he puts it, "philosophy is limited in its sources to the world as disclosed in human experience."[44] Both Whitehead and Descartes agree, then, that the world as disclosed in human experience is the primary data for philosophy. But Descartes, because he interprets human experience in substance/quality terms, must interpret what is disclosed as mere qualities and thus as universals, with the ultimate consequence being solipsism of the present moment. Whitehead argues that this consequence is avoided by making "relation to other actuality" the meaning of "enjoyment of experience." By generalization from conscious experiencing, other actualities are also characterized by such relations.

Whitehead starts with human subjectivity and seeks to develop a metaphysical system that characterizes all things. He strips away all characteristics that are not shared by other entities (such as rationality, consciousness, sentience, life), with the goal of arriving at those characteristics (that is, metaphysical characteristics) that truly make up all final real things. He holds that "any doctrine which refuses to place human experience outside nature, must find in descriptions of human experience factors which also enter into the descriptions of less specialized natural occurrences."[45] He then tests the results for their adequacy; they must characterize all conceivable experience. In approaching metaphysics in this manner, Whitehead reverses the usual approach of starting from the characterization of things in the world and then seeking to show how the metaphysical categories developed include human subjectivity. This approach frequently leads to the disastrous mind/matter dualism.

In generalizing from the actual entity that is an act of human subjectivity to the nature of all actual entities, we can ask: What is the conceivable nature of all actual entities such that acts of human subjectivity are among them? Phrasing the question this way (and indeed taking human subjectivity as our starting point) entails that there not be two generic classes of actual entities in accord with the requirement of coherence. Actual entities must be described in such a way that they include all final real things, including acts of human subjectivity. Given this, the metaphysical nature of actual entities must be such that they are either constituted by internal relations to others or are not constituted by internal relations to others. But "not constituted by internal relations to others" is ruled out because human subjectivity is not an instance of such non-relativity. Therefore, all actual entities must be constituted by relations. To be constituted by relations is to be the subject of experience because experience simply is "the way in which one actual entity is qualified by other actual entities."[46]

If Whitehead endorses the turn to the subject as the most promising place to begin the metaphysical inquiry, he also holds that "Descartes' discovery on the side of subjectivism requires balancing by an 'objectivist' principle as to the datum for experience."[47] The primary data for experience are not universals, but actualities. It is the past world, actualities that have completed their concrescence, that provide the initial data for the experiencing subject. Whitehead maintains that one metaphysical characteristic of all actual entities is that they have the potential to be an element in a real concrescence of the many entities into one actuality.[48] This is the metaphysically basic "principle of relativity." That past actual entities enter into the constitution of a concrescing actual entity is the objective side to the experience of an actuality. The real world enters into the constitution of every entity, so every actual entity is a potential for "'objectification' in the becoming of other actual entities."[49] Here, objectification refers to the particular mode in which one actuality is realized or becomes an object for another actuality. As Whitehead summarizes, "The 'objectifications' of the actual entities in the actual world, relative to a definite actual entity, constitute the efficient causes out of which *that* actual entity arises."[50]

As noted, Whitehead holds that every concrescing actuality is a subject. "The way in which one actual entity is qualified by other actual entities is the 'experience' of the actual world enjoyed by that actual entity, as subject."[51] So every actuality is a subject, and what it experiences is being qualified by other actualities. What are disclosed in the experience of a subject are other subjects, so there is no solipsism of the present moment. In sum, Whitehead maintains that "subjective experiencing is the primary metaphysical situation which is presented for metaphysical analysis,"[52] and that this experience is "the way in which one actual entity is qualified by other actual entities."[53] And this leads to the *reformed subjectivist principle:* "Apart from the experiences of subjects there is nothing, nothing, nothing, bare nothingness."[54]

Understanding actual entities as subjects of experience is one of the most startling, and finally one of the most fruitful, features of Whitehead's thought. This subjectivity concerns not only the fact of receiving something from the world but also the fact that the one experiencing must subjectively integrate these data from the past in order to become one thing. All actual entities are similar to acts of human subjectivity insofar as they are constituted by relations to the past and integrate these data into a unity. That these relations must be integrated is clear from the fact that they cannot integrate themselves. None of the many data could cause the synthesis of itself that is the concrescing subject. The many data cannot cause the "one" that is the unification of the data because this one is in addition to the many. Once we hold that actual entities are atomic, as they must be for anything to become; and we grant the readily apparent fact that things do become or that change is real, then the conclusion that they are acting agents seems inescapable. Subjects are agents. They unite the data received and thereby condition the world to come after them. It is this role of conditioning that brings Whitehead to call subjects of experience "superjects." The notion of subjects only makes sense if, at the same time, they are also su- perjects because there must be some point, some goal, some *telos*, in ac- cord with which the data are integrated. Actual entities are determined not only by *efficient causation* (inheritance from the past) but also by *final cau- sation* (subjectively responding to and creatively synthesizing the inherited elements into one complex unity in accord with some purpose or *telos*).

Insofar as subjects are superjects, or subjects are agents, they must, in some sense, create themselves. "Creativity," Whitehead holds, "is the uni- versal of universals characterising ultimate matter of fact. It is that ultimate principle by which the many, which are in the universe disjunctively, be- come the one actual occasion, which is in the universe conjunctively. It lies in the nature of things that the many enter into a complex unity."[55] Crea- tivity introduces novelty into the world insofar as the many are unified into a novel entity other than the ones given disjunctively. "The many become one and are increased by one."[56] All actual entities combine the many fac- tors that they inherit into a unity.

To be a subject of experience is to be creative. As Charles Hartshorne puts it, "*To be is to create.*"[57] Since actual entities cannot be completely de- termined by what comes before them, they must be creative. Indeed, to be creative can be understood to mean simply incompletely determined in advance and in some measure responsible for completing oneself.[58] Every final real thing is self-creative, *causa sui,* and so enjoys some measure of freedom. Moreover, freedom *is* self-creation, whatever else it may be. Sub- jectivity, creativity, and freedom, then, are fundamental and closely related notions in Whitehead's metaphysics. This creativity and freedom form the basis for the claim that all creatures have moral worth, and it is in sharp contrast to Thomas' claim that only human beings are *causa sui,* and, fi- nally, for Thomas, that only human beings have moral worth.[59]

Still, even if it is conceivable that all actual entities are the subjects of experience and, indeed, if it is the only conceivable metaphysical option, it still rests uneasily with many people's understanding of reality. That is, some may find implausible the notion that subjectivity exists at all levels of reality regardless of the metaphysical arguments marshaled to defend the claim. So I want to take a moment to discuss in more detail the plausibility of this extension of subjectivity to all levels of reality.

One of the most ready charges made against Whitehead's metaphysics is that of anthropomorphism. Whitehead overcomes anthropocentric value theory through anthropomorphizing the rest of creation. That is, things

are understood to be independent centers of value because they are understood to be relevantly like human beings. But, the critic argues, that is
ridiculous. It is so implausible as to be fantastic. We have absolutely no
evidence that rocks (or plants or lower animals) are free or creative.

Let us stick to rocks because Whitehead's scheme seems most implausible at this level of reality. If Whitehead's understanding of subjectivity
can be made plausible here, then its application to all levels of reality becomes much less problematic. To all appearances, rocks are inert lumps of
stuff. Can Whitehead, or an advocate for him, seriously contend that rocks
enjoy freedom the way human beings do? The short answer is "no." Whitehead is not contending that rocks are creative. But that the actual entities
that compose rocks are subjects of experience and so enjoy *some measure*
of freedom and creativity, Whitehead takes as the only viable metaphysical
option.

Besides the metaphysical argument about the lack of alternatives, the
criticism has failed to attend to two major issues relevant to Whitehead's
contention. First, his analysis must be applied at the proper level, that of
microscopic actual entities and not of macroscopic entities. (After all, for
instance, the appearance that rocks are inert lumps of stuff has been found
by modern science to be deceptive; a rock is composed of molecules in vi-
olent agitation, which are in turn composed of still more basic particles.)[60]
Second, on Whitehead's ontology, there are degrees of freedom/creativity/
mentality, ranging from the negligible creativity of inanimate nature to the
relatively richer freedom of plants and animals to the immense wealth of
the rational freedom of human beings all the way to the incomparably rich
creativity of God. On this understanding, freedom and creativity (and so
subjectivity) do not require consciousness. Indeed, consciousness is merely
the tip of the iceberg that is freedom, creativity, mentality. Whitehead maintains that "consciousness presupposes experience, and not experience consciousness."[61]

Whitehead does not naively believe that the actual occasions of which
rocks are composed display discernible flashes of novelty. On the contrary, he holds that they "are merely what the causal past allows them to
be. . . . As we pass to the inorganic world, [efficient] causation never for
a moment seems to lose its grip. What is lost is originativeness, and any
evidence of immediate absorption in the present. So far as we can see, inorganic entities are vehicles for receiving, for storing in a napkin, and for
restoring without loss or gain."[62] The higher, originative phases of concres-

cence are "lost" in the sense that "so far as our observations go, they are negligible."[63] For the most part, the self-creation of actual entities at this level merely repeats what is given from the past, without gain or loss. As Whitehead puts it, "The process is a slave to the datum. There is the individualizing phase of conformal feeling, but the originative phases of supplementary and conceptual feelings are negligible."[64] To be a subject of experience does not require consciousness. Rather, it merely requires that the entity in question, the subject, unify diversity and is incompletely determined by its past.[65] Diversity is always unified and so creativity is always present, but for the lowest grade occasions it is negligible.

The two mistakes noted—that experience is confined to conscious experience, and that abstractions are taken for metaphysically ultimate existents—lead to the disastrous division between "mind" and "matter." When the issues are properly understood, then the real difference between "mind" and "matter" can be seen. As Hartshorne writes, "It is not an absolute difference in kind of singulars, but (a) a relative difference in kind (between high and low kinds) of experiencing singulars, *this difference falling within mind in the broadest sense*, plus (b) a difference in kind, not between singular and singular but between singular and inadequately apprehended group, the latter being irreducibly object rather than subject, and irreducibly abstract, since what makes it a single entity is its being objectified by subjects which in principle are richer in determinations than any of their objects, singular or compound."[66] The purported duality between "mind" and "matter" is either a relative difference between high- and low-level experiencing singulars, or a difference in kind between a high-level experiencing singular and an inert aggregate to which the singular is inappropriately compared. This is another way of summarizing the two common errors associated with the objection to the thesis that subjectivity characterizes all levels of creation.

There is an important distinction between true individuals, who are the subjects of experience, and mere aggregates, which are not. Rocks are not true individuals but composites of individuals or actual entities; such composites are less unified and individual than their parts. In contrast, the animal body is an immensely complex organization that coordinates the activities of subordinate individuals to enable the emergence of a higher-level, compound individual. Any true individual is an entity that seems "to respond as a whole with a degree of spontaneity to its environment,"[67] and it does not have the same properties if it is divided. Compound individuals have "a unity of experience over and above that of their constituents."[68] We might agree, then, that rocks are not subjects of experience. But this is because they are not true individuals but, rather, aggregates of actual entities whose activities are largely uncoordinated and so do not order the environment of the rock (say, in the way an animal body does).

One important implication of this expansion of subjectivity to all levels of reality is that all true individuals can now be understood to be intrinsically valuable and worthy of moral consideration. To be a subject is to be a center of experience and an agent that acts. Subjects can be said to enjoy experience in themselves and for themselves. Indeed, according to Whitehead, "experience *is* [the] complete formal constitution"[69] of a concrescing actuality. The value of an actual entity exists independently of any other experiencer's imputation of value. It is objective in this sense. Just as human beings are valuable as subjects who enjoy experience, so all actual entities are valuable as subjects who enjoy experience.

Understanding subjectivity as occurring at all levels of reality expands the realm of intrinsic value and moral worth to all these levels. Just as there is *no ontological divide* between human beings and other creatures, so, too (and for the same reason), there is *no moral bifurcation* between human beings and other creatures. Indeed, one of Whitehead's goals in developing his metaphysics is to do justice to "the poetic rendering of our concrete experience" of nature. He takes this poetic rendering as evidence that "the element of value, of being valuable, of having value, of being an end in itself, of being something which is for its own sake, must not be omitted in any account of an event as the most concrete actual something. 'Value' is the word . . . for the intrinsic reality of an event. Value is an element which permeates through and through the poetic view of nature."[70] Further, value characterizes the intrinsic reality of an actual occasion. It is the concrete experience of an entity as an end in itself. The attainment of value, the reaching an end, is the realization of something that exists for itself.[71] For one seeking to build an ecological ethic, the depth and clarity of Whitehead's analysis of the value of all creation, coupled with his numerous and incisive criticisms of substance metaphysics and his defense of the notion that droplets of experience are metaphysically basic, combine to make this metaphysics an attractive foundation for such an ethic.[72] Still, as we will see, the fact that all actual entities have intrinsic value and moral worth does not entail that all actual entities are equally valuable.

Let us turn our attention to a closer examination of the process of becoming, beginning with the initial phase. "The first phase," for Whitehead, "in the immediacy of the new occasion is that of conformation of feeling. The feeling as enjoyed by the past occasion is present in the new occasion as datum felt, with a subjective form conformal to that datum."[73] As noted, the subjective form of the feeling is *how* the datum is felt.[74] In the initial phase, the datum is felt by the prehending actual entity conformally, or the feeling of a past actual entity is felt in the same manner as it was felt by the past actuality. This continuity of subjective form is the initial sympathy of the prehending subject toward the datum prehended. "In conformal feelings the *how* of feeling reproduces what is felt. Some conformation is necessary as a basis of vector transition, whereby the past is synthesized with the present."[75] This initial phase of primitive feeling is at a far lower level than the sense perception, which involves complex integration of feelings and massive simplification. Rather than sense perception, at one point, Whitehead calls this phase "sense-reception."[76] In the initial, conformal phase of concrescence, the feelings are called "physical feelings," so this phase is called the "physical pole" of the actuality. The datum of a physical feeling is always another (past) actual entity. Physical prehensions are prehensions of actual entities or "prehensions whose data involve actual entities."[77] The past actual entity is "objectified" for the actual entity in concrescence, where this objectification "refers to the particular mode in which the potentiality of one actual entity is realized in another actual entity."[78] It is the functioning of one actual entity in the self-creation of another.[79]

The past of simple, low-grade actualities, say, those that compose a rock, is relatively impoverished in comparison to the past inherited by a complex, high-grade actuality, such as a human being. An act of human subjectivity is able to integrate a far greater diversity of data than is possible for a low-grade occasion. Therefore, for low-grade occasions, whose aim is basically to repeat the past, much more of the world must be negatively prehended. The objective data then are relatively simple. The richness or meagerness of one's past sets the limits of possibility for one's future, which is to say that it sets the limits on the diversity of data that can be integrated (and so positively prehended) in any moment of experience.

Though the concrescing entity may, in later phases, integrate and reintegrate the data given in the initial phase in complex ways, and even use them to form novel possibilities, the fact remains that the initial data place a limit on the range of these novel possibilities. Even within our human existence, all other things being equal, the richer one's cultural, educational, and religious background, the richer the possibilities for the future. The richer the past, the more open the future. The impoverished past of those actual entities comprising a rock means that there is no possibility for that rock to go on and "do great things." The possibilities in their future are overwhelmingly dominated by mere repetition.

As discussed above, the data do not integrate themselves, and so an active subject is needed to effect this integration. Such integration requires some aim or *telos* or purpose in accord with which the data are to be integrated. Whitehead calls this aim or goal or *telos* of the concrescing entity its "subjective aim." Though this aim may be modified in the later phases of integration (especially of high-grade entities), it is helpful to introduce this notion now because it is necessary to make sense of there being any concrescence at all, and because its analysis brings out a crucial aspect of God's relation to creatures.

A subjective aim constitutes the final cause or lure for feeling, "whereby there is determinate concrescence."[80] The subjective aim "controls the becoming of a subject"[81] since it is that which the entity is seeking to become. It is the reason that the data are integrated in the way that they are. There must be an aim for there to be integration. As such, the subjective aim must be present throughout the process of integration. The data must be integrated according to some goal or purpose.

The feelings in a given phase are integrated in order to achieve the subjective end for that phase.[82] That is, prehensions are not independent of each other. "The relation between their subjective forms is constituted by the one subjective aim which guides their formation."[83] The inherited or conformal subjective forms of feelings are modified in accord with the subjective aim of the concrescing entity.[84]

Whitehead characterizes the subjective aim that actual entities pursue as "intensity of feeling (a) in the immediate subject, and (b) in the relevant future."[85] The concrescing subject seeks to become *one* and seeks maximal *intensity*, or, as Whitehead also puts it, maximal *beauty*. The many data are unified in such a manner as to attempt to achieve maximal beauty, which is just to repeat that the data are unified in accord with the subjective aim. Intensity refers to the nature of an actual entity's enjoyment of experience.

The intensity of feeling involved in conscious experience, for example, is greater than that of non-conscious experience. A more intense, richer experience integrates a greater diversity of data in patterned contrasts. I will have more to say about "intensity" below.

Since concrescence only occurs if there is a subjective aim, a *telos*, then there must be a subjective aim given in the initial phase of concrescence. For Whitehead, this initial aim must come from God because otherwise there is no ground for order in the universe, for the coordination of purposes (and so activities) of countless actual entities. Absent God's aim, the result would be sheer chaos, which is impossible. Therefore, Whitehead posits a conception of God that is dipolar. Like all actual entities, God has a conceptual pole and a physical pole. The conceptual pole is God's "primordial" nature, our concern at the moment. We will look at God's "consequent" nature, or physical pole, below.

God's primordial nature is that which is eternal in God; it is his essential nature. It includes, for example, the fact that God is unsurpassable by another, God's omniscience (but not the content of his knowledge), God's necessary love for all creatures who have existed or currently exist (but does not specify which exist or have existed), God's necessary existence, God's necessary goodness, God's absolute reliability and unwavering pursuit of the *telos* of beauty. In short, it includes much of the traditional list of divine perfections, with some modification necessary because of the alternative metaphysics on which this conception is based.[86]

In the initial phase of concrescence, prehensions are felt *conformally*. Therefore, initially, God's valuation of the possibilities[87] is felt conformally or in the same manner as God. This is the initial aim of that subject, given to it by God. This exemplifies Whitehead's understanding of God as working through persuasion rather than coercion because this initial aim can be embraced as well as modified or, in some actual entities, rejected in later phases of concrescence (though this is most relevant to high-grade occasions). With God's valuation or grading of possibilities some are thought to be more desirable; they are "lures for feeling."

God's aim orders possibilities in terms of value. That is, God values possibilities in such a way as to encourage the emergence of ever more intense forms of subjective experiencing. It is God's subjective aim, God's purpose, that orders and unifies the realm of possibilities. Without this ordering, there would be no order and no novelty in the world. There would only be bare, abstract possibilities, without the lure for concrescing actualities.[88]

God's valuation is felt in the initial phase of any concrescing actuality. With this gift of an initial aim, the prehending entity receives an appetition, a desire, for self-constitution that fulfills God's aim for maximal beauty or intensity of experience. The relevance of the possibility depends upon the past of the actuality in question. If this past is relatively disordered, then the only possibilities relevant will largely replicate the past. If this past is massively ordered, say, through an animal body, then the possibilities open to it will be far more significant. But in every case, the living immediacy of an actual occasion originates with the reception of an initial aim from God.

Gradations of Creaturely Value

I want now to focus on the "mental pole" of an actual entity. Before beginning our analysis, it bears mentioning that such a mental pole is mental in the broad sense that any actual occasion is the subject of experience that pursues a subjective aim, and in doing so is *causa sui;* every actuality is self-creative. Not only do actualities receive from the world (initial phase), but they also respond to it (supplementary phases). All actualities decide *how* to respond to the world. In making this (perhaps non-conscious) decision, they are deciding among possibilities to pursue. This requires valuation, and valuation can only be understood as a mental operation. As Whitehead puts it, "The mental pole introduces the subject as a determinant of its own concrescence. The mental pole is the subject determining its own ideal of itself by reference to eternal principles of valuation autonomously modified in their application to its own physical objective datum."[89] To repeat, this understanding of mentality does not entail that every actual entity enjoys consciousness or sensuous experience. Conscious and sensuous experience is only the tip of the iceberg. Experience extends much more deeply and broadly. Creatures may merely enjoy non-conscious, non-sensuous experience. In the lowest grades of actuality, the mentality is trivial, and the actuality merely repeats the past in thoughtless aesthetic adjustment.

I want here to introduce Whitehead's conception of the order of nature, where this includes gradations among actual entities and his understanding of "societies" as productive of this gradation. This further analysis will

enable us to understand in more detail the basis of value, or intrinsic goodness, in Whitehead's metaphysics as well as the relative ordering of goodness among diverse kinds of creatures.

Whitehead maintains, "[W]e discern four grades of actual occasions,
grades which are not to be sharply distinguished from each other. First,
and lowest, there are the actual occasions in so-called 'empty-space'; secondly, there are the actual occasions which are moments in the life-histories
of enduring non-living objects, such as electrons or other primitive organisms; thirdly, there are the actual occasions which are moments in the life-
histories of enduring living objects; fourthly, there are the actual occasions
which are moments in the life-histories of enduring objects with conscious
knowledge."[90] While not precisely the same, we might note the similarity
between Whitehead's distinctions between these grades of actual occasions
and Thomas' distinctions between inanimate objects, vegetables, and animals. There are, however, certain differences.

First, and for our purposes the least important, Whitehead adds the category of "actual occasions in empty space." Second, Whitehead sees continuity where Thomas sees discontinuity (or differences in essence). This is
especially the case when we consider the discontinuity or generic difference between immaterial substances and material substances in Thomas'
thought. For Whitehead, not even God differs generically from other actual entities. The third difference is Whitehead's distinction between "living" and "conscious" rather than "vegetable" and "animal." Presumably,
some animals, say single-cell organisms, lack consciousness. The bound-
aries are difficult to draw in any case, and Whitehead sees the difference
between plants and animals as less significant than that between life
and consciousness. Fourth, Whitehead views the actual occasions as "moments" rather than themselves enduring objects. This, as we have seen,
is the crux of the difference between process metaphysics and substance
metaphysics. (We might note that the actual occasions that Whitehead is
concerned with here are those that "dominate" a given enduring object,
wherever such domination occurs. The passages that follow this schema
make that clear.)[91] Finally, other than entities in empty space, these actual
occasions are moments "*in* the life-histories of enduring objects" of one
sort or another. These enduring objects (which are Thomas' "primary substances") are what Whitehead calls "societies," and it is because of the order
provided by these societies that the actual entity in question can have the

intensity of experience that it does. In other words, the integrative (and perhaps reintegrative) phase of concrescence is what it is because of the society that orders (or is the order of) the environment of the actuality in question.

Let us consider what Whitehead means by society and how these societies affect the experience of diverse actual entities. He uses the term "society" to specify the order existing among actual entities. Societies have a "defining characteristic," which Whitehead maintains is akin to Aristotle's understanding of "substantial form."[92] This is helpful because it explains how the objects of our everyday experience fit into Whitehead's metaphysical scheme. These objects are groupings of actual occasions, each of which exemplifies a common element of form. Furthermore, Whitehead argues, a society is self-sustaining because the reproduction of the common form is due to the relations between the actualities that make up the society.[93] In sum, a society is an environment with some element of order (for its members) that persists because of the relations between its own members.[94]

Reality is composed of layers of social order. No society exists in isolation. According to Whitehead, "Every society must be considered with its background of a wider environment of actual entities, which also contribute their objectifications to which the members of the society must conform."[95] The background environment contributes the general characteristics that a specialized society presupposes for its members. So every society needs a social background, of which it is a part. The widest societies— the extensive continuum, the geometrical society, and the electromagnetic society—cannot provide adequate order for the production of individual actual occasions with peculiarly intense subjective experiences. For this, more specialized societies are needed because these societies are the vehicles of such order.[96] As Whitehead maintains, "The most general examples of such societies are the regular trains of waves, individual electrons, protons, individual molecules, societies of molecules such as inorganic bodies, living cells, and societies of cells such as vegetable and animal bodies."[97] And here we come to those societies presupposed by Whitehead's grading of actual occasions. Presupposing the most general kinds of societies, we can now turn to those that are of interest in this chapter.

Whitehead holds that the everyday things we see around us are societies: "The real things that endure are all societies. They are not actual occasions."[98] As we have had occasion to discuss, substance metaphysics has been thwarted by its confusion of "societies with the completely real things which are the actual occasions. A society has an essential character, whereby it is the society that it is, and it has also accidental qualities which vary as circumstances alter."[99] This allows us to see in greater detail why Whitehead calls taking societies as the final real things an example of "the fallacy of misplaced concreteness." Substance metaphysics confuses a society, which is a complex composition of actual entities, with the actual entity itself. A society is an abstraction from that which is most concrete. Taking societies as metaphysically fundamental can only result in confusion, such as the confusion that ontologically separates "mind" from "matter" or cannot truly account for change or yields solipsism of the present moment.[100]

As noted, what societies contribute to an environment is order. Indeed, that is what a society is—an environment with some degree of order for its members.[101] But "the evocation of intensity,"[102] not the establishment of order, is the final goal or *telos;* it is God's aim at beauty. Mere order could be stultifying and involve trivial repetitiveness. Still, as Whitehead says, "The intensity of satisfaction is promoted by the 'order' in the phases from which concrescence arises and through which it passes; it is enfeebled by the 'disorder.'"[103]

Let me now offer a brief sketch of the meaning of "intensity of subjective experience" and how this notion relates to societies, order, and novelty. Whitehead's treatment of the notion of intensity is complex, and I shall not attempt to give a complete rendering of it.[104] That which is intrinsically valuable is subjective experience. This value is aesthetic, with "beauty" understood as "the mutual adaptation of the several factors in an occasion of experience."[105] These factors must be adapted or harmonious, which is to say that they must be unified. So far, this says nothing more than beauty is unity in diversity or the unifying of diversity. All experience unifies diversity, and, insofar, all experience has some degree of beauty, some degree of aesthetic value.

Great aesthetic value requires not only harmony but also intensity, which depends upon contrasts.[106] Whenever diverse data are unified, there is a real synthesis of the elements into a single feeling. This synthesis, now a single thing, is a contrast. And the feeling is infected with "the individual particularities of each of the relata,"[107] which enhances its richness. In the simplest case, there will be only two relata. But far richer experience arises from unifying much more complex data. The wider the diversity of data that is integrated, the more complex the contrasts, the richer the aesthetic experience, the more intense the subjective experience, the greater the aesthetic beauty, the more open the future, and the greater the intrinsic value.

Novelty is also essential to intense subjective experience. As Whitehead puts it, "Spontaneity, originality of decision, belongs to the essence of each actual occasion. . . . Freshness, zest, and the extra keenness of intensity arise from it. In a personal succession of occasions the upward path towards an ideal of perfection, with the end in sight, gives a thrill keener than any prolonged halt in a stage of attainment with the major variations completely tried out. . . . Each occasion in a society of occasions, and more particularly each occasion in a personal society seeks this zest by finding some contrast between Appearance [or possibility] resulting from the operations of the mental pole and the inherited Realities of the physical pole."[108] Intensification of experience depends upon enhanced functioning of the mental pole because this allows for the formation of the novel possibility that a concrescing occasion might seek to actualize. Experience is intensified by integrating the contrast between appearance and reality, by feeling and actualizing some novel possibility.

Still, just as order is not the goal, neither is novelty for its own sake the goal. Novelty as such can be destructive as well as creative. Consider what would happen if all the societies that make up the human body pursued novel possibilities independently of the needs of the whole body. The lack of coordination would soon result in destruction of the whole. Likewise, anarchy in society might be novel, but it is also destructive. The *telos* of the universe is not toward novelty as such, but toward beauty and the evocation of intensity. Novelty adds to beauty and intensifies experience, but intensity also depends upon order. Part of what novelty does is to evolve new forms of order as old forms become decadent with their major possibilities played out.

With this interplay of novelty and order, we can consider Whitehead's statement: "What is inexorable in God, is valuation as an aim towards 'order'; and 'order' here means 'society permissive of actualities with patterned intensity of feeling arising from adjusted contrasts.'"[109] We see that what is inexorable in God is God's aim at beauty, and this aim is served by aiming at the emergence of societies that produce actualities capable of intense subjective experience. "The universe achieves its values," Whitehead writes, "by reason of its coordination into societies of societies, and in societies of societies of societies."[110] It is no accident that he uses the word "values." What is valuable is subjective experience, the unifying of diversity. But great value is achieved and great novelty is possible only if great order is presupposed. Societies provide *ordered diversity*, diversity that can be unified.[111]

The interplay of novelty and order is necessary to evoke intense experience. Societies are important for ordering the data and so making possible novel, and intense, experience. The intensity of the subjective experience depends upon the diversity that is integrated. That is, the diversity admitted in the physical pole of an occasion dictates the richness of experience possible for that occasion. This diversity must be capable of unification, and societies provide the needed ordered diversity. So what is admitted into feeling (and the rest must be negatively prehended) is determined by the past of the occasion in question—including especially the society of which it is a part—and its subjective aim at intensity. And that brings us back to a consideration of the supplemental phase of concrescence.

With this understanding of what Whitehead means by society, let us turn to a more detailed discussion of his gradations of actual entities. When an actual occasion is only part of the most general societies (for example, of extension and of geometry) and not part of a more specialized structured society, its intensity of experience will be negligible. The actuality is dominated by its physical pole, and the mark of the physical pole is repetition and conformity. So for the simplest grade of actuality ("the actual occasions in so-called 'empty-space'"), "the process is deficient in its highest phases; the process is a slave to the datum. There is the individualizing phase of conformal feeling, but the originative phases of supplementary and conceptual feelings are negligible."[112] Beyond the novelty of its own particularity, novelty plays no role in this simplest grade.

The next grade of actual entities ("actual occasions which are moments in the life-histories of enduring non-living objects") is influenced not only by the widest societies—the extensive continuum, the geometrical society, and the electromagnetic society—but also by some more specialized society. This grade includes all occasions in non-living or inorganic societies. These occasions, or at least the vast majority of them, terminate their concrescence with some unconscious valuation of the worth of a possibility, which is abruptly chosen. The degree of novelty in the relevant alternative possibilities is so small as to be negligible. Nevertheless, that such alternatives exist, and are sometimes decided upon, Whitehead believes accounts for the "vibration and rhythm [that] have a dominating importance in the physical world."[113] And only this selection of alternative possibilities could account for the rise of such tremendous diversity and richness of inorganic forms. The non-conscious, non-sensuous decisions of an uncountable number of actual occasions of this variety are the reason why the laws of nature are only statistical or probabilistic rather than deterministic. There is some minimal degree of freedom or indeterminism even in the inorganic realm.

The transition from the second to the third grade of actuality marks the transition from non-living to living, from inorganic to organic. Although the boundary line is not sharp, this transition is significant. Before continuing with an elaboration on the third and fourth grades, I want to consider Whitehead's understanding of what constitutes something as "living." In a society that is living, life may characterize some set of occasions, though not necessarily all of them, in the society. Whitehead argues that complex, structured societies enable heightened intensity of experience, but, because of the need for a specialized environment, survival becomes a problem. While inorganic structured societies secure stability amid environmental novelties by "elimination of diversities of detail," living societies deal with the problem of survival by an "origination of novelties of conceptual reaction,"[114] by initiative in the mental pole. "The purpose of this initiative," Whitehead notes, "is to receive the novel elements of the environment into explicit feeling with such subjective forms as conciliate them with the complex experiences proper to members of the structured society. Thus in each concrescent occasion its subjective aim originates novelty to match the novelty of the environment."[115] In higher organisms this initiative amounts to thinking, while in lower organisms it amounts merely to the thoughtless adjustment of aesthetic emphasis in order to keep the specialized environment in harmony with the external environment so that life within the society can continue. This creative impulse originates a self-preservative reaction that affects the entire society. The mental pole, then, takes on an increased importance in living societies.[116]

The mental spontaneities throughout the occasions of a living society must be coordinated, so that the reaction of the society as a whole is coordinated. The entire society must respond in a coordinated way to a prehended possibility that is valued. There is a teleological introduction of novelty. It is this introduction together with coordination of purpose

throughout the society that marks living societies.[117] With this characterization of living societies, which applies to those that include the third and
fourth grades of actual occasions, let us return to Whitehead's gradation of
actual entities.

Occasions of the third grade ("actual occasions which are moments in
the life-histories of enduring living objects") are influenced not only by the
widest societies and various inorganic societies but also depend upon a
highly specialized living body, a living society. All living bodies contain at
least some occasions that are non-living, but of concern here are the "living occasions" of any living body, from a single-cell organism to the aston-
ishingly complex animal body.

The enhanced freedom of living over inorganic entities consists in the
integration of a greater diversity of data. For living occasions, the "many"
in "many become one and are increased by one" are more than for non-
living occasions. That is, the past of such occasions is richer and their aim
is not simply repetition, but perhaps growth and flourishing within its
kind. The data admitted in the physical pole will then be considerably
greater than that admitted by non-living occasions. The greater unity in diversity depends upon an extension of the supplemental phase. Societies of
which living occasions are a part provide ordered diversity, or great diversity that is not merely a welter but diversity that also can be unified—that
is, aesthetically ordered diversity. With the supplemental phases, the living
occasion that takes in this relatively massive data simplifies and orders
the data.

For creatures whose mentality does not reach the level of consciousness
(that is, actualities of the third grade), the concrescence terminates with
the realization of an unconscious purpose. Satisfaction is reached. The
purpose is unconscious because the subjective reaction to the "lure" of the
possibilities is unconscious. The valuation *is* the choosing of a purpose.

This analysis in terms of final end or purpose is, on Whitehead's account, necessary to explain such things as the novelty of growth in living
societies as well as the self-preservative actions taken by such societies in
response to novel conditions in their environments. For instance, if we
take the living occasions in the cell of a tree leaf in spring, the goal is not
simply to repeat the past but also to survive and grow. As Whitehead
puts it, "the predominant aim with the organism is survival for its own
coordinated expressiveness."[118] Accordingly, those relevant possibilities are

chosen that enable these occasions to achieve that aim to the extent possible. The quantity of data that must be prehended is more massive than if such an occasion was simply aiming at repeating the past. The intensity of its subjective experience is correspondingly higher than that of an occasion that is a moment in the life history of an inorganic object.

We turn then to the fourth grade of actual entity ("actual occasions which are moments in the life-histories of enduring objects with conscious knowledge"). A conscious actual entity feels the difference between "is" and "might not be"—that is, feels the "affirmation-negation contrast"—and this feeling is consciousness.[119] "Consciousness," Whitehead says, "is the way of feeling [a] particular real nexus [the physical prehension], as in contrast with imaginative freedom about it [possibilities in relation to the given reality]. The consciousness may confer importance upon what the real thing is, or upon what the imagination is, or both."[120] Consciousness allows the concrescing occasion to judge a possibility before committing to it. The subjective form of the integral feeling that integrates a possibility and an actual fact (physical prehension) involves a judgment.[121] "A judgment is a critique of a lure for feeling."[122]

A conscious creature is dominated by a personally ordered society of entities that more or less directs the operations of its living body. Such creatures, through their bodies, must prehend massive amounts of data from their physical environment. The animal body is the structured society that is especially relevant to ordering the welter of data that is prehended in the physical phase. For the dominant occasion in a sheep, for example, to judge that a wolf is dangerous, to determine if it is too far away to be a threat, that the protection of dogs and a human is nearby, that it needs to run, requires the input of a terrific amount of data from the environment, with the most immediate environment for this occasion being the animal body of the sheep. What is taken in is determined by the past of the sheep and its aim. This aim can be quite complex; beyond seeking survival it may seek its favorite food, it may seek to rest in its favored spot. These aims are well beyond what seems possible for non-conscious occasions. Whitehead writes, "The animal grade includes at least one central actuality, supported by the intricacy of bodily functioning. Purposes transcending (however faintly) the mere aim at survival are exhibited. For animal life the concept of importance . . . has a real relevance."[123]

The data that are admitted in the conformal phase require a tremendous amount of ordering and simplification for the dominant occasion to obtain useful information about its environment. For example, it needs to recognize the macroscopic objects relevant to its well-being, and not the microscopic entities that compose these objects. It must abstract from the details in order to focus on the structural elements of the environment that are important for the achievement of its aim. For this massive simplification and concentration on the systematic elements of its environment (rather than on the minute details), the structured society of the animal body is necessary. This structured society makes possible the unification of an immense input and so enables a conscious creature to enjoy a greater intensity of subjective experience, greater unity in diversity, than is possible for non-conscious creatures.

When we come to rational knowing, or self-consciousness, we reach a new level of complexity. While the judgments formed by conscious, non-rational creatures are wholly concerned with the self-constitution of the creature, rational judgments are also concerned with the truth of the propositions themselves. Whitehead would concur with Thomas that rationality allows the judgment of our judgments. Human beings not only *live* their lives, they also *lead* them in accord with accepted ideals or possibilities. "The conceptual entertainment of unrealized possibility," Whitehead maintains, "becomes a major factor in human mentality. In this way outrageous novelty is introduced, sometimes beautified, sometimes damned, and sometimes literally patented and protected by copyright."[124]

In some significant respects, Whitehead agrees with Thomas' characterization of the human mind. It is capable of consciously entertaining universals, of criticizing our judgments. So far as we can tell, this capacity is not present in other creatures, at least not to the extent that it is in human beings. This capacity introduces outrageous freedom, the capacity to deliberate consciously and choose among purposes. The intensity of our subjective experience is unparalleled in the world. We are provident over our actions to an extent that other creatures are not. And for this reason, religion and morality become relevant to us in a way in which they do not appear to be for other creatures.

The two thinkers, of course, finally diverge irreconcilably. For Thomas, the difference between human beings with their rational soul and non-rational creatures is the generic difference between immaterial and material substances. *Only* human beings are provident over their actions. *Only* human beings are *causa sui*. All other creatures must be moved to their ends by another; they are slaves, suitable merely to be instruments for the human good. For Whitehead, the difference between human beings and other creatures can only be one of degree. There is no sharp division between types. All creatures are *causa sui* to some extent; all creatures are related to possibility and move themselves to their own ends; all creatures are subjects of experience, and so all have moral worth.

Still, there is a gradation in the capacity for rich experience among actual entities that provides the basis for developing a value hierarchy, so important for a viable ecological ethic. The above analysis, with its explication of the grades of actual entities, provides the basis for developing that hierarchy. And at the highest reaches of this hierarchy, the rationality of the human being calls into question the very meaning of existence. This is finally a religious question, which Whitehead addresses through his development of the "consequent" nature of God.

Before turning to that discussion, it bears mentioning that, on this alternative metaphysics, the human psyche is capable of self-conscious reflection because of the massively ordered data inherited from the human body with which it is intimately related. This psyche is what Thomas calls the "human soul." But, on Whitehead's alternative account, the psyche arises out of the environment of the body and the immensely complex relations that the body orders. We have a "soul" or a "psyche" because of our marvelously complex bodies (which is not to gainsay that we ourselves can further develop this psyche and ourselves). On this metaphysics, then, the soul is understood not as something separate from or "added to" or existing apart from the body. Of course, this raises the difficult and important question of whether human beings can be understood to enjoy subjective immortality on neoclassical grounds. Although I will not enter into an extended discussion of this debate, in my judgment, any positive answer to this question would lean heavily on the conception of God's "consequent" nature. I want to turn now to this "consequent" nature—God's prehension of the world—in order to flesh out more fully God's relation to the world.

God's "primordial" nature provides the ground of experience, the foundation of order, and the goad toward novelty. God's "consequent" nature provides the meaning of existence and the final ground of the world's value. God's primordial nature concerns God as the ultimate source of the world. And God's consequent nature concerns God as the ultimate end of the world. God is the source and the end of all that is.

Reality as a Realm of Value and Meaning

Whitehead holds that "'order' and 'novelty' are but instruments of God's subjective aim,"[125] which, as noted, is the "evocation of intensity."[126] It is finally because of God's subjective aim that we, as rational creatures, are able to enjoy an intensity unsurpassed (so far as we know) in the world. But this intensity comes at a cost. We are consciously aware of the tragedy, the evil, the suffering in our world. We are faced with the existential question of the meaning of it all. Are tragedy, evil, and suffering the last word? Does all goodness pass away forgotten; in the long run, is it without efficacy? We experience not only goodness and vitality and heroism and beauty but also the persistence of evil and suffering and malice and loss. What, finally, is the character of reality? Is it all absurdity? Is life, as Shakespeare's Macbeth has it, "but a walking shadow, a poor player that struts and frets his hour upon the stage, and then is heard no more, . . . a tale told by an idiot, full of sound and fury, signifying nothing"?

This is the religious problem of the meaning of existence, and it is where metaphysics meets religion most intimately. That what we do is meaningful, that the good we do really matters, is not always clear in human life. Evil often seems to triumph and goodness often seems to disappear into the sands of time. Whitehead puts the problem in the following way: "The most general formulation of the religious problem is the question whether the process of the temporal world passes into the formation of other actualities, bound together in an order *in which novelty does not mean loss*. The ultimate evil in the temporal world is deeper than any specific evil. *It lies in the fact that the past fades, that time is a 'perpetual perishing.'*"[127] If all that we do finally passes away, then are all of our efforts but "a passing whiff of insignificance"? Addressing this issue has important implications for understanding the value of creatures.

In his answer to this problem, Whitehead introduces his own understanding of God's consequent nature, the ultimate end and final purpose of the universe. But here Whitehead faces an interesting issue. Whatever determination he makes regarding God's character must be tested against human experience. The aspect of experience that is most relevant here is religious experience, where claims are made about encountering God.[128] This means that Whitehead must turn to religious experience and must depend on particular religious intuitions in developing his understanding of God's consequent nature. But then Whitehead must decide to which tradition of religious intuitions he should turn, and what interpretation he should give them.[129]

Whitehead begins by pointing out the primary options, all of which he rejects. "In the great formative period of theistic philosophy . . . three strains of thought emerge which, amid many variations in detail, respectively fashion God in the image of an imperial ruler, God in the image of a personification of moral energy, God in the image of an ultimate philosophical principle. Hume's *Dialogues* criticize unanswerably these modes of explaining the system of the world."[130] Whitehead associates these understandings of God with various historical religions. He believes, for example, that "when the Western world accepted Christianity, Caesar conquered."[131] That is, when Christianity became dominant, the "brief Galilean vision of humility" was overshadowed by an understanding of God as "divine Caesar," an imperial ruler. But, for our purposes, the important point is that Whitehead is rejecting these three understandings of God's character, which he takes Hume to have refuted.

Whitehead turns to what he takes to be the most profound alternative— the God revealed in the life and work of Jesus. "There is . . . in the Galilean origin of Christianity yet another suggestion which does not fit very well with any of the three main strands of thought. It does not emphasize the ruling Caesar, or the ruthless moralist, or the unmoved mover. It dwells upon the tender elements in the world, which slowly and in quietness operate by love; and it finds purpose in the present immediacy of a kingdom not of this world. Love neither rules, nor is it unmoved; also it is a little oblivious to morals. It does not look to the future; for it finds its own reward in the immediate present."[132] This is the vision against which Whitehead would have his understanding of God's character tested.

This vision also feeds his metaphysical reflection on the "consequent" nature of God. He states that "we must investigate dispassionately what the metaphysical principles, here developed, require on these points, as to the nature of God. There is nothing here in the nature of a proof. There is merely the confrontation of the theoretic system with a certain rendering of the facts. But the unsystematized report upon the facts is itself highly controversial, and the system is confessedly inadequate."[133] Whitehead warns us from the outset that the deductions reached in this sphere of thought cannot be viewed as more than mere suggestions as to how the problem is transformed in view of the system. The facts against which this understanding is to be tested (and which help shape the understanding itself) are those that he takes to be the profoundest vision of God's nature available to us—Jesus' vision.[134]

Let us turn now to Whitehead's understanding of God's nature. He begins by pointing out "God is not to be treated as an exception to all metaphysical principles, invoked to save their collapse. He is their chief exemplification."[135] God is an actual entity, generically like other actual entities. In his primordial nature, God is deficiently actual for two reasons. First, "his feelings are only conceptual and so lack the fullness of actuality."[136] An actual entity is constituted not only by a mental pole but also by a physical one. Without the physical pole, God, who is merely "the unlimited conceptual realization of the absolute wealth of potentiality,"[137] lacks actuality. Second, "conceptual feelings, apart from complex integration with physical feelings, are devoid of consciousness in their subjective forms."[138] God without consciousness would fail the test against the "facts" of religious intuition with which Whitehead begins. God must know and love the world. The religious vision that Whitehead takes to be most profound demands this. And it is necessary in order for God to be the answer to our deep need for meaning in life.

God, as we have seen, is presupposed by every actuality in the world. And, "by reason of the relativity of all things, there is a reaction of the world on God."[139] Just as for creaturely actualities, to be actual is to be involved in the double relation of the actuality inheriting the past world and the actuality bequeathing itself to future actualities in the world, so, too, God's actuality depends on this principle of relativity. Just as with other actual entities, God's nature is dipolar. God enjoys physical as well as conceptual prehensions.[140]

God experiences how creaturely actualities have reacted to the possibilities received from his primordial nature. God prehends every actuality in the world *without loss*. So, for God, the initial data are the same as the objective data. God feels, without loss, what each occasion of experience feels; he undergoes perfectly and everlastingly each experience of every creature.[141] The world offers God actualized value. Each occasion actualizes some value, chosen from among its relevant possibilities. And it becomes a "novel element" in God's experience because it decided to actualize just *this* value in its actual situation in the world. In the conformal phase, the subjective form of God's feeling conforms to that of the creatures prehended, the data of God's physical prehension. That is, God feels what the prehended occasion felt as God's feeling of that creature's feeling. To be clear, God feels perfectly the sadistic pleasure of a sadist but feels that feeling *as the feeling of that individual entity*. Likewise, God feels joy and hope and despair and boredom and indifference as creatures feel them, as the creatures' own feelings.

These data are integrated and reintegrated with the conceptual prehensions of God's mental pole, so that God experiences the whole universe as unified. This phase is also part of God's consequent nature, which, Whitehead maintains, "is the realization of the actual world in the unity of his nature, and through the transformation of his wisdom."[142] The conformally felt subjective form is transformed by integration with God's conceptual prehensions unified by God's subjective aim at beauty.[143] The actual facts in the world are now felt and evaluated by (or judged by) God in relation to his prehensions of possibility.

In the following, Whitehead attempts to give his vision of what it means to say that God's consequent nature is "the realization of the actual world in the unity of his nature, and through the transformation of his wisdom."[144] Here, he is clearly influenced by his understanding of Jesus' vision:

> The perfection of God's subjective aim . . . issues into the character of his consequent nature. In it there is no loss, no obstruction. The world is felt in a unison of immediacy. . . . The wisdom of subjective aim prehends every actuality for what it can be in such a perfected system—its sufferings, its sorrows, its failures, its triumphs, its immediacies of joy—woven by rightness of feeling into the harmony of the universal feeling, which is always immediate, always many, always one, always with novel advance, moving onward and never perishing. The revolts of destructive evil, purely self-regarding, are dismissed into their triviality of merely individual facts, and yet the good they did achieve in their individual joy, in individual sorrow, in the introduction of needed contrast, is yet saved by its relation to the completed whole. The image—and it is but an image—under which this operative growth of God's nature is best conceived, is that of a tender care that nothing be lost. [God] saves the world as it passes into the immediacy of his own life. It is the judgment of a tenderness which loses nothing that can be saved. It is also the judgment of a wisdom which uses what in the temporal world is mere wreckage.[145]

It seems clear that in this characterization of God's nature, Whitehead draws not only on his metaphysical system but also on his religious intuitions. The language derives its strength and evocative power from these underlying intuitions. God "is the poet of the world, with tender patience leading it by his vision of truth, beauty, and goodness."[146] Whitehead's understanding of God refuses the images of him as imperial ruler, moralist, or philosophical principle. To be sure, God is not an exception to metaphysical principles, but this God is a God of love and tenderness, who saves the world through his own immediate and everlasting experience of its deepest sorrows and greatest joys, its darkest despair and its brightest hopes. This is a God who in his own nature answers the deepest religious longings of humanity; a God who loves and leads creatures; a God who feels their struggles and triumphs; a God who not only powerfully affects the world but is also affected by the world.

This understanding of God's concrete experience is the final ground securing the value of the world, saving the activity of worldly actualities from becoming "a passing whiff of insignificance." The fact that every experience is everlastingly taken up into the divine experience, and thereby makes a difference to God, means that every experience has abiding significance. Every creature in every moment contributes everlastingly to the good of the universe. It is this abiding significance of the actions of subjects that is the guarantor of their value. Without God's prehension of the world, nothing could finally be of value. If all achievement of value is temporary, then, in the long run, no value is, in truth, achieved. [147]

Let me close with a quote from Whitehead on "the dim foundation of experience"[148] that captures much of the point of this chapter: "At the base of our experience is the sense of 'worth.' . . . It is the sense of existence for its own sake, of existence which is its own justification."[149] He maintains, "Everything has some value for itself, for others, and for the whole. *This characterizes the meaning of actuality.* By reason of this character, constituting reality, the conception of morals arises. *We have no right to deface the value experience which is the very essence of the universe.* Existence, in its own nature, is the upholding of value intensity. Also no unity can separate itself from the others, and from the whole. And yet each unit exists in its own right. It upholds value intensity for itself, and this involves sharing value intensity with the universe."[150]

Chapter Six

Intrinsic Value and Moral Worth

In this chapter, I summarize the foundation for an ecological ethic that can be built on neoclassical metaphysics. I then demonstrate that the value theory embodied in this ecological ethic provides a basis for an understanding of intrinsic value that incorporates the best insights of, and avoids the problems that plague, two of the leading theorists in contemporary ecological ethics, Holmes Rolston III and J. Baird Callicott.

Foundation for an Ecological Ethic

To form the basis for an ecological ethic in the neoclassical tradition, I begin by comparing some central concepts in the thought of Thomas and Whitehead. In particular, an area of significant overlap exists between the two philosophers' understanding of goodness. For both Thomas and Whitehead, the world is enchanted, drenched with value and suffused with goodness. The core of reality is not so much facticity as it is valuation. Because the world is good in its deepest reaches, reality in all of its parts is good. For Thomas, goodness is convertible with being. For Whitehead, the subjective experience of all creatures is the value of creation.

Yet there is an important difference between these thinkers. For Thomas, the ontological goodness of creatures does not entail that they have moral worth; ultimately, in his conception, only human beings have moral worth.

This moral bifurcation is based upon the ontological divide between material and immaterial creatures. For Whitehead, any such ontological divide is ruled out as creating an incoherent metaphysical scheme. The absence of such a divide means that the ontological goodness of creatures does, in Whitehead's metaphysics, affirm the moral worth of all creatures. Once subjectivity is understood to characterize all levels of reality, there can be no arbitrary boundary for the attribution of intrinsic value and moral worth. In other words, because there is continuity between the levels of creation, if intrinsic value exists at any level it exists at every level. Both the intrinsic value and moral worth of all creatures are founded upon their capacity for, and enjoyment of, subjective experiencing.

However, this does not mean that all creatures are of equal value in Whitehead's metaphysics; he establishes a hierarchy based upon a creature's capacity for rich or intense experience—the greater a creature's capacity for intense experience, the greater its moral worth. This conceptualization corresponds to our intuitions regarding the value of creatures, with living creatures being of greater worth than non-living ones, conscious creatures being of greater worth than non-conscious ones, and self-conscious creatures (that is, human beings) being of greater worth than those that are merely conscious. As a guide for action, any ethic developed in light of this metaphysics must balance a creature's intrinsic value (its being for itself, or its capacity for rich experience) with its instrumental value (its usefulness to other creatures).[1]

As noted, the intrinsic value or moral worth of all creatures is grounded in their capacity for, and enjoyment of, subjective experience. The *telos* of creatures is to enhance this experience, to create beauty in the universe. Another way to characterize this *telos* is in terms of God's experience. Creatures, in pursuing their own *telos*, contribute to God's experience. God prehends completely and retains everlastingly whatever value is achieved by creatures. Therefore, to say that all creatures pursue the *telos* of maximizing unity in diversity is to say that the *telos* of all creatures is to contribute to the richness of God's experience, which finally secures the value of the world. God's experience is made richer by creaturely experience being richer. That is why the *telos* of the universe is the evocation of intensity.

This understanding sharply contrasts with Thomas' view of God and God's relation to the world. For Thomas, God is wholly actual and completely perfect, without need of addition. There is no way for creatures to contribute to the divine experience; God's experience is the same whether or not the universe exists. This view raises troubling questions, as the value of the entire universe is indifferent to the existence or non-existence of the world.[2]

While Thomas argues that the diverse grades of species are necessary to most fully *reflect* the divine goodness, Whitehead believes that the diversity of species is necessary to most fully *contribute* to the divine experience. In Whitehead's metaphysics, there is no ultimate divergence of final ends between diverse creatures, as there is for Thomas. According to Whitehead, every creature contributes here and now to the divine experience to the extent that it can. This view offers a further rationale for the value of diversity (in addition to the rationale that it is needed for individual creatures to have a rich experience). Each different kind of creature realizes a different kind of value. For example, the experiences of a proton, a tree, a wolf, and a human being offer diverse values to God that others could not offer. Further, the unity of the final end of all creatures ensures that this account of the need for diversity does not ultimately collapse, as does Thomas' divergent account of the final ends of rational and non-rational creatures.

I offer, in sum, an alternative conception of intrinsic value and moral worth based on neoclassical metaphysics, which holds that subjectivity characterizes creatures at all levels of reality, from non-conscious to conscious to self-conscious. Put more precisely, metaphysically fundamental units of reality, the ultimate ontological units of existence (or "actual entities"), are all alike *subjects* of experience constituted by internal relations to past subjects, which they integrate into one felt whole, thereby conditioning the future.

This understanding runs counter to the usual way of considering subjectivity, and a complete defense of this position is beyond the scope of this work. But the argument to support this conclusion runs as follows. If human beings are subjects, then the only way to avoid an untenable metaphysical dualism—the only way to truly maintain the continuity of creation—is to argue that *all* metaphysically fundamental entities are subjects of experience. To be a subject requires that an entity integrate its experience with some degree of autonomy, however trivial. (Note that I am discussing metaphysically ultimate units of existence, not aggregates such as rocks or oceans.) To argue that the world is divided into subjects with experience and objects without experience includes the assertion of a strictly negative existential claim—namely, that there are "mere objects" devoid of experience or subjectivity. Such a claim is without meaning, as any *meaningful* claim or thought must have an object. To posit that there are entities utterly devoid of experience is to offer an existential statement about reality that does not (even by implication) have positive content. Sheerly negative existential claims are meaningless because they offer no object of thought. Further, the argument that subjectivity characterizes all levels of reality is supported by the empirical evidence. Contemporary science, for instance, has arguably shown that reality is fundamentally indeterminate, rather than mechanistically determined, as classical physics would have it. This finding coheres nicely with the claim that all final real things determine themselves to some degree.

The interrelatedness and interdependency of all creatures must be central to any ethic developed using neoclassical metaphysics as a guide. The web of life can be given concrete meaning as a web of internal relatedness between creatures. An ethic developed on the basis of this metaphysics would place emphasis on such relationality. Its first principle is the instruction to seek to enhance the richness of experience for all creatures in the relevant future.[3]

The crucial importance of a creature's environment, as constitutive of the creature itself and as necessary for the richness of its experience, underscores the capacity of such an ethic to offer a rationale for considering the health of entire ecosystems as morally relevant. Because creatures cannot be understood in isolation, this ethic would emphasize the well-being of the entire community.

The Contemporary Debate

In this section, I demonstrate the relevance of the value theory grounded in neoclassical metaphysics to some of the most pressing problems in the current debate over how to articulate and justify an ecological ethic. This debate involves two of the most prominent value theorists, Holmes Rolston III and J. Baird Callicott, who argue, in different ways, for nonanthropocentric value theories. These thinkers agree that not all (intrinsic) value is centered in the human being. The fundamental difference between Rolston and Callicott lies in their disagreement over whether the intrinsic value of other creatures is objective and autonomous or subjective and attributed. Rolston argues that there is objective, non-anthropocentric, non-anthropogenic value in the natural world, value that is utterly and completely free from human evaluation or even human existence. Indeed, he believes that such value may be free from all subjectivity; it exists in nature, and human beings ought to respect it. Unable to make sense of value that exists independently of valuers, Callicott casts his own theory in subjective terms, specifically, in terms of human beings valuing non-human creatures intrinsically, without further contributory reference (for example, to human utility, pleasure, aesthetic enjoyment). In this theory, such creatures are valuable for themselves but not in themselves; value is anthropogenic, or generated by human beings, but not anthropocentric, as other creatures can be valued intrinsically, for their own sake. Human beings are the source, but not the sole locus, of value.

By contrast, Rolston rejects any suggestion that human beings are the source of value. He believes that such a theory is not only mistaken but also ultimately arrogant.[4] For Rolston, the intrinsic value of non-human creatures is utterly independent of human valuation. In this, he is right. Callicott holds that the only philosophically defensible value theory is one in which the ascription of value requires a subject capable of valuing. In this, he is right.

Rolston and Callicott are each right where they take themselves to disagree, but wrong where they agree. By challenging their point of agreement, we can develop a theory that unifies their seeming disagreements. These thinkers share the belief that valuing requires consciousness or, put differently, that subjectivity coincides with consciousness, so that valuing and subjectivity "go down" only so far as consciousness. For Rolston, who seeks an objective value theory, this entails that intrinsic value must not depend on subjectivity. For Callicott, who cannot make sense of such a theory, this entails that intrinsic value must be conferred by subjects (and, finally, by human subjects).

My thesis is that subjectivity is a metaphysical variable that is a necessary condition for creatures to have intrinsic value that entails moral worth. As "metaphysical," subjectivity is understood to characterize all levels of reality, from inanimate (say, electrons) to non-conscious living creatures, to conscious living creatures, to self-conscious creatures (human beings). As a "variable," subjectivity, which entails the capacity for experience, is understood to vary between different kinds of creatures; that is, different kinds of creatures would have diverse capacities for richness of experience, from the trivial to the outrageous. This thesis meets Callicott's legitimate demand that value requires a valuer. And because such subjectivity "goes all the way down," or characterizes creatures at all levels of reality, it meets Rolston's legitimate concern that the intrinsic value of non-human creatures be utterly and completely independent of human valuation.

Let us take a closer look at these thinkers' understanding of intrinsic value, beginning with Rolston, a pioneer who thought hard and fruitfully about the central problems of "environmental ethics" long before most other philosophers had even heard of the field. The foundation of Rolston's environmental ethic centers especially on his axiology: his argument for the objective intrinsic value of non-human creatures and systems.

Rolston's objective value theory ultimately rests on his defense of the intrinsic value of creatures that, in his judgment, lack subjectivity. This is because first, he defends a non-subjective value theory; second, his defense of the notion of "systemic value" only has merit if there is something of value that is produced; and third, his defense of the intrinsic value of non-biotic things or places rests on his notion of the value of the system that created them and the value of the life that depends upon them. Consequently, in offering a brief outline of Rolston's value theory, I focus on his discussion of the value of organisms that he considers to be below the level of sentience.

"Two different philosophical perspectives are possible," Rolston maintains, "when a valuing agent (a valuer) encounters an x in the world: (a) what is x good for? and (b) what is x's own good? The first is a question about instrumental value, the second about intrinsic value."[5] With this distinction as a starting point, Rolston's central argument in his value theory is simple. "Beyond dispute," he states flatly, "animals and plants defend a good of their own, and use resources to do so. . . . They promote their own realization. . . . Every organism has a *good-of-its-own*; it defends its kind as a *good kind*."[6] He makes this value claim explicit: "A life is defended for what it is in itself, without necessary further contributory reference. . . . There is intrinsic value *when a life is so defended*. That is ipso facto value in both the biological and the philosophical senses, intrinsic because it inheres in, has its focus within, the organism itself."[7] Rolston assumes that the demonstration that something has intrinsic value entails that it has moral worth or is worthy of direct moral consideration. "Whatever has such resident value *lays a claim* on those who have standing as moral agents when they encounter such autonomous value."[8] Thus, if we can show that a creature has a good of its own or can give a cogent answer to the question, "What is x's own good?" then that creature has intrinsic value. Rolston maintains that whatever has such value likewise has moral worth. Thus, since all living things defend their own lives, they have a good of their own and therefore have intrinsic value and moral worth.

Rolston argues at length that things are also good in terms of their roles in communities; from this, he derives the notion of "systemic value" discussed above. But the primary point here is that, according to Rolston, "we can speak of objective intrinsic value wherever a point event—a trillium—defends a good (its life) in itself."[9] This notion of intrinsic value applies to all living things, whether sentient or not. Therefore, Rolston can argue that "value attaches to a nonsubjective form of life, but is owned by a biological individual, a thing-in-itself. These things count, whether or not there is anybody to do the counting. They take account of themselves."[10] Nonsentient creatures "may have no autonomous options, but they defend a life as a good-of-its-kind."[11] Therefore, they are intrinsically valuable. Clearly, this value theory is strongly objectivist; unexperienced values— the *intrinsic* value of creatures utterly devoid of experience—can exist. According to Rolston, the value exists whether or not a valuer is present to appreciate it.[12]

Rolston at least implicitly assumes a dualism in his search for objective intrinsic value existing in nature, value in *objects* utterly independent of subjectivity. There is, he asserts, "subjective life" and "objective life." Subjects are living things that are also centers of experience with at least some degree of autonomy. Living objects are living things that are not centers of experience and are devoid of autonomy.[13] One of Rolston's goals, arguably his primary goal, is to demonstrate that objective life has intrinsic worth and so is worthy of direct moral consideration.

However, Rolston's dualism vitiates his claim to have secured the moral worth of objective life. This dualism makes tenuous the link between the *intrinsic goodness,* or the goodness a creature has in and for itself, and *moral worth,* or the moral demand that human beings consider the good of that creature in their actions. In other words, on Rolston's ontology, moral worth does not necessarily follow from intrinsic goodness. Rolston seeks an understanding of intrinsic value that directly entails that a creature having such value is worthy of direct moral consideration or has moral worth.

This inference is forthcoming only presupposing an adequate metaphysics. It is possible to view Rolston's articulation of the intrinsic value of all living creatures as an empirical reflection of a metaphysic similar to that of Thomas. For Thomas, the fact that all creatures are ontologically or intrinsically good means that they seek to preserve and augment their *own* being; this is so because being is convertible with goodness and because only the good seek the good. Thus, in his ontology, Thomas affirms the goodness of all creatures: "[E]very being, as being, is good."[14] But, in his moral theory, Thomas makes it clear that non-rational creatures are strictly instrumental to the human good; it is morally permissible for human beings "to make use of [animals], either by killing them or in any way whatsoever,"[15] and he forbids cruelty to animals only because such cruelty might be harmful in our relations with other human beings.[16] Once we grant his own dualism, Thomas can consistently hold that all creatures are ontologically (or intrinsically) good *and* that only human beings have moral worth. Similarly, there is no reason not to hold, on Rolston's grounds, that all living things are intrinsically good (in the sense that each thing seeks its own good) and that only (perhaps) subjective life has moral worth.

A crucial similarity between Rolston and Thomas is that they both understand creatures below a certain level to be devoid of experience, to be mere objects. This dualism is central to Thomas' claim that all creatures are ontologically good and that only human beings have moral worth. Creatures are ontologically or intrinsically good insofar as they seek to preserve and augment their own being. But this dualism has no implications for how human beings ought to treat other creatures; that is, it tells us nothing about these creatures' moral worth. Still, the notion that some creatures are mere objects does lend itself to the conclusion that they are suited to be mere instruments for human beings and therefore do not have moral worth.

Rolston's claim that a living thing defends its life as a good-of-its-kind may, depending on the underlying metaphysics, imply that that thing is ontologically or intrinsically good, but there is no reason to conclude that it has moral worth or that human beings are likewise obligated to defend that thing's life or seek its good. One might endorse all that Rolston has to say about objective life without ever drawing his inference that "[w]hatever has such resident value *lays a claim* on those who have standing as moral agents when they encounter such autonomous value."[17] One need not infer that creatures with intrinsic value have moral worth. Their existence may be for the sake of another, as Thomas argues. The bare notion that something has a good of its own, or intrinsic value, is not necessarily the same as having moral worth.

It is precisely Rolston's dualism that opens up the possibility of separating intrinsic value from moral worth. Rolston argues that any living thing is a good kind and a good of its kind because it seeks to preserve and enhance its own existence. Also, "Biology has steadily demonstrated how subjective life is a consequence of objective life, the one always the necessary sponsor of the other. Why not value the whole process with all its product organisms, rather than restrict valuing to the upper, subjective level? Certainly, the emergence of eyes, ears, and cognitive psychological experience is quite a miracle, but why is not the pursuit of vital, though unconscious self-identity a value event objectively as well?"[18] Rolston then asks, Why is subjective life, or a living thing that is a center of experience, valuable, but not objective life, or a living thing that is not a center of experience? After all, they are first, a necessary precursor of subjective life; and second, they, too, defend a good of their own.[19] The short answer is that the dominant paradigm is correct: value requires a valuer *if the value in question is to entail moral worth.*[20]

Ernest Partridge offers the following helpful analysis: "without minimal feeling and awareness, nothing can 'matter' to a being. . . . '[M]ere things' may be said to be 'good' in the sense of having properties 'deemed good' by others. But 'goodness *of*' these beings cannot be 'goodness *for*' them, if that 'goodness' makes no difference to them. To make a difference to them that is a good (or bad) for them (for them to have 'sakes' or 'interests'), beings must have what [Joel] Feinberg calls 'rudimentary cognitive equipment.'[21] Conversely, nothing that happens to X *matters* to X, if X is irrevocably insentient and non-conscious."[22] To this, I would make one correction: namely, metaphysically ultimate units of existence are subjects of experience but not necessarily conscious. It is subjectivity, not consciousness, that is required for something to be "goodness for," or for something to matter to, an entity. With this correction, Partridge's insistence that subjectivity is required for something to matter to another thing, and thus for the ascription of moral worth to that thing to be sensible, is on target.

Rolston has failed to make his case, and it is difficult to see what kind of metaphysics would allow him to do so if he denies that all final, real things are subjects. Subjectivity, understood as a metaphysical variable, allows for the development of an understanding of intrinsic value that does entail that a creature having such value has moral worth. In neoclassical metaphysics, every creature is a subject that pursues the same telos of creativity, each according to its own capacity; each creature is in some measure free and creative. Since creativity, as the *telos* of the universe, is the good to be pursued, for human beings the pursuit of creativity is rationally required; it is the *moral law*. This moral law binds human beings to seek to maximize the conditions necessary for the exercise of creativity as such, so that any entity that is self-creative or in some measure free falls under the moral law or has moral worth. Subjectivity characterizing all levels of reality is necessary to secure the *moral worth* of all creatures; it is necessary to secure the link between intrinsic goodness and moral worth.

Insofar as Rolston's theory fails to hold that subjectivity characterizes entities at all levels of creation, it fails to secure moral worth for creatures below what he assumes to be the level of subjectivity. With this failure, Rolston's attempt to demonstrate the moral worth of all living beings (and, derivatively, some non-biotic portions of creation) fails. Because of the bifurcation between subject and object, we have no reason to affirm that the intrinsic goodness (defined in terms of a creature seeking to defend and augment its own life) of objective life has any moral significance for human beings.

If Rolston fails to secure the link between intrinsic value and moral worth, then the same cannot be said of Callicott. For Callicott, a necessary condition for something to have intrinsic value is that it be valued "intrinsically" (or for itself) by human beings. Intrinsic value (or, as Callicott calls it, "inherent value") is conferred by human beings who value something for what it is in itself, and not for anything that it can contribute to other creatures, including human beings. In Callicott's ethic, properly understood, the moral worth of creatures simply is their being valued intrinsically.

However, the same thing that secures the link between intrinsic value and moral worth is also the central problem for Callicott's ethic. Callicott understands the intrinsic value of something as necessarily conferred *by* subjects (and, ultimately, human subjects) rather than a thing that is intrinsically valuable because it is a subject. This understanding of intrinsic value leads to an untenable relativism, which Callicott attempts to escape by covert appeal to transcendental standards of assessment. This appeal undermines his entire empirically based ethic by grounding the moral judgments in reason, whether reason itself (as in Immanuel Kant) or some reality that reason can discern (as in Thomas).[23]

Callicott offers a summary moral maxim of his land ethic: "A thing is right when it tends to disturb the biotic community only at normal temporal and spatial scales. It is wrong when it tends otherwise."[24] His axiology provides the justification for this maxim. According to Callicott's subjective and affective value theory, whose roots he traces to Hume and Charles Darwin, there cannot be any intrinsic value that is "objective and independent of all valuing consciousness."[25] He insists that "there is no value without a valu*er* . . . Something *has* value, in other words, if and only if it is value*d*."[26] Consequently, Callicott's position is that "intrinsic value is subjectively conferred—that is, if there existed no valuing subjects, nothing would be of value, intrinsic or otherwise."[27]

It is here that Hume's theory of the moral sentiments comes in, when he grounds morality in empirical feelings. "According to Hume," Callicott writes, "one may have a strong emotional attachment to one's own interests, but such an attachment is entirely contingent. It is possible, indeed, that one may also have strong feelings for the interests of other beings."[28] Thus, human beings may value other beings for themselves, or intrinsically. This valuing is the source of the intrinsic value of non-human creatures or ecosystemic wholes. Callicott offers this statement of his axiology: "the *source* of all value is human consciousness, but it by no means follows that the *locus* of all value is consciousness itself or a mode of consciousness like reason, pleasure, or knowledge. In other words, something may be valuable only because someone values it, but it may also be valued for itself, not for the sake of any subjective experience (pleasure, knowledge, aesthetic satisfaction, and so forth) it may afford the valuer. Value may be subjective and affective, but it is intentional, not self-referential."[29] Intrinsic value has its source in human consciousness, not in extracognitive reality. Callicott maintains that "nonhuman natural entities and nature as a whole may be valued not only for what they do for us, but . . . also . . . for their own sakes."[30] As he states, he tries "to pass this altruistic species of value off as 'truncated intrinsic value.' . . . Truncated intrinsic value [Callicott's understanding of the only kind of intrinsic value that can be philosophically validated] is the value *we* ascribe to something *for* itself even if it has— since nothing does . . .—no value *in* itself."[31] The intrinsic value of an entity or a whole depends solely upon human beings valuing something for its own sake.[32]

One of the primary strengths of a Humean, sentiment-based ethic, from Callicott's point of view, is that it provides for the possibility of intrinsically valuing "wholes," such as human communities or biotic communities or ecosystems. Callicott maintains that holism is this ethic's principal asset.[33] Hume, he argues, provides a theory according to which "wholes," such as species, ecosystems, and the biotic community, can be valued intrinsically and thus have intrinsic value.[34] If this ethical theory is grounded in empirical feelings or sentiments, then does the ethic collapse into relativism? As Callicott puts it, "If ethics, as Hume . . . says, is ultimately a matter of taste (!), then there can be no objective standards of conduct, no moral norms. The issue [concerns] . . . the very possibility that any uniform norms of conduct at all can be cut from the fickle fabric of feeling. A sentiment-based ethic seems to collapse into the most decadent emotivism and the rankest relativism."[35] But, Callicott argues, this is not the case. Rather, the universality of the sentiments—the "consensus of feeling"— provides the equivalent of objective moral standards.

Here, Callicott brings in Darwin's theory of the origin and evolution of ethics. "For Hume," Callicott maintains, "the 'universality' of human moral dispositions was an ad hoc fact. Darwin completed Hume's theory by explaining how such a standardization came about. Like the complex of normal human physical characteristics, normal human psychological characteristics, including the moral sentiments, were fixed by natural (and perhaps by sexual) selection."[36] That is, Callicott explains, the "social sentiments" were naturally selected because they enhanced the inclusive fitness of the individual and the group. Individuals depended on each other for survival and well-being; the larger and more internally peaceable the group—that is, the more developed its social sentiments—the greater its chances of surviving and prospering. "Now, to be sure," he continues, "inherited social feelings and moral sentiments may vary from person to person. But they vary within a range of normalcy, not unlike physical characteristics. . . . Thus, upon Darwin's account, we can explain how ethical dispositions vary, as obviously they do, while insisting that neither are they radically relative."[37] Therefore, a sentiment-based ethic finds a normative dimension in a "consensus of feeling." Callicott argues again and again that emotions, or the sentiments, are the "ground" or "foundation" of ethics.[38] Presumably, this refers to that which makes a moral claim valid. In Callicott's ethic, what makes a moral claim valid, "the final court of appeal of moral judgments,"[39] is a "consensus of feeling," and that consensus is the result of evolution or natural selection.[40]

The "normative dimension" of the moral sentiments is, as Callicott acknowledges, like the normativity of medicine or physiology. In moral theory, this seems to leave us with an unacceptable biological determinism that leaves no room for moral praise or blame. Indeed, Callicott's critics have powerfully advanced the argument that his ethic lacks "normative force" in this sense.[41] Callicott nicely summarizes the point of these critiques: "[T]he theory provides us no means of criticizing the medical-like descriptive norms derived from common innate moral sentiments. There may be a consensus of feeling that murder is evil, but there also seems to be a consensus of feeling that only people are worthy of moral considerability. . . . If the final court of appeal of moral judgments is a consensus of feeling, how can we possibly argue that although something is generally felt to be right or good, say, speciesism, it *ought* not to be?"[42]

Callicott rejects what he calls "a particularly strong sense of 'normative force' . . . [which holds] that a proper ethic should *rationally coerce* a moral agent into doing something or into leaving something undone, irrespective of her feelings."[43] Normative force, in this sense, means logically compelled on the pain of self-contradiction.[44] A couple of critical comments are in order here. First, Callicott's position demands that he reject this understanding of normative force. To adopt it would be to ground ethics in reason (either reason itself or some reality that reason can discern) rather than in empirical sentiments, and therefore to jettison the entire edifice so carefully built by Callicott on the basis of Hume's theory of the moral sentiments. That is, if this understanding of strong normative force is correct, then reason, not the sentiments, is the final court of appeal. Second, the reason that this is the only appropriate understanding of normative force in moral theory is not because it is Kantian, but because Kant argues convincingly that only on this understanding can an ethic avoid an untenable relativism;[45] the moral law must bind the will unconditionally. If this is correct, then Callicott's rejection of this understanding of normative force is beside the point, because failure to adhere to this understanding means that the resulting ethic must finally be relativistic. And, indeed, such is the case with Callicott's ethic.

To demonstrate this point, let us return to Callicott's response to the charge that his ethic lacks normative force. For Callicott, the moral sentiments are not themselves the whole of ethics. Indeed, "the moral sentiments are in themselves underdetermined and plastic."[46] So, while "[e]thics is grounded in naturally selected feelings, . . . there is also a large cultural component of morality that gives shape and direction to our selfless sentiments. In general, we may say, culture informs the moral sentiments."[47]

At this point, the urge to charge this ethic with "a normatively deficient cultural relativism"[48] is almost irresistible. After all, if it is cultural representations that determine the proper objects of the moral sentiments, and if these cultural representations vary from culture to culture, then it seems that what is moral in one culture may be immoral in another, and that which objects count as worthy of moral consideration (or as having intrinsic worth) in one culture may differ from those that count as worthy of moral consideration (or as having intrinsic worth) in another. With a value theory in which intrinsic worth is conferred by human sentiments and the proper objects of these sentiments is *fixed by*[49] cultural representations, Callicott is apparently in the strange position of advocating an ethic that holds that which objects have intrinsic worth varies depending upon the culture under discussion. Clearly, such a view renders an ethic impotent (especially in the face of global environmental problems) because it endorses the view that mutually incompatible moral schema are legitimate.[50]

But, Callicott insists, such relativism is emphatically not his position. "A culture," he states, "is, among other things, a shared worldview. A culture's values and ethical ideals rest upon and are justified by suppositions of fact and supposed relations among supposed facts. . . . We condemn racism and attempt to purge it from our own culture—or from any other for that matter—principally by debunking the alleged 'facts' on which it is based and by which it is justified."[51] Callicott holds that "a culture's value and ethical ideals" rest upon and are justified in accord with reason or "by suppositions of fact and supposed relations among facts." And he here appeals to a universalistic understanding of reason. That is, since "facts" can be "debunked" across cultures, there must be standards of assessment for what counts as successfully "debunking"—standards that transcend any and, thus, every culture.

Let us examine these claims. If values can be justified by facts, and these facts can be known in accord with universal standards of reason, then we have a universal standard of values. Because the debunking of relevant facts occurs across cultures or transcends the worldview of any given culture, so, too, do the values justified by facts that cannot be debunked. That is, there must be transcendental standards of assessment that are binding on all rational agents.[52] If these standards of assessment are themselves determined in the debate between differing worldviews, then in accordance with what standard are *these* standards assessed? If the standards of assessment were themselves to be determined in debate between cultures, we would be left with an infinite regress ("In accordance with what standard should the standards of assessment be assessed? In accordance with what standard should the standards that assess these standards of assessment be assessed?" and so on) or with the arbitrary choice of some standard. If there are no transcendental standards of assessment, then the standards are either culturally relative or, to say the same thing, chosen arbitrarily.

Callicott's dilemma is twofold: if he states that values are fixed by evolution, then he can claim the "equivalent of objective moral standards," but at the cost of making these standards immune to rational criticism; and if he states that values are justified by reason, then he can claim that his ethic is not rationally arbitrary and has normative force, but at the cost of jettisoning his empirical sentiment-based ethic. He wants it both ways: an ethic grounded in empirical sentiments and values justified by reason. But his covert appeal to a universalistic understanding of reason undermines his empirical sentiment-based ethic.

Once it becomes clear that Callicott undermines his own "grounding" of ethics in the moral sentiments, we have no good reason to hold, with him, that the intrinsic value of non-human creatures is conferred by human consciousness. Callicott's mistake, I think, is the belief that the following two statements are equivalent: "there is no value without a valuer"; and "there is no value without a *conscious* valuer." Once valuing becomes the domain of conscious creatures, so that only such creatures can be the source of value, then if there is no value without a valuer, one must resort to a theory in which human beings project or confer value on such creatures. This explains why Callicott cannot make sense of Rolston's theory of intrinsic value. Rolston holds that there can be value without an experiencer or a valuer. In this sense, Callicott is correct: there can be no value without a valuer. In this sense, Rolston is correct: intrinsic value does not depend upon human consciousness or, indeed, upon consciousness. The key to uniting these insights into a single theory is to posit subjectivity that characterizes all levels of reality, thereby allowing non-conscious subjects of experience, or non-conscious valuers, as in neoclassical metaphysics.

Analyzing the locus of failure of Rolston and Callicott's value theories offers insight into the shape of a viable value theory. Rolston's theory fails because he bifurcates creation into subjects and objects. Once this bifurcation is made, there is no reason to conclude, on his grounds, that the value of objects has any moral relevance for human beings. Callicott's theory fails because he insists that any intrinsic value in the world find its source in the empirical moral sentiments of human beings. Once a moral theory is built upon these empirical grounds, there is no escape from an untenable relativism.

A viable value theory, then, might take the form of a *metaphysical* scheme (rather than an empirical account) in which all creatures are understood to be subjects (rather than bifurcating creation into subjects and objects). It is such a value theory, built upon neoclassical metaphysics, that I have espoused. This theory not only avoids the problems that plague those of Rolston and Callicott but also incorporates their best insights. With Callicott, such a theory holds that there can be no value without a subject capable of valuing; it is a subjective value theory in the sense that value depends upon subjectivity. With Rolston, such a theory holds that intrinsic value characterizes all levels of reality and does not depend upon human valuation; it is an objective value theory in the sense that value is independent of human subjectivity.

Conclusion

The deteriorating state of the natural environment is among the foremost problems facing humanity at the dawn of the twenty-first century. It is on our actions that the fate and, indeed, the very survival of much planetary life depend. We are entering unchartered waters, where the gradual accretion of alterations to our planet is exerting ever-increasing pressures on its life-support systems. This pressure threatens to alter these systems fundamentally, and changes may occur in an abrupt and non-linear manner, resulting in the massive dislocation of human beings as well as other creatures. We need an ethic of life both to sustain us in hope and to guide us in revising our very ways of seeing and of being. We need an ethic in which human beings are understood to be fundamentally united with other creatures and bear moral responsibility for our actions that cause harm to other creatures as well as to unborn generations of human beings.

One of the central thrusts of this book is that a felt sense of responsibility and care finds barren soil in dualistic metaphysics, where separations are posited between God and the world and between human beings and other material creatures. As long as God is understood to be wholly complete and separate from our planetary travail, and thus unaffected by the world, then the full extent of the effects of our activities remains opaque to us because we do not see them as affecting God's own experience. In understanding God as the universal individual who shares without loss the experience of every creature in the world, we gain insight into the significance of our actions both toward other human beings and toward non-human creatures. In coming to endorse Jesus' saying, "that which you do to the least of my brothers, that you do unto me," as the literal reality of God's experience, we can come to a deeper appreciation of the value and worth of all creatures. Every creaturely achievement of value is savored everlastingly by God. With this felt tie between human beings and other living things, mediated through an understanding of God's love for creatures and his enjoyment of every achievement of creaturely value, human beings can come more readily to love and savor the world as well. We can gain a richer understanding of the meaning of creaturely existence.

As long as we see ourselves as separate from the rest of creation, different in kind and with a *telos* that differs in kind, it seems difficult to imagine an effective response to the problems that we face. This separation too easily lends itself to the view that the rest of creation exists exclusively for human use. As we saw when examining the work of Thomas (with the distinction between "ontological goodness" and "moral worth"), it is this separation—and only secondarily the view of the rest of creation—that is crucial in legitimating an instrumentalist attitude. We need to view the rest of creation not only as good but also as being worthy of direct moral consideration. Though a value hierarchy is needed in order to avoid paralysis, such a hierarchy need not, and ought not, entail a dichotomy. There are morally legitimate distinctions to be made between types of creatures with different potentialities. But these are distinctions within continuity.

To address properly how we ought to live within ecological limits, then, requires a rethinking of the human place on our home planet. I offer this work as part of the effort to rethink that place, to defend the view that *all* creation is continuous and suffused with a goodness that entails its moral worth. The healing of our fragile planet on which life depends would be well served by a view of human beings as truly continuous with the rest of creation and by an understanding of God as truly affected by creaturely activity. A well-known quote from Senegalese conservationist Baba Dioum states the idea nicely: "In the end we will conserve only what we love, we will love only what we understand and we will understand only what we are taught." I argue that a critical component in this learning is coming to see the continuity between God, ourselves, and the world of creatures.

Much remains to be done, of course. For instance, if the critical appraisal of Thomas' view of the soul can be sustained, then how can a satisfactory alternative understanding of the human soul and the end times—conceptions central to the Christian tradition—be articulated? Presumably, to be satisfactory such an alternative would preserve the continuity of creation while also addressing deep concerns in Christianity about the future life. Perhaps an understanding of all things as returning to

God in such a way that they exist forever in the divine life could be sustained on the alternative metaphysics articulated above. And perhaps a satisfactory account of human subjective immortality could be defended on the basis of God's perfect and everlasting experience of every creaturely experience. Such a thorough and thoughtful work would lean heavily on fleshing out how God's consequent nature might be articulated in a manner consistent with subjective immortality, if, indeed, this can be done.

Still, there is one understanding of the end times, the eschaton, which is positively excluded on this alternative metaphysics. There is no final closure. Though human beings and the earth itself may pass away, the world of creatures will remain eternally as God's companions in the unending cosmic adventure. There will be no "end of time." The reconciling of all things to God is ongoing and everlasting. So, too, is God's judgment of things through his awareness both of actual creaturely choices and what might have been. So, too, is God's mercy through his perfect and everlasting experience of each and every actualization of creaturely value. God integrates these many experiences into one felt whole that is the universal experience—God's experience. There is no final judgment day in which all things are "set aright." *In each and every moment*, God pursues justice, shows mercy, and loves the world. God, in every instant, seeks to persuade all creatures to work for the true good of themselves, each other, and the whole.

An understanding of the eschaton as a final cataclysmic event in which God intervenes, takes over, and ends human history finally undermines true creaturely freedom and the moral responsibility that human beings have to work for the good of our home planet and all its inhabitants. As long as the eschaton is present as the horizon of our activities, there is a safety net and an escape hatch that undermines our truly taking our responsibility—and our freedom—with the seriousness, and the joy, that they deserve. After all, with this understanding of a cataclysmic end time, it is not actually in our hands but in God's. Our responsibility, and with it our freedom, is forfeit. By making freedom finally illusory, this understanding of God—as wholly perfect and complete, as wholly powerful, and without need of the world—shields us from the fear of accepting our responsibility for the world that we have made. While this understanding assumes a patina of humility before the awesome power of God, a strong case could be made that it is a reflection of fear and a search for comfort in a world that seems far beyond our control. Humility is, in the end, better cultivated by a full awareness of the awesomeness of the task that God has set for us. Freedom is indeed a gift from God, but it is a gift that comes with a terrific price—true responsibility for what we do, which includes living with the consequences.[1]

The meaning of existence does not depend upon God bringing a catastrophic end to history. It depends, rather, on his experiencing with, and savoring everlastingly, what fragmentary value we do achieve. God's love for us, God's desire for us, God's savoring of us, lends life its final meaning. By the same token, it lends meaning to the whole cosmic adventure, to all creaturely activity. It all has meaning in the cosmic play of the universe, and there is no need for some explosive end. Its meaning is in the here and now, in the very achievement and enjoyment of value.

We are at a time in history when the fundamental choice is between fear and love. Fear threatens us—fear of the unknown, fear of terrorists, fear of economic or environmental collapse, fear of meaninglessness as modern life is fragmented and the sacred canopy is shredded, fear of running out of fossil fuel. Fear causes us to hunker down, to protect what is "ours," to lash out at the Other, to seek solace in rationalizations that bolster the importance of the self in the face of any perceived onslaught. Above all, fear refuses vulnerability. Love is open, love reaches out and embraces, love takes chances and so makes us vulnerable. Love embraces freedom and is confident in the final goodness of creation. Fear cannot risk and so is willing to trade freedom for security. Love risks and is never willing to make this trade, for such a trade is to forfeit that which makes life worth living and that which is the basis of human dignity, our very capacity to express ourselves creatively. Our conception of the divine individual both reflects and reinforces our basic orientations toward fear or love. Understanding God as fundamentally open to creaturely experience encourages an openness in us that can nurture our love for others. Understanding God as unaffected by the plight of the world and as having dominating and complete control offers us security, plays on fear, and encourages the view that human beings are separate from the rest of creation.

There is much to be done to flesh out these issues in a sustained, and satisfactory, manner. There are also some practical, but equally important, issues that this work only lays the foundation for addressing. One might show, for instance, how the moral law articulated in this value theory ("so act as to maximize the conditions for the exercise of freedom") can be used to generate a norm capable of assessing consumption patterns of individuals in industrialized nations, which patterns are among the foremost

drivers of ecological degradation. On this value theory, the ethical assessment of human development hinges not only on how such development
impacts the expansion of human freedoms or capabilities but also on how
it impacts the capacity of other creatures to exercise their freedoms or capabilities. Taking this route would allow for the evaluation of commodity
possession on the basis of its effects on the exercise of both human and
non-human capabilities. Further, understanding the meaning of what we
do and who we are in terms of our contribution to the divine life in the
here and now (through our contributions to the lives of other creatures)
takes the onus off defining ourselves in ecologically destructive ways that
require excessive consumption driven by the need to find meaning in terms
of comparing ourselves (and, by extension, our possessions) with others.

The question of how a vision becomes effective is complex and multi-
faceted. Much depends on factors such as education, religion, cultural and
social background, and the perceived problems with the natural environment. One way of addressing this question is to offer for public debate this
alternative conception of the relation between human beings and the rest
of creation and between God and the world. For instance, if such an understanding of God, as permeating and truly affected by the created order,
were to become widespread and deeply felt, then it might help to change
attitudes and behaviors, to help us become more sensitive to the effects of
our activities on other creatures and on ecosystems more generally.[2]

This work itself is devoted to the more foundational project, on which
these other projects would be built, of articulating and defending an understanding of value and moral worth in creation that extends the entire
breadth and depth of the created order. Thomas Aquinas, to his credit,
made the best use of the resources available to him. His genius, his gener-
osity, and his penetrating insight are perhaps unsurpassed in the Christian
tradition. But that should not blind us to the real problems that plague the
position he has staked out. Nor should it serve as a shield to prevent reflection upon a real alternative when it is presented to us. Alfred North Whitehead presents such an alternative, and it deserves to be taken seriously. On
his alternative metaphysic, creation is permeated with goodness and is
worthy of our moral consideration. It is my hope that someday soon, a vision such as this might come to be widely shared and permeate our very
way of thinking about, talking about, and, especially, walking on the earth.

Spiritual Change and Materiality

In Thomas' thought, natural existence can be material, such as dogs
or trees or colors, or immaterial, such as angels or the human soul. Interestingly, properly understood, intentional (or, understood as specified
above, "immaterial") existence can also be material (that is, sensory knowledge) or immaterial (that is, intellectual knowledge). This results in three
possible relations between spiritual change and the material/immaterial
distinction. If the cognizer is a material entity capable of sensory knowledge, then both the natural mode of existence of the thing known and the
intentional existence of that thing in the sense organs are material. If the
cognizer is an immaterial entity and the thing known is also an immaterial
entity,[1] then both the natural mode of existence of the thing known and the
intentional existence of that thing in the sense organs are immaterial. If the
cognizer is a material entity capable of intellectual knowledge (a category
to which only human beings belong), then the natural mode of existence of
the thing (naturally) known is material while the intentional existence
of that thing in the intellect is immaterial. I propose to examine here the
first two cases in order to flesh out Thomas' theory of cognition and to elucidate the nature of the change that brings about knowledge. The third case
is addressed in the text of chapter 3.

In sense knowledge, as noted, the natural mode of the thing known and
the intentional existence of the thing in the sense organs are both material.
All sensing occurs through corporeal organs. There are both external and

internal senses or sensitive powers. The exterior senses for Thomas include the traditional list of sight, hearing, smell, taste, and touch. He argues that an exterior sense "is a passive power, and is naturally immuted by the external sensible."[2] So an exterior sense is a power that is immuted or changed in some way by a sense object. Let us consider first the passivity of the exterior senses and then consider the nature of this immutation or change. "[S]ense is related to the sensible thing as a patient to an agent, because the sensible thing alters the sense."[3] For example, "seeing is accomplished by the fact that the visible species is received in sight; and this is a sort of passivity or suffering."[4] Since the agent—the sensible object in act—that reduces the sense to act, or actualizes it, has actual existence outside the soul, there is no need for any activity on the part of the exterior senses; there is no need for any "agent sense." The sensible species of the sensible object exists in the medium, such as air or water, between the object and the sense faculty, and it impresses itself upon the sense faculty that is in potency to that particular species. Sensible species are completely sufficient for bringing about cognition in the exterior sense faculties. The faculties themselves are in potency to particular kinds of sensation. For example, the faculty of hearing is in potency to sound. When a sensible object is in act, it transmits its sensible form through the air to the ear, imprints itself on that organ, and thus hearing the sound of the sensible object results.

Let us now consider the nature of the change that occurs in the sense organ. As noted earlier, a mere material change is not sufficient for sensing; otherwise all change would be sensed by the body experiencing the change. For knowledge, spiritual or intentional change must take place. With some of the senses, such as touching and tasting, a material or natural change occurs in addition to the intentional one. With others, such as sight, no material change occurs at all; there is only an intentional change.

The sensible species is simultaneously the sensible in act and the sense faculty in act. As Thomas puts it, "the likeness of a sensible thing is the form of the sense in act."[5] (As we will see, this notion has its parallel in the intellect.) The species of the external object is the form of the actualized sense. One operation, sensation, is caused by the sensible object and received by the senses. In this operation the object is active and the senses are passive.[6] The sense organs have a form that is a sensitive potency; it is in potency to further forms by which the senses gain sensitive knowledge. For example, sight is the sensitive potency that is the form of the eye. The sensible object, or more precisely the sensible species of the sensible object, acts directly on the eye and at the same time informs this potency, so that the cognizer actually sees.

The form that informs the sensitive potency is the form of the sensible object. So there is a formal identity between the sensible and the sense. "The sensible in act is the sense in act."[7] We are able to have sensory knowledge of external things because our sensory knowledge is formally identical with those things. The sensitive species becomes the form of the sense in act and is the principle by which sensation occurs. This species can be viewed as a property or state of both the sensible in act and the sense organ in act. It is in virtue of this state that the sense organs produce the appropriate intentional content.[8] Because the sensitive powers are potencies, such a species is necessary actually to sense.

On my reading, Thomas is not saying that intentional being in the senses is some kind of ghostly, spiritual existence within an otherwise material organ. On the contrary, when they receive the intentional form, the sense faculties, as material organs, undergo the only kind of modification they can—material modification. If this reception of form did not bring about material modification, then Thomas would be left to explain what it means to produce an immaterial change in a material organ, and, if this is possible, why a material organ then cannot receive universals or, more precisely, intelligible species.[9] Still, this material modification is not "material change" in the technical sense because it produces knowledge. The change is "spiritual or immaterial." If this reading is correct, then the senses undergo material modification since they are material organs and cannot undergo any other kind of modification. But this modification does not cause the organ to become literally like the naturally existing form of the thing that brought about the change. Instead, this modification produces sense knowledge, and the sensible species is the ontological state or property of the sense organs that produces this sensitive cognition.[10]

Before turning to the discussion of the human intellect, I want to provide a brief characterization of the interior senses (and especially the imagination), which serve as a bridge between the sense and the intellect,[11] and of the way in which immaterial entities know one another. Imagination is an interior sense whose function is to retain and preserve the forms received by the exterior senses. Thomas characterizes the imagination or fantasy as "a storehouse of forms received through the senses,"[12] and he maintains that "those animals have imagination in the precise sense of the term which retain a distinct image of things even while they are not actually sensing things."[13] So imagination allows human beings to recall the forms that once impressed themselves upon the exterior senses even though the exterior object is no longer acting on the senses. The imagination can also create images of things never actually witnessed by combining in new ways what has been experienced. For example, "the imagination from the preconceived images of a mountain and of gold can form the likeness of a golden mountain."[14] The image produced by the imagination is called a phantasm.[15] To identify things not merely as absent (which the imagination does) but also as past, the memory is needed. Memory and imagination are similar, but memory always places its object in a temporal context as something experienced in the past. Imagination does not do this. Further, memory complements the third interior sense, the cogitative power, by preserving the intentions that it apprehends. The cogitative power apprehends the useful or harmful character of things as intentions that are not received through the senses.

Having demonstrated that when the cognizer is a material entity capable of sensory knowledge both the natural mode of existence of the thing known and the intentional existence of that thing in the sense organs are material, I want now to turn to the way by which one immaterial entity knows another. We will see that both the natural mode of existence of the thing known and the intentional existence of that thing in the sense organs are immaterial. This becomes clear through a consideration of Thomas' discussion of how one angel knows another. An objector argues that one angel cannot know another: "It cannot be said that one angel knows the other by a species; because that species would not differ from the angel understood, since each is immaterial."[16] Thomas responds, "One angel knows another by the species of such angel existing in his intellect, which differs from the angel whose image it is, not according to material and immaterial nature, but according to natural and intentional existence. The angel is himself a subsisting form in his natural being; but his species in the intellect of another angel is not so, for there it possesses only an intelligible existence."[17]

It is not the immateriality of the species that is the relevant distinction here because angels both naturally existing and intentionally existing (that is, an angel as known by another angel) are immaterial. If immateriality alone picked out both naturally existing and intentionally existing angels, then it is hard to see how one angel could know another. In that case, it would seem that the only way by which one angel could be informed by the form of another would be to become that angel (that is, to undergo substantial change). No knowledge could be had of one angel by another. So Thomas explains that in every angel, "there was impressed the form of his *own* species according to both its natural and its intelligible condition, so that he should subsist in the nature of his species, and understand himself by it."[18] He continues, "the forms of *other* spiritual and corporeal natures were impressed in him only according to their intelligible natures, so that by such impressed species he might know corporeal and spiritual creatures."[19] The relevant distinction here is between natural and intentional existence. Natural existence is the extra-mental existence of an immaterial entity, and intentional existence is the cognitive existence of this same being in the mind of another. The intentionally existing form produces knowledge, but never substantial change. In this case, both the naturally existing and the intentionally existing forms are immaterial.

Appendix B

God's Nature

The Controversy

Among those who take their philosophical bearings from White-head, there is an important controversy concerning the nature of what he calls God's "primordial nature." Whitehead maintains, "The primordial fact is the unconditioned conceptual valuation of the entire multiplicity of eternal objects."[1] If God primordially envisages all possibility, then God is, in some sense, "before" all actuality. This means that, unlike worldly actu-alities (the datum of God's physical prehensions), God's conceptual pole is prior to his physical pole. God's envisagement of all eternal objects in their relation to one another must be prior to any relation to the world because it is not affected by the actual ordering of eternal objects in the world. As unconditioned by the actual world in this primordial envisagement, God must be in everlasting concrescence; otherwise, the divine ordering of pos-sibilities would be conditioned by the world. Since there is no end to God's concrescence and since time is defined by a transition between actualities, God is, in a sense, outside of time.

Charles Hartshorne, in particular, objects strenuously to this under-standing of God's nature, which he finds riddled with problems. Most fun-damental among them is that it seems to make God an exception to the metaphysical categories. The "category of the ultimate" is that "the many become one and are increased by one." This does not apply to God, whose concrescence never reaches satisfaction, so the many are not, in this singular case, increased by one.[2] Insofar as this understanding of God's nature puts God outside the metaphysical categories that apply to all other actual entities, then, on Hartshorne's reading, it creates the very dualism that Whitehead's metaphysics was developed to avoid.

In order to remedy this situation, Hartshorne maintains that we should jettison Whitehead's understanding of God's primordial nature as the primordial envisagement of *all* possibilities or universals. Instead, Hartshorne holds that "all specific qualities, i.e., those of which there can be negative instances in experience, are emergent, and only the metaphysical universals are eternal."[3] All non-metaphysical universals emerge in the creative advance. "The ultimate principle is experience as partly free or self-creative, and this principle, being ultimate, accounts for definiteness without help from any other principle."[4] There is no need for God to primordially envisage all possibility because these possibilities, or universals, can emerge from the creativity of worldly entities. If this were not the case, "then there could be no emergent novelty at all."[5] That is, God could not truly be the ground of novelty if there really is no novelty, if God had already envisioned every possibility.

Once universals or forms of definiteness are understood to be emergent, then God can be understood not as a single actual entity, but as a personally ordered society or individual. Like other actualities, God's concrescence would start with prehensions of the past—the world and God's own. The category of the ultimate, the many become one and are increased by one, is then strictly metaphysical.[6] God's nature would be utterly reliable because God would inherit, without loss, his everlasting purpose from all past divine actualities. (Although some, including Hartshorne, do not like the term "eternal object," I will use it in order to preserve clarity in our conversation. Nevertheless, with proper qualification, the term "universal" or "possibility" can also be used in its place.)

Given this understanding of God, what is required for Hartshorne to affirm the notion that God gives all actualities an initial aim is that this aim be kept sufficiently general, perhaps as general as "aim at the greatest possible unity in diversity." That is, each occasion inherits the divine aim and its own past, and it has some degree of freedom as to what to do with them. (Hartshorne would also qualify this understanding of the initial aim in terms of the divinely imposed generic laws for any cosmic epic, which laws impose constraints or bounds on the pursuit of purposes.)[7] Hartshorne's critics have pointed out that his understanding of divine experience implies that there is a universal simultaneity of time, and this is ruled out in principle by contemporary physics.[8] Hartshorne responds that the perspective of the physicist is particular or localized and so may not be applicable to the divine perspective. Perhaps "*God here now* is not the same concrete unit of reality as God somewhere else 'now.'"[9] This may seem to compromise God as a cosmic individual, but this may be the case simply because we have stretched too far the analogy of God's experience with human experience.

Notes

Introduction

1. See, e.g., Population Reference Bureau (www.prb.org, 2005); The Millennium Assessment Synthesis Report (www.millenniumassessment.org, 2005); Andrew Goudie, *The Human Impact on the Natural Environment*, 5th edition (Cambridge, Mass.: The MIT Press, 2001); Allen L. Hammond et al., eds., *World Resources 1994–95: A Guide to the Global Environment* (New York and Oxford: Oxford University Press, 1994); and Lester Brown et al., *The State of the World* (New York: W. W. Norton and Company, 1997).

2. See, e.g., The Millennium Assessment Synthesis Report.

3. Never mind that this argument appears to avoid the hard and painful choices that face those of us in industrialized countries concerning the institutionalized injustice that allows the top 20 percent of humanity to consume 86 percent of the earth's resources while the 20 percent at the bottom of the scale consume a mere 1.3 percent (*Business Week*, October 25, 1999, with data from the UN Population Fund).

4. I use the term "direct moral consideration" to distinguish from what might be called the moral consideration that arises indirectly. Consider that Thomas Aquinas holds that human beings ought not to be cruel to animals. This belief appears to give animals moral consideration. But the reason that human beings ought not to be cruel to animals, according to Thomas, is because such cruelty might have harmful effects on people's relations with other humans (that is, they themselves may simply become cruel). So, if this prohibition can be termed "moral consideration" (and perhaps it cannot), it can only be *indirect* moral consideration—moral consideration that is given to one creature because of the direct moral consideration due to another creature. Moral worth, on my usage, means worthy of direct moral consideration. Creatures worthy only of indirect moral consideration have only instrumental goodness or value.

Part I.   Created Goodness and Moral Worth

1. As we shall see, the pivotal point on which this moral separation depends is the human capacity consciously to relate to universals. It is this capacity that makes possible rational freedom, knowledge of God, and proofs for the immortality of the human soul. For a contrary view, see Judith Barad, "Thomas' Inconsistency on the Nature and Treatment of Animals," *Between the Species: A Journal of Ethics* 4 (Spring 1988): 102–111. Barad's interpretation of Thomas is strained, and she fails to examine thoroughly Thomas' rationale for the moral separation between human and non-rational creatures. See also Robin Attfield, *The Ethics of Environmental Concern* (New York: Columbia University Press, 1983). Attfield argues, "The Thomistic metaphysic, indeed, does not require the despotic attitude to animals held by Thomas himself" (p. 54). I argue that Thomas' metaphysic and his moral stance are mutually consistent and systematically interwoven.

2. Several recent books offer rich analyses of the biblical and traditional sources for the dominant Christian conception of the soul and the modern scientific approach to the study of the human being as well as how this scientific approach provides some fundamental challenges to the dominant Christian concept. See Warren S. Brown, Nancey Murphy, and H. Newton Murphy, eds., *Whatever Happened to the Soul? Scientific and Theological Portraits of Human Nature* (Minneapolis: Fortress Press, 1998). The theme that unites this work is "nonreductive physicalism," which attempts to overcome mind/body dualism, holding that statements that science makes about the physical nature of the human being correspond with statements that religion makes about his spiritual nature. In part, this work seeks to motivate a rereading of biblical texts and theological traditions through the lens of a monistic or unified understanding of the human being. And, in part, it seeks to offer a perspective that can reunite science and religion. Nancey Murphy's essay, in *Whatever Happened to the Soul?* and also separately published ("Physicalism without Reductionism: Toward a Scientifically, Philosophically, and Theologically Sound Portrait of Human Nature," *Zygon* 34, no. 4 [December 1999]: 551–571), offers the most in-depth philosophical defense of nonreductive physicalism. Two other books that further the conversation on the human soul in relation to the Christian tradition and contemporary science are Joel B. Green, ed., *What about the Soul? Neuroscience and Christian Anthropology* (Nashville: Abingdon Press, 2004), and Malcolm Jeeves, ed., *From Cells to Souls—And Beyond: Changing Portraits of Human Nature* (Grand Rapids, Mich.: Eerdmans, 2004). For a more environmentally focused analysis of the human soul in the Christian tradition, see Anna Peterson, *Being Human: Ethics, Environment, and Our Place in the World* (Berkeley and Los Angeles: University of California Press, 2001).

3. Peterson, *Being Human*, p. 29.

4. Peterson also draws attention to some of the destructive impacts of this understanding. For example, exclusive definitions of humanness have been used to establish hierarchies within and between societies. This was perhaps most evident during the period of colonialism. Ibid., see p. 42.

5. Peterson seems to take exception to the idea of any hierarchy of value between human beings and non-rational creatures. (See, e.g., ibid., chapters 2 and 3, pp. 28–76.) To my way of thinking, this is misguided. There can, I argue later, be hierarchies that make important value distinctions. The crucial point is that there is moral continuity, not moral separation, between human beings and other creatures. Attempts to eradicate value hierarchies cannot, I believe, be conceptually sustained. These attempts also lead to practical paralysis.

6. Peterson asserts that "there is no way to prove one has a soul" (ibid., p. 29). If this view is taken critically, it might be a justified statement. Still, Peterson means it descriptively, and Thomas attempts just such a proof. The middle portion of this work offers a critical look at these proofs for the subsistence of the human soul.

7. See, e.g., Andrew Linzey, *Christianity and the Rights of Animals* (New York: Crossroad, 1987), pp. 22–27; Peter Singer, *Animal Liberation* (New York: Random House, 1975), pp. 193–196; and Paul Santmire, *The Travail of Nature: The Ambiguous Ecological Promise of Christian Theology* (Philadelphia: Fortress Press, 1985), pp. 84–95. Santmire's analysis is nuanced and enlightening. He notes the ambiguity in Thomas' thought, which finally gives way to an instrumentalization of non-rational creatures.

8. See, e.g., Jill Le Blanc, "Eco-Thomism," *Environmental Ethics* 21, no. 3 (Fall 1999): 293–306; and Peter Drum, "Thomas and the Moral Status of Animals," *American Catholic Philosophical Quarterly* 64, no. 4 (Autumn 1992): 483–488.

9. Andrew Tardiff, "A Catholic Case for Vegetarianism," *Faith and Philosophy: Journal of the Society of Christian Philosophers* 15, no. 2 (1998): 210–222. While Tardiff does not explicitly take a stand on the moral status of animals in Thomas, it seems to me that his argument is successful only if one assumes that, for Thomas, animals have moral worth.

10. Attfield seems to hold such a view.

11. According such moral worth would be a challenge to Thomas' view that divine providence directly preserves all "grades of goodness" (or species) in existence.

12. For further discussion of this issue, see, e.g., Michael Northcott, *The Environment and Christian Ethics* (Cambridge and New York: Cambridge University Press, 1996); Larry Rasmussen, *Earth Community, Earth Ethics* (Maryknoll, N.Y.: Orbis, 1996); Santmire, *The Travail of Nature;* and Attfield, *The Ethics of Environmental Concern.*

13. That is, for Thomas, God's will is necessarily carried out through God's own agency. Thomas claims that God maintains species in existence so that the divine

will for the universe will be fulfilled. There is nothing that human beings can do to thwart the divine will.

Chapter One.   The Metaphysical Grounding of Goodness

1. A "first substance" is an individual something, a *hoc aliquid*. A "second substance" is a universal, a genus or species. See, e.g., *Commentary on the Metaphysics of Aristotle,* trans. John P. Rowan (Chicago: Regnery, 1961), VII. L.13:C 1583. That is, Book VII, Lesson 13, Commentary, Section 1583.

2. *Questions on the Soul,* 1.

3. For a discussion on the relation between matter and potency, see, e.g., *Commentary on the Metaphysics of Aristotle* VIII. L.4:C 1735–1736; 1753; 2438.

4. The two basic kinds are material substances and immaterial substances.

5. Thomas also specifies "particular matter," e.g., this arm or this branch, and "common matter," e.g., arms in general or branches in general. In both cases, the matter under discussion is informed matter.

6. *On Spiritual Creatures,* trans. M. C. Fitzpatrick (Milwaukee: Marquette University Press, 1951), chap. 1.

7. Ibid., VII. L.7:C 1419.

8. *Summa Theologiae,* trans. English Dominicans (New York: Christian Classics, 1981), IIIa, Question 77, Article 2. Or, again, as Thomas says in *On Spiritual Creatures,* "matter is the principle of individuation, inasmuch as it has not the natural capacity of being received in something else. But forms which have the natural capacity of being received in a subject cannot by themselves be individuated; because so far as their own character is concerned, it is a matter of indifference to them whether they are received in one or in many" (*On Spiritual Creatures,* 5, 8).

9. *Summa Theologiae* Ia, 67.

10. The efficient cause is an extrinsic moving cause and is "that from which the first beginning of change or of rest comes" (*Commentary on the Metaphysics of Aristotle* V. L.3:C 765). The final cause is the thing's end, "that for the sake of which something is done" (ibid., V. L.3:C 771). These two mutually cause each other.

11. See John Wippel, "Thomas Aquinas on Creatures as Causes of *Esse,*" *International Philosophical Quarterly* 40, no. 2 (June 2000): 200. Also see *Summa contra Gentiles,* trans. English Dominicans (London: Burns, Oates, and Washbourne, 1934), Book I, Chapter 27; and II, 68.

12. In material creatures, there is a twofold composition: *esse* and essence; and form and matter. And our focus now is on the latter.

13. *Summa Theologiae* Ia, 76, 4. See also *Questions on the Soul,* 9.

14. See *Questions on the Soul,* 19.

15. *On the Power of God,* trans. English Dominicans (London: Burns, Oates, and Washbourne, 1932–1934), Book I, Question 3, Article 8. See also *Commentary on*

the Metaphysics of Aristotle VII. L.7:C 1423. Here, Thomas is arguing that the composite and not the form is generated: "a form is said to exist in matter, although a form does not [properly] exist, but a composite exists by its form. Thus the proper way of speaking is to say that a composite is generated from matter according to such and such a form. For forms are not generated, properly speaking, but are brought from the potency of matter, inasmuch as matter, which is in potentiality to form, becomes actual under some form; and this is to produce a composite." It is on the basis of this Aristotelian understanding of form that Anthony Kenny criticizes Thomas' attempt to argue that a form can be subsistent. See Anthony Kenny, *Thomas on Mind* (London and New York: Routledge, 1993).

16. See, e.g., Etienne Gilson, *The Christian Philosophy of St. Thomas Aquinas* (Notre Dame, Ind.: University of Notre Dame Press, 1956), p. 31.

17. See, e.g., Rudi A. te Velde, *Participation and Substantiality in Thomas Aquinas,* revised from the Dutch with the help of Anthony P. Runia (Leiden: E. J. Brill, 1995), p. 8; and James Weisheipl, *Friar Thomas d'Aquino: His Life, Thought, and Works* (Washington, D.C.: The Catholic University of America Press, 1974), p. 134.

18. Quoted from Thomas Aquinas, *An Exposition of the 'On the Hebdomads' of Boethius,* trans. Janice L. Schultz and Edward A. Synan (Washington, D.C.: The Catholic University of America Press, 2001), L.3.B1–10. Note that I am following the translators' notation for citations. "L" refers to the Leonine edition of the Latin text. The number following the "L" refers to the chapter. When the chapter number is followed by a "B," the text is from Boethius' work. When the chapter number is followed by an "A," the text is from Thomas' commentary. The final digits refer to the line numbers in the Leonine edition.

19. See, e.g., Jan Aertsen, "Good as Transcendental and the Transcendence of the Good," in *Being and Goodness: The Concept of the Good in Metaphysics and Philosophical Theology,* ed. Scott MacDonald (Ithaca: Cornell University Press, 1991), pp. 56–73, for a discussion of this issue. See especially pp. 57–58.

20. Quoted from Thomas Aquinas' *Commentary on Aristotle's 'Nicomachean Ethics,'* trans. C. I. Litzinger (Notre Dame, Ind.: Dumb Ox Books, 1993), 1094a1–3.

21. *Commentary on Aristotle's 'Nicomachean Ethics,'* Book I, Lecture 1, Section 9.

22. Thomas quickly goes on to explain two things. First, "There is no problem from the fact that some men desire evil. For they desire evil only under the aspect of good, that is, insofar as they think it good" (ibid., I, 1, 10). Second, "The saying '. . . what all desire' is to be understood not only of those who knowingly seek good but also of beings lacking knowledge" (ibid., I, 1, 11). Those things that do not have knowledge are moved under the direction of the divine intellect, and this natural tendency to good is called desire for good. (See also, for example, *Summa contra Gentiles* IIIa, 24.)

23. *Commentary on Aristotle's 'Nicomachean Ethics'* I, 1, 9.

24. This is probably better translated: "To be (*esse*) is the actuality (*actualitas*) of all things."

25. *Summa Theologiae* Ia, 5, 1.

26. See ibid., Ia, 13, 4.

27. Ibid., Ia, 5, 1.

28. Ibid.

29. Ibid., IIaIIae, 132, 4.

30. *Disputed Questions on Truth,* vol. 1 trans. Robert William Mulligan, vol. 2 trans. James V. McGlynn, vol. 3 trans. Robert W. Schmidt (Chicago: Regnery, 1952–1954), Question 21, Article 3.

31. *Summa Theologiae* Ia, 5, 1.

32. Ibid.

33. See Jan Aertsen, "The Convertibility of Being and the Good in St. Thomas Aquinas," *The New Scholasticism* 59 (1985): 449–470. See, e.g., p. 457.

34. *Summa Theologiae* Ia, 5, 2 ad 4.

35. *Summa contra Gentiles* I, 28.

36. *On the Power of God* III, 7, 2 ad 9, italics added.

37. Ibid., Ia, 5, 3. Whatever is, is good. This belief may seem to deny the existence of evil; certainly as a metaphysical notion, it does just that. Since good is a transcendental, evil cannot have ontological existence. However, Thomas does not deny the reality of evil, which he understands as a privation of being. Something is evil insofar as it lacks an actuality that it ought to have. (See, e.g., *Summa Theologiae* Ia, 48, 5 ad 1.)

38. Ibid., Ia, 5, 1, obj 1.

39. Ibid., Ia, 5, 1 ad 1.

40. See Aertsen, "Good as Transcendental and the Transcendence of the Good," p. 67.

41. See Jan Aertsen, "Thomas Aquinas on the Good: The Relation between Metaphysics and Ethics," in *Aquinas's Moral Theory: Essays in Honor of Norman Kretzmann,* ed. Scott MacDonald and Eleonore Stump (Ithaca and London: Cornell University Press, 1998), pp. 235–253.

42. See *Summa Theologiae* Ia, 5, 6.

43. Ibid., Ia, 5, 2 ad 2.

44. Every creature, Thomas maintains, is itself a final cause only by relation to God, who is the final cause of the universe. Each is a final cause only in the sense that they are related to, and directed toward, the final cause of everything that exists. (See, e.g., *Disputed Questions on Truth,* 21, 1 ad 1; or 21, 5.)

45. See, e.g., *Disputed Questions on Truth,* 21, 5.

46. I have found the following articles especially helpful in clarifying Thomas' understanding of participation as well as the debates that swirl around it. George Lindbeck, "Participation and Existence in the Interpretation of St. Thomas Aquinas I," *Franciscan Studies* 17 (1957): 1–22; George Lindbeck, "Participation and Ex-

istence in the Interpretation of St. Thomas Aquinas II," *Franciscan Studies* 17 (1957): 107–125. This two-part article is particularly helpful in setting the parameters of the debate. Cornelio Fabro, "The Intensive Hermeneutics of Thomistic Philosophy: The Notion of Participation," *The Review of Metaphysics* 27 (1974): 449–491. This article is a summary of some of the central ideas in Fabro's influential and insightful book, *Participation et Causalité*. Sister Helen James John, "Participation Revisited," *The Modern Schoolman: A Quarterly Journal of Philosophy* 39 (1962): 154–165. This article offers a sketch of Fabro's larger work. Sister M. Annice, "Historical Sketch of the Theory of Participation," *The New Scholasticism* 26 (1952): 46–79. The title says it all. Keith Buersmeyer, "Predication and Participation," *The New Scholasticism* 51 (1981): 35–51. This article seeks to show the interconnection between Thomas' logical predication and ontological participation. John Wippel, "Thomas Aquinas and Participation," in *Studies in Medieval Philosophy*, ed. John Wippel (Washington, D.C: The Catholic University of America Press, 1987), pp. 117–158. This article offers a helpful analysis of Thomas' understanding of the modes of participation as well as guidance on where to turn in Thomas to most readily discern his understanding of participation. Rudi te Velde, *Participation and Substantiality in Thomas Aquinas*. Written as a dissertation, this thorough and thoughtful analysis offers a wealth of penetrating insight. Ralph M. McInerny, "Saint Thomas on *De hebdomadibus*," in *Being and Goodness*, ed. Scott MacDonald (Ithaca: Cornell University Press, 1991), pp. 74–97. Though only tangentially concerned with participation, this article helps to clarify participation in Thomas' commentary on Boethius' work.

47. For a more extended treatment of this issue, see, e.g., Aertsen, "Good as Transcendental and the Transcendence of the Good," pp. 56–73.

48. *Summa Theologiae* Ia, 5 and 6; *Disputed Questions on Truth*, 21.

49. *Disputed Questions on Truth*, 21, 4.

50. *Summa Theologiae* Ia, 6, 4.

51. See, e.g., *Summa contra Gentiles* II, 44 and 45; II, 83; IIIa, 69; and *Summa Theologiae* Ia, 47, 2.

52. The point at which Plato is mistaken can be seen from Aristotle's critique of Plato's conception of the idea of the good, a critique that Thomas follows. (See, e.g., *Disputed Questions on Truth*, 21, 4.) Plato's understanding of an "idea" holds that it is the nature or essence of all things that partake of the idea, so there cannot be one idea of things not sharing a common nature. Things in different categories do not share a common nature. Good, however, is found in every category. (See, e.g., *Commentary on Aristotle's 'Nicomachean Ethics'* I, 6, 81.) Therefore, Plato's understanding of the separated good as the formal goodness of all things cannot be correct, because diverse things do not have the same formal goodness. For example, in quality, good is predicated of the virtuous, which makes its possessor good. In relation, good is predicated of the useful, which is good relative to the proper end, and so on. There is no good that is the common nature of all goods. Otherwise,

good would only be found in one category rather than in all of them. Thus, good is not predicated univocally of things in different categories. But neither is good predicated of things in diverse categories in a purely equivocal manner. Rather, it is predicated analogically. Thomas distinguishes these types of predication as follows: "Univocal terms mean absolutely the same thing, but equivocal terms absolutely different; whereas in analogical terms a word taken in one signification must be placed in the definition of the same word taken in other senses; as, for instance, 'being' which is applied to 'substance' is placed in the definition of being as applied to 'accident'; and 'healthy' applied to animal is placed in the definition of healthy as applied to urine and medicine. For urine is the sign of health in the animal, and medicine is the cause of health" (*Summa Theologiae* Ia, 13, 10). We will see below how analogical predication applies when speaking of the goodness of creatures and of the Creator.

53. See, e.g., *Commentary on the Metaphysics of Aristotle*, I. L.17:C 259; or I. L.10:C 153.

54. See, e.g., Joseph Owens, *An Interpretation of Existence* (Milwaukee: Bruce Publishing Co., 1968), pp. 102–103.

55. *An Exposition of the 'On the Hebdomads' of Boethius* L.1.A70–80.

56. Ibid.

57. See, e.g., Wippel, "Thomas Aquinas and Participation," p. 119.

58. The first mode of participation concerns the way in which a species (e.g., human) participates in a genus (animal), or an individual (e.g., Socrates) participates in a species (human). It is the way that "human being is said to participate in animal because it does not possess the intelligible structure of animal according to its total commonality; and in the same way, Socrates participates in human" (*An Exposition of the 'On the Hebdomads' of Boethius* L.1.A70–80). Something of less extended intelligibility participates in something of more extended intelligibility. Unlike Plato, Thomas does not draw any ontological implications from this type of participation. Socrates is said to participate in human nature not because the species has independent existence. Rather, Thomas' point is simply that Socrates is not identical with his human nature. The species participates in the genus, or the individual participates in the species, only when these terms are understood logically rather than ontologically. If understood in an ontological sense, then we have turned from Aristotle to Plato. With Plato, there is a necessary opposition between what is said essentially and what is said by participation. With Aristotle, in this first mode of participation, this need not be the case. As Thomas explains, since "a human is truly that which is animal—the essence of 'animal,' as it were, not existing outside the differentiating note 'human'—nothing prohibits that what is said through participation also be predicated substantially" (ibid., L.2.A60–70). That is, "human" participates in "animal," so "animal" is predicated of "human" by participation. But "animal" is also predicated essentially of "human." Therefore, with this

first mode, what is said through participation can also be predicated substantially or essentially.

The second mode of participation is the way "a subject participates in an accident, or matter in form, because a substantial form, or an accidental one, which is common by virtue of its own intelligible structure, is determined to this or that subject" (ibid., L.2.A70–80). Such forms are universal in their intelligible contents, or as considered simply in themselves, but are restricted when received in a subject. When a form is received, an ontological composition of that form and the receiving subject is formed. The received form is a perfection of the subject, which shares in or takes part in (and so participates in) the form without being identical to it or exhausting it. A subject participates in a form insofar as many subjects can share the same perfection and none is identical to it. A subject receives the perfection from another partially (i.e., is not identical to it) and so is said to participate in it. With this mode of participation, essential predication, or "to be through essence," and predication by participation, or "to be through participation," are opposites. As Thomas explains, this is because "an accident is outside the substance of a subject, and form is outside the very substance of matter" (*An Exposition of the 'On the Hebdomads' of Boethius* L.2.A50–60). Only that which is of the substance of the subject (or of matter) can be predicated of it essentially.

59. Ibid., L.2.A80–90.

60. *Summa Theologiae* Ia, 4, 3.

61. As a secondary matter, the second mode is also relevant to an understanding of how creatures are good by participation. To anticipate our discussion, it is according to the third mode that creatures are substantially good or good relatively, good insofar as they have substantial being. It is according to the second mode that creatures are accidentally good or good simply, good insofar as they actualize the potentialities, or achieve the perfection, appropriate to their kind.

62. *Disputed Questions on Truth,* 21, 4. He maintains that this is "also because of the first goodness taken as the exemplar and effective cause of all created goodness" (ibid.).

63. *On the Power of God* III, 7, 5. Thomas continues, "and this is the case in all univocal causes: thus man begets a man, and fire generates fire" (*On the Power of God* III, 7, 5). Univocal causes can also communicate in form according to the same formality but not according to the same measure, as when fire heats iron. A univocal cause is a particular, rather than universal, cause. It cannot be the cause of the form as such because then it would be the cause of its own form, insofar as the form of the agent is essentially the same as the form of the effect. See also, e.g., *Summa Theologiae* Ia, 13, 5 ad 1.

64. *Disputed Questions on Truth,* 5, 8 ad 8.

65. See, e.g., *Summa Theologiae* Ia, 104, 1. See also Wippel, "Thomas Aquinas on Creatures as Causes of *Esse,*" especially p. 210.

66. *Summa Theologiae* Ia, 13, 5. See also, e.g., *Disputed Questions on Truth*, 10, 13 ad 3; *Summa Theologiae* Ia, 104, 1; and *Summa contra Gentiles* IIIa, 65.

67. Thomas states that "things generated by the sun's heat may be in some sort spoken of as like the sun, not as though they received the form of the sun in its specific likeness, but in its generic likeness" (*Summa Theologiae* Ia, 4, 2).

68. Ibid., Ia, 4, 3.

69. Ibid.

70. Note that Thomas, at times, calls analogical causes "equivocal causes." But in *Summa Theologiae* Ia, 13, 5 and 5, 1, he clarifies that such causes are not absolutely equivocal; otherwise they would not be able to produce their own likeness. Rather, they are analogical or according to proportionality.

71. *Summa Theologiae* Ia, 104, 1.

72. See Wippel, "Thomas Aquinas on Creatures as Causes of *Esse*." This fundamental difference between God and creatures is expressed in the way we predicate attributes of God and of creatures. As Thomas states, "Nothing is predicated of God and creatures as though they were in the same order, but, rather, according to priority and posteriority [i.e., analogically]. For all things are predicated of God essentially. For God is called being as being entity itself, and He is called good as being goodness itself. But in other beings predications are made by participation, as Socrates is said to be man, not because he is humanity itself, but because he possesses humanity" (*Summa contra Gentiles* I, 32). There can be no attribute that is predicated univocally of God and creatures. God is self-identical; God is what God has. Any perfection predicated of God is essential in the sense that it is identical with God. This is not true of any creature. This statement can be understood in terms of the simplicity of God and the composite nature of creatures. Since God is absolute form or absolute being and since in form itself or being itself there is nothing besides itself, then in God there is nothing besides God's essential self. Whatever we predicate of God must be predicated essentially. God does not participate in anything and has no accidents. A creature is not self-identical. A material creature is composed of matter and form as well as essence and *esse*, while an immaterial creature is composed of essence and *esse*. By the very fact of being created, a creature must be a composite since it cannot be *ipsum esse*. (See *Summa Theologiae* Ia, 3, 7.)

73. *Summa contra Gentiles* II, 15. See also ibid., IIIa, 66.

74. *Summa Theologiae* Ia, 4, 2.

75. Still, one might argue that, in the end, the argument is viciously circular if what is taken for granted is not simply that contingent creatures exist but that the world itself is contingent and thus requires a cause. One might argue that this premise is not self-evident but, rather, itself finally depends on Thomas' understanding of God. At any rate, this is a discussion that we can circumscribe for the purposes at hand.

76. *Summa Theologiae* Ia, 44, 1.

77. Ibid., Ia, 4, 2.

78. For additional arguments, see, e.g., ibid., Ia, 11, 3 and 4; and *Summa contra Gentiles* II, 52.

79. See, e.g., ibid.

80. A brief exploration of Thomas' understanding of how creatures imitate God can lend clarity to his understanding of the goodness of creatures. God is the *efficient cause* of creatures because creatures are the effects of God's creative agency. God is the *exemplary cause* of creatures insofar as creatures receive a similitude of God, imitate God in some way, and reflect the divine goodness.

Because God is an analogical cause, it is helpful to investigate what it means to say that creatures imitate God. Since, Thomas holds, the world was not made by chance, "there must exist in the divine mind a form to the likeness of which the world was made" (*Summa Theologiae* Ia, 15, 1). But "there cannot be an idea of any whole, unless particular ideas are had of those parts of which the whole is made. . . . So, then, it must needs be that in the divine mind there are the proper ideas of all things" (ibid., Ia, 15, 2). This is not repugnant to the divine simplicity because these ideas exist in the divine as things understood by it. God knows God's own essence "not only as it is in itself, but [also] as it can be participated in by creatures according to some degree of likeness" (ibid.). Since the divine essence contains all perfection in a simple unity, this essence is the sufficient exemplar of everything existing. But since it is infinite, it is not this universal essence of God that is itself the idea of each thing. Rather the exemplary forms or ideas of creatures are the divine essence *as it is known by divine wisdom to be imitable by other things*. To repeat, each exemplary form is the divine essence as known by God as the model or likeness of a given species of creature. For example, Thomas maintains that "by conceiving His essence as imitable in respect of life and not of knowledge, it conceives the proper form of a plant: or again as imitable in respect of knowledge but not of intellect, it conceives the proper form of an animal, and so on" (*Summa contra Gentiles* I, 54).

Things are distinguished by species according to their characteristic mode of being. Each type of thing's diverse relation to being, the way it imitates God's essence, rather than any formal hierarchy of essences as such, is what distinguishes creatures. Any given created nature has being in a finite way, and the way it has being is what defines that kind of creature or determines it to a given species and not some other. The essence of a thing is simply the way that thing has being.

81. *Summa contra Gentiles* I, 54.

82. *Disputed Questions on Truth*, 21, 5.

83. Ibid.

84. Ibid.

85. *Summa Theologiae* Ia, 6, 4, italics added.

Chapter Two.   **The Moral Bifurcation of Creation**

1. As we will have occasion to note, there is also a sense in which rational and non-rational creatures have divergent final ends.

2. *Summa contra Gentiles* IIIa, 19.

3. See ibid., IIIa, 3. Again, Thomas argues, "every action and movement are for the sake of some perfection" (ibid., IIIa, 3). And what is perfect is a good, so every action and movement are for the sake of a good.

4. Ibid., IIIa, 24.

5. See ibid., IIIa, 18.

6. *Summa Theologiae* Ia, 65, 2.

7. Ibid.

8. For the sake of clarity it might be pointed out here that, on Thomas' account, there is a twofold good of order in the universe: "one consisting in the whole universe being directed to that which is outside the universe [i.e., God], just as the army is directed to the commander-in-chief: while the other consists in the parts of the universe being directed to each other, as the parts of an army: and the second order is for the sake of the first" (*Summa contra Gentiles* I, 78). Having discussed the first, we consider the second below after considering what it means for each creature to exist for its own perfection.

9. See, e.g., Le Blanc, "Eco-Thomism," pp. 305–306.

10. See, e.g., *Summa contra Gentiles* II, 44.

11. Ibid., II, 45. Or, again, a plurality of goods is better than any one finite good because this plurality contains this good and more besides. All creaturely goodness is finite and so falls short of the infinite goodness of God. "Therefore the universe of creatures, if they are of many degrees, is more perfect than if things were of but one degree" (ibid.).

12. See, e.g., *Summa Theologiae* Ia, 47, 2.

13. *Summa contra Gentiles* IIIa, 22.

14. Two common arguments employed by Thomas draw on the order of generation and the order of preservation that he takes to be evident in nature. In the generation of things, he argues, there is a procession from the imperfect to the perfect. Since everything moved tends, as toward a divine likeness, to be perfect in itself, everything seeks to become actualized by way of movement. So the more perfect an act, the more the appetite of matter (which is in potentiality to form) inclines toward it. The less perfect creature strains toward, so to speak, the more perfect. Thomas' hierarchy of being is dynamic; all beings strain, so to speak, toward actuality. "Certain grades are to be found in the acts of forms. For primary matter is in potentiality, first of all, to the elemental form. While under the elemental form, it is in potentiality to the form of a mixed body: wherefore elements are the matter of a mixed body. Considered as under the form of a mixed body, it is in potentiality to

a vegetative soul: for the act of such a body is a soul. Again, the vegetative soul is in potentiality to the sensitive, and the sensitive to the intellective" (*Summa contra Gentiles* IIIa, 22. See also, e.g., *Summa Theologiae* Ia, 96, 1). The same conclusion is forthcoming if we consider how creatures keep themselves in existence: the more perfect make use of the less perfect. "Mixed bodies are preserved by the qualities becoming to the elements: plants are nourished by mixed bodies; animals derive their nourishment from plants; and [those] that are more perfect and powerful [derive their nourishment] from the imperfect and weak. Man employs all kinds of things for his own use" (ibid; see also, e.g., *Summa Theologiae* Ia, 96, 1). This argument is perhaps Thomas' most common for explaining the hierarchical ordering of creatures. In his *Summa Theologiae,* he adds, "the hunting of wild animals is just and natural, because man thereby exercises his natural right" (*Summa Theologiae* Ia, 96, 1).

15. *Summa contra Gentiles* IIIb, 112.

16. See, e.g., *Summa Theologiae* IaIIae, 64, 1; Ia, 96, 1; and *Summa contra Gentiles* IIIb, 112. By the very fact that human beings possess a rational soul, they have an essential perfection that is in addition to the perfections enjoyed by any other material creature. Human beings are at the apex of the material world. Seemingly, since higher creatures use the lower creatures throughout the hierarchy of being, the fact that human beings are at the apex of material creation by itself justifies instrumentalizing other creatures to the human good. To the modern interpreter of Thomas, this may be troubling since he seems to have blatantly violated what has become enshrined as the "is/ought" distinction. That is, he appears to have drawn morally relevant conclusions from empirical descriptions of, or facts about, the world. The notion that creatures understood on Thomas' ontology to be more perfect make use of those that are less perfect, or the claim that the less perfect are ordered to the more perfect in the order of generation, does not justify the strict instrumentalization of "less perfect" creatures. One cannot legitimately draw an inference from what other creatures (or human beings) *do* to what human beings *ought* to do precisely because human beings are moral creatures, capable of consciously relating to universals and so exercising rational freedom. Simply put, the very perfection that places human beings at the apex of material creation—the rational soul—problematizes any inference from what other creatures (or human beings) *do* do to what human beings *ought* to do. It is only because human beings are moral creatures that the issue of the moral status of other creatures becomes relevant.

One might maintain that for Thomas the issue is definitional, so there is no need to justify argumentatively his view that non-rational creatures are strictly instrumental to the human good. That is, for Thomas, one might argue, it is simply definitionally the case that if creature X is ordered to creature Y in a hierarchy of being, then X is of only instrumental significance to Y. Then it immediately follows that, assuming Y is capable of making moral choices, Y *ought* to treat X as of only instrumental value, since this is to treat X in accord with X's own nature. On this reasoning, Thomas' moral conclusion would not be reached merely by inferring it from descriptions of the way that creatures do, in fact, behave. Rather, they behave that way because of their natures, which are ordered in a hierarchy, and so forth. This position is problematic if it takes Thomas to be making a bare definitional assertion (concerning the strict instrumental ordering of other creatures to human beings) without need of support. We can ask what it is about creaturely natures that renders them suitable for such instrumental ordering. As we will see, on Thomas' account, there are, in fact, what he takes to be good reasons for the strictly instrumental ordering of one creature to another.

17. Besides freedom and immortality, Thomas offers various other reasons for the separation of human beings from non-rational creatures. For example, human beings "attain to the end" of "knowing and loving" God, while non-rational creatures cannot do so. Human beings are also "principal parts" of the universe, "more akin to the whole," and are immortal (*Summa contra Gentiles* IIIb, 112).

18. *Summa contra Gentiles* IIIb, 112.

19. Ibid., italics added.

20. *Summa Theologiae* IaIIae, 64, 1 ad 1.

21. Ibid., italics added.

22. Ibid.

23. *Summa contra Gentiles* IIIb, 112.

24. Thomas follows with a similar argument: "That which has dominion over its own act, is free in its action, because he is free who is cause of himself: whereas that which by some kind of necessity is moved by another to act, is subject to slavery. Therefore every other creature is naturally under slavery; the intellectual creature alone is free" (ibid.).

25. *Disputed Questions on Truth*, 24, 2.

26. Ibid.

27. Ibid.

28. *Summa contra Gentiles* II, 48. See also *Disputed Questions on Truth*, 24, 2.

29. *Summa contra Gentiles* II, 48. See also *Disputed Questions on Truth*, 24, 2.

30. See *Summa contra Gentiles* II, 48. For some of Thomas' discussions on that which is free being its own cause, see *Summa Theologiae* Ia, 83, 1ad 3; IaIIae, 108, 1 ad 2; IIaIIae, 19, 4; *Summa contra Gentiles* I, 72; and *Commentary on the Metaphysics of Aristotle* V, L.16:C 1000.

31. See *Summa Theologiae* Ia, 83, 1 ad 3.

32. *Summa contra Gentiles* IIIb, 112.

33. William French, "Christianity and the Domination of Nature" (Ph.D. diss., University of Chicago, 1985), p. 513.

34. Ibid., pp. 513–514.

35. Ibid., p. 514.

36. To be sure, as noted, one gets into some tricky issues here with the difference between Thomas' understanding of species and the modern understanding. But, as long we are concerned with living creatures, it is enough for our discussion that on both accounts, the greater the number of species, the greater the diversity of life on earth.

37. *Summa Theologiae*, Ia, 47, 1.

38. See, e.g., *Disputed Questions on Truth*, 5, 3.

39. Thomas sometimes puts this in terms of "a certain perpetuity." See, e.g., *On the Power of God* I, 3, 10.

40. *Disputed Questions on Truth*, 5, 3.

41. And, indeed, Thomas does maintain that species are maintained "for their own sakes" because they are necessary for the perfection of the universe. (See, e.g., ibid.)

42. *Summa Theologiae* Ia, 23, 7.

43. Ibid., Ia, 15, 2.

44. Ibid., Ia, 73, 1.

45. Ibid.

46. *On the Power of God* II, 5, 5.

47. Ibid., II, 5, 7.

48. Ibid., II, 5, 7 ad 17.

49. Ibid., II, 5, 9.

50. Ibid., italics added.

51. Thomas' explanation for why the human body continues in existence is as follows: "By its perfect union with God the soul will have complete sway over the body: so that although matter, if left to itself, is corruptible, it will acquire incorruption by the power of the soul" (*On the Power of God* II, 5, 10 ad 3).

52. *On the Power of God* II, 5, 9.

53. See also, e.g., Thomas' response to the objection that elements are required for their service to humans during their time on earth as wayfarers, so too, then, should plants and animals be similarly rewarded. Thomas counters: "The elements are said to be rewarded not in themselves, because in themselves they had no merit; but because men will be rewarded in them, inasmuch as their brightness will conduce to the glory of the elect. As to plants and animals they will be of no use to man like the elements which will be as it were the place of their glory: hence the comparison fails" (ibid., II, 5, 9 ad 9).

54. Ibid., II, 5, 9.

55. Vernon Bourke, "Is Thomas Aquinas a Natural Law Ethicist?" *The Monist: An International Quarterly Journal of General Philosophical Inquiry* 58 (1974): 52–66.

56. Ibid., p. 53.

57. A useful way to put the contrast drawn here between diverse understandings of natural law is to suggest a development in Thomas' own thought from an

emphasis on precepts naturally implanted in the human being to an emphasis on right reason in discerning the objective order. In his early commentary on Peter Lombard's *Sentences,* Thomas writes, "Natural law is *nothing* other than a notion naturally implanted in man, whereby he is fittingly directed to perform proper actions, either in accord with his generic nature (such as procreating, eating, and so on), or in accord with his specific nature (reasoning, and the like)" (*Scriptum in IV Sententiarum,* ed. Pierre Mandonnet and M. F. Moos [Paris: Lethielleux, 1933], 33, 1, 1, c; quoted in Bourke, "Is Thomas Aquinas a Natural Law Ethicist?" p. 60). Thomas is here claiming that certain precepts of natural law are innate. In his later works, he comes to emphasize right reason rather than innate precepts in his discussion of proper human action. This can be seen, for example, in the following passage, where human reason (and not natural law) is juxtaposed with the eternal law. "The due order to an end is measured by some rule. In things that act according to nature, this rule is the natural force that inclines them to that end. . . . Now in those things that are done by the will, the proximate rule is the human reason, while the supreme rule is the Eternal Law. When, therefore, a human action tends to the end, according to the order of reason and of the Eternal Law, then that action is right: but when it turns aside from that rectitude, then it is said to be a sin" (*Summa Theologiae* IaIIae, 21, 1). On the reading given here, this juxtaposition of human reason and the eternal law makes good sense because the precepts of natural law are what right reason discerns about what is fitting, given God's rational ordering of the universe. This is why Thomas says that natural law is the "participation of the eternal law in the rational creature" (ibid., IaIIae, 91, 2).

58. Ibid., IaIIae, 94, 2.

59. Ibid., italics deleted.

60. Ibid., IaIIae, 94, 2.

61. Ibid., italics deleted.

62. Ibid.

63. See, e.g., Ralph M. McInerny's discussion in chapter 3 of *Ethica Thomistica: The Moral Philosophy of Thomas Aquinas,* revised edition (Washington, D.C.: The Catholic University of America Press, 1997).

64. *Summa Theologiae* IaIIae, 94, 3.

65. Ibid., IaIIae, 71, 6 ad 4.

66. Ibid., IaIIae, 4, 3.

67. See, e.g., ibid., IaIIae, 100, 3 ad 1.

68. See ibid., IaIIae, 72, 4.

69. Ibid., IIaIIae, 64, 1.

70. *Summa contra Gentiles* IIIb, 112.

71. *Summa Theologiae* IaIIae, 91, 2.

72. Ibid., IaIIae, 91, 1.

73. *Disputed Questions on Truth,* 14, 2.

74. *Summa Theologiae* IIaIIae, 47, 6 ad 3.

75. Ibid., IIaIIae, 47, 6 ad 1.

76. Ibid., IaIIae, 55, 1.

77. See, e.g., ibid.

78. See, e.g., ibid., IaIIae, 58, 3.

79. Let me briefly justify my decision to focus on justice. In the following, Thomas offers an overview of his understanding of the role of the different virtues in the moral life. I shall interrupt this quotation at several places to provide commentary. "Human virtue . . . is that which makes a man good, and renders his work good. Now man's good is to be in accordance with reason. . . . Wherefore it belongs to human virtue to make man good, to make his work accord with reason. This happens in three ways: first, by rectifying reason itself, and this is done by the intellectual virtues" (ibid., IIaIIae, 123, 1). The most relevant intellectual virtue is prudence, which occupies a sort of middle ground between the intellectual and the moral virtues. Its *subject* is the intellect, so it is essentially an intellectual virtue. But "considered on the part of its *matter*, it has something in common with the moral virtues: for it is right reason about things to be done. . . . It is in this sense that it is reckoned with the moral virtues" (ibid., IaIIae, 58, 3 ad 1, italics added). Thomas often treats prudence as a moral virtue, though it is actually so only in a qualified sense, insofar as it is concerned with human activity. Prudence is concerned with reasoning about the *means* to achieve a given end. Therefore, an analysis of this virtue cannot tell us whether respecting the moral worth of other creatures is among the *ends* relevant to pursuit of the human good. (See, e.g., ibid., IaIIae, 58, 4 and IIaIIae, 47, 6.) I mention prudence, then, in order to set it aside. It is the moral virtues, properly so called, that concern habituation toward the end that is appointed by reason.

Let us return to Thomas' remarks on the second way the virtues make human works accord with reason, namely, "by establishing the rectitude of reason in human affairs, and this belongs to justice" (ibid., IIaIIae, 123, 1). Justice is the virtue whose subject is the rational appetite, the will. Justice orients the will toward those goods that relate us to others, which transcend the individual's good (though, to be sure, this orientation is necessary for the achievement of the individual good as well). Before taking up the discussion of justice, I first want to look briefly at the sensitive appetite and the virtues that rectify it, again in order to demonstrate that these virtues are not directly relevant to our conversation.

The sensitive appetite responds not only to reason but also to the senses, memory, and imagination. Sensual pleasure or pain can sway the sensitive appetite either to seek or to avoid objects in a manner contrary to the dictates of reason. By this attraction or repulsion, the sensitive appetite can hinder the will from following the rectitude of reason, pursuing instead that which is counter to our true good. Continuing with the quotation above, Thomas maintains that the third way the virtues make our activity accord with reason is "by removing the obstacles to the establishment of this rectitude in human affairs" (ibid., IaIIae, 123, 1). He goes on, "Now the human will is hindered in two ways from following the rectitude of reason. First, through being drawn by some object of pleasure to something other than what the rectitude of reason requires; and this obstacle is removed by the virtue of temperance. Secondly, through the will being disinclined to follow that that is in accordance with reason, on account of some difficulty that presents itself. In order to remove this obstacle fortitude of the mind is requisite" (ibid.). The sensitive appetite of the soul can be considered to have two aspects: the concupiscible, which seeks what is pleasurable; and the irascible, which seeks to avoid what is painful. In order to moderate these passions of the sensitive appetite, which rebel against reason chiefly by lack of moderation (see, e.g., ibid., IaIIae, 141, 3), so as to be in accord with reason, it is necessary that the sensitive appetite be perfected by the virtues of temperance and fortitude. Temperance, "which denotes a kind of moderation, is chiefly concerned with those passions that tend towards sensible goods" (ibid., IaIIae, 141, 3). Fortitude denotes a "firmness in bearing and withstanding those things wherein it is most difficult to be firm, namely in certain grave dangers" (ibid., IaIIae, 123, 2). The sensitive appetite requires habituation to dispose it to respond in accord with reason. With such habituation, one's immediate response to a given situation will, under most circumstances, reliably direct one to action that is appropriate or accords with reason or truly perfects. Temperance and fortitude are cardinal virtues that incline the sensitive appetite to follow the dictates of reason by removing the obstacles of concupiscence and fear, which passions can withdraw the will from following reason. (See, e.g., ibid., IaIIae, 47, 7 or IaIIae, 61, 2.)

The virtues of the sensitive appetite primarily concern the good of the virtuous individual since they involve the proper internal ordering of the passions. To refrain from gluttony, to be courageous in the face of danger, etc., enable one to actualize one's own potentialities to an extent that is not possible for someone who lacks temperance or fortitude. Therefore, these virtues, as ordering internal passions, cannot be directly relevant (though they may be indirectly so) to the issue before us—whether Thomas' moral theory allows for the possibility of according moral worth to non-rational creatures. As Thomas says, "[W]e are not directed immediately to another by the internal passions" (ibid., IaIIae, 58, 9).

80. Ibid., IaIIae, 58, 12.

81. Still, we need to be careful not to overstate this aspect of the difference between justice and the virtues of the sensitive part (i.e., the good of the individual versus the individual being properly related to the good of others) because, for Thomas, there is a unity of the virtues. Nevertheless, justice is clearly the virtue most relevant to our relation with others, and so most relevant to the topic at hand.

82. See *Summa Theologiae* IaIIae, 56, 6. See also Jean Porter, *The Recovery of Virtue: The Relevance of Thomas for Christian Ethics* (Louisville, Ky.: Westminster/ John Knox Press, 1990), p. 124.

83. Following Aristotle, Thomas holds that there are two kinds of justice: general, and particular. Our focus is on particular justice, as "specified or enumerated with the other virtues" (*Summa Theologiae* IIaIIae, 58, 5 ad 1). Particular justice "directs man in relation to other individuals" (ibid., IIaIIae, 58, 7). General justice "directs man immediately to the common good" (ibid.). Thomas also calls general justice "legal" because it is the purpose of law to direct human beings to the common good. I focus on particular justice because this is the cardinal virtue that is listed with the other moral virtues. All the virtues can be considered in terms of general justice because, for example, insofar as a virtue directs one to one's own or another's individual good and insofar as the individual good is a component in the common good, then all acts of virtue pertain to general justice. As Thomas says, "The good of any virtue, whether such virtue direct man in relation to himself, or in relation to certain other individual persons, is referable to the common good, to which justice directs: so that all acts of virtue can pertain to justice, in so far as it directs man to the common good" (ibid., IIaIIae, 58, 5). The moral worth of non-rational creatures can only fall under the ambit of *general* justice if *particular* justice makes a moral demand on us in our relation to these creatures. Commitment to the common good as such cannot entail such a demand because, at least so far as the moral relevance of this issue goes, the good of the entire changeable universe is finally at the service of the human good. The point and purpose of material creation is the generation of the requisite number of the elect. Once it has served its purpose, this order will pass away. This point can also be seen in the equation of general justice with legal justice. Law is directed to the common good, but (valid) human law is derived from natural law; and, as we have seen, natural law leaves no room for the direct moral consideration of non-rational creatures. As Thomas explicitly states, "[L]egal justice is referred to the *human* common good" (*Summa Theologiae* IIaIIae, 59, 1 ad 1).

84. Ibid., IIaIIae, 57, 1.

85. Ibid., IaIIae, 114, 1.

86. Ibid., IIaIIae, 79, 1.

87. Ibid., IIaIIae, 61, 2 ad 2.

88. Ibid., IIaIIae, 80, 1. See also, e.g., ibid., IIaIIae, 117, 2 ad 3 and 62, 2.

89. Porter argues cogently that "normative equality" between human beings is the basis of Thomas' understanding of the virtue of justice. This commitment itself is based, she maintains, on the anthropological thesis that all persons either are capable of moral virtue or have the intellect and will that are proper to our species. See Porter, *The Recovery of Virtue*, pp. 135–141.

90. *Summa Theologiae* IIaIIae, 80, 1, italics added.

91. Ibid., IIaIIae, 58, 3 ad 3, italics added.

92. Ibid., IIaIIae, 58, 11, italics added.

93. See note 79.

94. *Summa Theologiae* IIaIIae, 79, 1.

95. Ibid., IIaIIae, 80, 1.

96. Ibid., IIaIIae, 61, 1.

97. Ibid.

98. Ibid.

99. Ibid., IIaIIae, 61, 2.

100. Ibid.

101. Ibid., IIaIIae, 64, 1

102. Ibid.

103. Indeed, as noted, the basis of the claim that transactions between individuals morally bind each one to treat the other with justice, to render each his due according to equality, to give in equal measure as has been received, is the ontological equality of participants in the transaction. This ontological equality can only be the equality of rational agents. Without presupposing such equality, the equality of justice cannot itself be justified. Outside the relations between human beings little sense can be made of this equality of (commutative) justice. Therefore, commutative justice, as a species of particular justice, cannot be employed to accord moral worth to non-rational creatures.

104. See *Summa Theologiae* IIaIIae, 61, 1 ad 4.

105. Ibid., IIaIIae, 61, 2.

106. Ibid., IIaIIae, 63, 1.

107. Ibid.

108. To repeat, the equality of justice in distributive justice is "not according to equality between thing and thing, but according to proportion between things and persons: in such a way that even as one person surpasses another, so that which is given to one person surpasses that which is allotted to another" (ibid., IIaIIae, 61, 2).

109. Ibid., IIaIIae, 61, 4 ad 2.

110. Ibid., IIaIIae, 80, 1.

111. Ibid.

112. Ibid.

113. Ibid., IIIa, 85, 3 ad 2.

114. One might note the parallel here with our earlier discussion of natural law as participation in the eternal law.

115. *Disputed Questions on Truth,* 23, 6.

116. Ibid.

117. Ibid., italics added.

118. Ibid.

119. Ibid.

120. Ibid. Thomas qualifies this response in a characteristic way: "It might, however, conceivably be said to have the note of justice because of the ordination of the thing made to the will. For it is of obligation from the very fact that God wills it that everything which God wills be done. But in the fulfillment of this ordination it is wisdom which does the directing as the first rule" (*Disputed Questions on Truth,* 23, 6). The positing of God's absolute goodness, coupled with God's omnipotence (such that everything God wills is infallibly done), has caused some to question whether Thomas can consistently hold that God *freely* creates the world. That is, absolute goodness coupled with omnipotence seems to *dictate* that God create, if that is best (or not create, if that is best).

Although it is not our direct concern here, a fascinating and illuminating discussion on this issue took place in the late 1940s between Arthur O. Lovejoy, Henry Veatch, and Anton C. Pegis. See Henry Veatch, "A Note on the Metaphysical Grounds for Freedom, with Special Reference to Professor Lovejoy's Thesis in 'The Great Chain of Being,'" *Philosophy and Phenomenological Research* 7, no. 3 (March 1947): 391–412; Arthur O. Lovejoy, "The Duality of the Thomistic Theology: A Reply to Mr. Veatch," ibid., pp. 413–438; Veatch, "A Rejoinder to Professor Lovejoy," *Philosophy and Phenomenological Research* 7, no. 4 (June 1947): 622–625; Lovejoy, "Analogy and Contradiction: A Surrejoinder," ibid., pp. 626–634; Anton Pegis, "*Principale Volitum*: Some Notes on a Supposed Thomistic Contradiction," *Philosophy and Phenomenological Research* 9, no. 1 (September 1948): 51–70; and Lovejoy, "Necessity and Self-Sufficiency in the Thomistic Theology: A Reply to President Pegis," ibid., pp. 71–88. This exchange continued through another three articles. In addition to clarifying the issues at stake in the debate about whether an omnipotent, absolutely good God can freely create, this debate also illustrates nicely how the differing sets of presuppositions (indeed, the differing worldviews) of the participants make settling these issues extraordinarily difficult.

121. *Disputed Questions on Truth,* 23, 6.

122. Ibid., 23, 6.

123. Ibid., 23, 7.

124. Ibid.

125. See, e.g., *Summa Theologiae* IaIIae, 87, 8; IIaIIae, 64, 2; 64, 4; 65, 3; 67, 3; and *On the Power of God* II, 6, 1.

126. *Summa contra Gentiles* IIIb, 112.

127. Ibid.

128. *Summa Theologiae* IaIIae, 21, 1.

129. Ibid., IaIIae, 21, 1 ad 1.

130. Ibid., IIaIIae, 25, 3.

131. Ibid.

132. Ibid.

133. Ibid.

Chapter Three.   Thomas' Conception of the Human Soul

1. James H. Robb, "Introduction," in Thomas Aquinas, *Questions on the Soul,* trans. James H. Robb (Milwaukee: Marquette University Press, 1984), p. 30.

2. Robb, "Introduction," p. 30.

3. See *Summa contra Gentiles* II, 57. For further arguments, also see Anton Pegis, *St. Thomas and the Problem of the Soul in the Thirteenth Century* (Toronto: Pontifical Institute of Mediaeval Studies, 1978), pp. 158–160.

4. See, e.g., Pegis, *St. Thomas and the Problem of the Soul,* p. 128.

5. *Questions on the Soul,* 1.

6. See Kenny's *Thomas on Mind,* pp. 148–151, for an interesting critique of Thomas' position. According to Kenny, the concrete understanding of "form" that is necessary for a form to be subsistent is incompatible with the abstract Aristotelian understanding of form as that by which the composite has existence. Kenny argues that Thomas' response to objectors who question the very possibility of subsistent forms is entirely inadequate since Thomas merely assumes the very possibility that the objector denies. Kenny is specifically addressing Thomas' discussion in question 76, article 1 of the *Summa Theologiae* Ia, but, to the best of my knowledge, the same problem occurs whenever Thomas discusses the notion of a subsistent form.

7. See, e.g., *Summa contra Gentiles* II, 51; 57; and 68. Also see Pegis, *St. Thomas and the Problem of the Soul,* pp. 168–169.

8. *Summa Theologiae* Ia, 75.

9. Ibid.

10. Ibid.

11. Both Anthony Kenny and Norman Kretzmann make similar points on this matter. See Kenny, *Thomas on Mind,* pp. 129–131; and Norman Kretzmann, "Philosophy of Mind," in *The Cambridge Companion to Thomas,* ed. Norman Kretzmann and Eleonore Stump (Cambridge and New York: Cambridge University Press, 1993), pp. 128–159, especially pp. 128–131.

12. *Questions on the Soul,* 1. See also, e.g., *Summa contra Gentiles* I, 98.

13. *Questions on the Soul,* 14 ad 8.

14. As implied by the statement, "to live is the 'to be' of living things," Thomas rejects the notion of a plurality of substantial forms—e.g., one by which a body is, one by which it is living, one by which it is rational. As he says, "[S]ince a soul is a substantial form because it constitutes a human being in a determinate species of substance, there is no other substantial form intermediate between a soul and prime matter; but it is the soul itself which perfects a human being according to diverse levels of perfection, so that he is a body, and a living body, and a rational animal" (*Questions on the Soul,* 9). This rejection of a plurality of substantial forms is important (and faced considerable opposition in Thomas' day). It is only on the

basis of this rejection that the conclusion that the soul is the substantial form of the living body follows from his definition of the soul as the first principle of life. That is, if the soul is the first principle of life and is the substantial form by which the body is animated, and there is only one substantial form of the human (or of the body), then it follows that the soul is the substantial form of the human (or of the body). Thomas rejects the plurality of substantial forms because, he argues, if a substance had more than one substantial form, the substance would not, in truth, be *one*. (See, e.g., *Summa Theologiae* Ia, 76, 3; and *Questions on the Soul,* 10 and 11.) Thomas offers numerous other arguments to support his view of this substantial unity. For example, he holds that this account of the soul as the substantial form of the body is the only way to explain how this action of understanding is the action of this particular person. (See *Summa Theologiae* Ia, 76, 1 for details.)

15. *Questions on the Soul,* 14 objs. 9, 10, and 11.

16. Ibid., 14 ad 11.

17. *Disputed Questions on Truth,* 19, 1.

18. See John Wippel, "Thomas Aquinas and the Axiom 'What Is Received Is Received According to the Mode of Knower,'" in *A Straight Path: Studies in Medieval Philosophy and Culture, Essays in Honor of Arthur Hyman.* ed. Ruth Link-Salinger et al. (Washington, D.C.: The Catholic University of America Press, 1988), pp. 279–289.

19. *Summa Theologiae* Ia, 14, 1. Since Thomas clearly means to designate both sensitive and intellectual creatures by the term "cognoscentia," the term "knowing" or "cognitive" might be better employed than the term "intelligent," which seems to specify only intellectual creatures. (The Blackfriars translation uses the term "knowing subjects" and "non-knowing subjects," instead of "intelligent beings" and "non-intelligent beings.") Following Robert Pasnau, I generally use the terms "cognitive beings" or "cognizers" and "non-cognitive beings" or "non-cognizers."

20. *Commentary on Aristotle's 'De Anima',* trans. Kenelm Foster and Silvester Humphries (reprint, Notre Dame, Ind.: Dumb Ox Books, 1994), II. L.14:C 418.

21. While it is tempting to say that natural existence is the existence had by things outside the mind, the problem with this definition is that it implies that the intellect (which has natural existence) is outside the mind, and that is a rather odd conclusion. I thank Chris Gamwell for pointing this out.

22. See *Summa Theologiae* Ia, 56, 2 ad 3.

23. Ibid., Ia, 84, 2.

24. See Appendix A, "Spiritual Change and Materiality," for details.

25. Yves Simon, *Introduction à l'ontologie du Connaître* (Paris, 1934), p. 17. Quoted in John N. Deely, "The Immateriality of the Intentional as Such," *The New Scholasticism* 42 (1968): 293–308, see especially pp. 298–299.

26. See Appendix A for a discussion of sensitive knowledge and of an immaterial creature's (an angel's) knowledge of other immaterial creatures (angels).

27. *Summa Theologiae* Ia, 79, 3.

28. *Questions on the Soul,* 2.

29. *Summa Theologiae* Ia, 87, 1.

30. Ibid.

31. *Disputed Questions on Truth,* 8, 6.

32. *Questions on the Soul,* 7.

33. *On Spiritual Creatures,* 1. See also *Summa Theologiae* Ia, 84, 3 ad 2.

34. *On Spiritual Creatures,* 1.

35. *Commentary on Aristotle's 'De Anima'* II. L12:C 380 .

36. See, e.g., Robert Pasnau, *Theories of Cognition in the Later Middle Ages* (Cambridge and New York: Cambridge University Press, 1997), pp. 191–194.

37. Thomas summarizes this in various places, such as *Summa Theologiae* Ia, 77, 3.

38. Ibid.

39. *Questions on the Soul,* 4, 1. For understanding to occur, the intellect must mentally abstract the intelligible species from the phantasm. See, e.g., *Summa Theologiae* Ia, 85, 1 ad 1 and ad 4, for Thomas' explanation of abstraction.

40. Thomas summarizes this in ibid., Ia, 77, 3.

41. Sensible forms are unable to act on the possible intellect. (See *Disputed Questions on Truth,* 10, 6 ad 1; or *Summa Theologiae* Ia, 85, 1 ad 3.)

42. *Summa Theologiae* Ia, 17, 3.

43. The act of understanding is this assimilation of known to knower. As Thomas says, "the intellect by the very act of understanding is made one with the object understood" (ibid., Ia, 27, 1).

44. Ibid., Ia, 54, 1, ad 3.

45. Ibid., Ia, 14, 4, italics added.

46. See, e.g., ibid., Ia, 14, 5 ad 3; 84, 3; and *Questions on the Soul,* 7 ad 1.

47. *Summa Theologiae* Ia, 84, 3.

48. See, e.g., Bernard J. Lonegran, *Verbum: Word and Idea in Thomas* (Notre Dame, Ind.: University of Notre Dame Press, 1967), p. 176.

49. *Summa Theologiae* Ia, 14, 14. Or, again, "[I]t is because the intelligible species, which is the form of the intellect and the principle of understanding, is the image of the external object, that the intellect in consequence forms an intention like that object: for such as a thing is, such is the effect of its operation. And since the understood intention is like a particular thing, it follows that the intellect by forming this intention understands that thing" (*Summa contra Gentiles* I, 53). Also see, e.g., *Summa Theologiae* Ia, 58, 2.

50. *Summa contra Gentiles* II, 98.

51. Ibid., II, 98. See also *Disputed Questions on Truth,* 10, 8. Or, again, see *Commentary on Aristotle's 'De Anima'* III. L.9:C 724; or *Summa contra Gentiles* II, 98.

52. *Disputed Questions on Truth,* 10, 8 RpCn 9, italics added. See also *Summa Theologiae* Ia, 87, 1.

53. As Thomas says, "the species by which the intellect is informed so that it can actually understand is the first means by which understanding takes place; and because the intellect is brought into act by means of this form, it can now *operate and form* quiddities of things, as well as compose and divide. Consequently, the quiddities formed in the intellect, or even the affirmative and negative propositions, are, in a sense, products of the intellect, but products of such a kind that through them the intellect arrives at the knowledge of an exterior thing" (*Disputed Questions on Truth*, 3, 2, italics added).

54. See, e.g., *On the Power of God* III, 9, 5.

55. The distinction between the nature of the intelligible species and the nature of the universal is important to the discussion in chapter 4, where I call into question the philosophical legitimacy of arguing from the nature of one to the nature of the other.

56. As Thomas says, "[R]ather a human soul is in potency to intelligible species since it is like a wax tablet on which nothing has been written. . . . Consequently it must acquire intelligible species from things outside itself through the mediation of sense powers, which cannot accomplish their appropriate operations without bodily organs" (*Questions on the Soul*, 8).

57. As Thomas summarizes the point, "Although a soul depends on its body to the extent that without its body a soul does not attain the fullness of its nature, yet a soul is not so dependent on its body that a soul cannot exist apart from its body" (ibid., 1 ad 12). The soul needs the body to be a substance in the complete sense. (See also ibid., 15.)

58. As Thomas summarizes, "A soul is united to its body both for a good that is a substantial perfection, namely, that its specific nature might be achieved, and also for a good that is an accidental perfection, namely, that a soul might be perfected in achieving intellectual knowledge, which a soul acquires through the senses" (ibid., 1 ad 7).

59. *On the Power of God* III, 8, 1, italics added.

60. See, e.g., *Commentary on the Metaphysics of Aristotle* VII. L.13:C 1570. The universal can be used to signify the substance of a thing, or it can be taken to signify what many share.

61. I am making these distinctions for the sake of clarity. While Thomas himself often adheres to this demarcation, such is not always the case. He sometimes employs the term "intelligible species" to refer to the inner word and sometimes "universal" to refer to the form by which the possible intellect is actualized.

Chapter Four.   The Soul as an Entity

1. David R. Foster, "Thomas' Arguments for Spirit," *American Catholic Philosophical Quarterly* 65 (1991): 235–252, see especially pp. 236–239.

2. Here, I follow Foster's argument. See Foster, "Thomas' Arguments for Spirit."

3. *Questions on the Soul,* 14.

4. See also Foster, "Thomas' Arguments for Spirit," pp. 236–238.

5. For a more detailed discussion of sensitive knowledge, see Appendix A.

6. *Questions on the Soul,* 14.

7. See, e.g., *Summa Theologiae* Ia, 75, 6.

8. For arguments that bear on this same issue, see Robert Pasnau, "Thomas and the Content Fallacy," *The Modern Schoolman* 75 (1998): 293–314; and Joseph A. Novak, "Thomas and the Incorruptibility of the Soul," *History of Philosophy Quarterly* 4 (1987): 405–421. I have been instructed by these articles. Still, my own approach differs from these two authors. Like Novak and unlike Pasnau, I am exclusively concerned with this problem as it relates to Thomas' arguments for the incorruptibility of the soul. However, unlike Novak, I go beyond Thomas' explicit arguments from our capacity to know universals to include some of Thomas' other types of arguments for the soul's incorruptibility. With my discussion of Thomas' theory of cognition, I have also tried to nail down more precisely than these authors the locus of the problem in these arguments. Further, the use to which I am putting my argument and the context in which I discuss it differ from those of these authors. Finally, I tie this problem in Thomas' thought to his broader metaphysics in a different manner than do Pasnau or Novak because the problem itself is the focus of their articles. I am interested also in its implications for the human relation to non-rational creation.

9. See, e.g., *Summa Theologiae* Ia, 79, 5 ad 2.

10. See, e.g., *Summa contra Gentiles* IIIa, 42.

11. Perhaps this interpretation is also indicated when Thomas writes that these universals "are considered" (*considerantur*), since this term seems more likely to refer to the inner word that is consciously entertained (in the sense that we make use of it whenever we understand anything, though not necessarily in the sense that we are explicitly aware that we are making use of it). The intelligible species, however, requires a special act of attention to consider it.

12. *Summa contra Gentiles* II, 30.

13. See *Summa Theologiae* Ia, 76, 2 ad 3.

14. Ibid., Ia, 76, 2.

15. Ibid., Ia, 76, 2, obj 3.

16. Ibid., Ia, 76, 2, ad 3.

17. Ibid., italics added.

18. Ibid.

19. See, e.g., ibid., Ia, 85, 1.

20. Or he may be arguing to the nature of the activity of the intellect, a possibility that I discuss below.

21. *Disputed Questions on Truth*, 10, 8, italics added to emphasize the inference between representative and ontological immateriality. See also, e.g., *Summa Theologiae* Ia, 50, 2.

22. See *Summa Theologiae* Ia, 57, 2; *On Spiritual Creatures*, 5 ad 7; or *Disputed Questions on Truth*, 2, 5 ad 17.

23. *Questions on the Soul*, 14.

24. See, e.g., Pasnau, "Thomas and the Content Fallacy," p. 299, for a similar discussion.

25. See, e.g., *Summa Theologiae* Ia, 50, 2.

26. I am grateful to Chris Gamwell for this formulation.

27. *Summa Theologiae* Ia, 75, 5.

28. Note that step 3 is necessary because it is possible for wholly immaterial forms to be received into material things (though not vice versa). Therefore, the effect of the form in producing the universal is also needed for the conclusion that the intellect is immaterial or an absolute form.

29. Note that if step 2 was taken to refer to the form that exists in the intellect intentionally, then the transition from step 4 to 5 might be effected by the phrase, "For if the intellectual soul were composed of matter and form, the forms of things would be received into it as individuals." But this reading falls prey to the conversion criticized above. It moves between the ontological and the representative (without suitable justification) insofar as it fails to address the issue of why it is the case that material apprehension can only represent things materially or as singulars.

30. *Summa Theologiae* Ia, 75, 6. See also, e.g., *Summa contra Gentiles* II, 55.

31. See *Summa Theologiae* Ia, 70 and 97.

32. Ibid., Ia, 75, 6.

33. *Summa contra Gentiles* II, 50.

34. *Commentary on the Metaphysics of Aristotle* III, L.11:C 759.

35. *Summa Theologiae* Ia, 75, 6.

36. I believe that a similar critique can be developed against the type of argument that maintains that the senses can be destroyed by too great a sensory input while the intellect cannot be destroyed by too great an intellectual input.

37. *Summa Theologiae* Ia, 88, 1. Our knowledge of immaterial entities must be by remotion (that is, by negation) or by reasoning from effect to cause or by comparison. See also *Summa Theologiae* Ia, 84, 7 ad 3.

38. Ibid., Ia, 50, 1.

39. *The Division and Methods of the Sciences, Questions V–VI of the Commentary on Boethius' De Trinitate*, trans. Armand Maurer (Toronto: Pontifical Institute of Mediaeval Studies, 1953), Question 6, Article 3.

40. See, e.g., *Commentary on the Metaphysics of Aristotle* X. L12:C 2141–2142.

41. *Commentary on Boethius' De Trinitate*, 6, 3.

42. See, e.g., *Commentary on the Metaphysics of Aristotle* X. L12:C 2141–2142, in which material/immaterial can be substituted for corruptible/incorruptible without a change in meaning.

43. For an interesting discussion on this issue that argues on the basis of the abstract understanding of form in Aristotle versus the concrete understanding of form necessary for there to be a form that is subsistent, see chapters 11 and 12 of Anthony Kenny's *Thomas on Mind*. If forms are abstract and defined as that by which something is, then to posit forms as concrete entities requires some argument to sustain the legitimacy of this move.

44. Although Thomas was convinced that he had successfully demonstrated the existence of God and thus established the existence of both material and immaterial beings, the many arguments that the human soul is an immaterial entity suggest that he thought that this conclusion could be reached without taking the immaterial existence of God as an explicit premise. Given that the existence of God and thus of immaterial entities can be demonstrated, in other words, Thomas seems to have believed that there must be independent arguments for the conclusion that the human soul is such an immaterial entity. Nothing of what I have said so far, then, ought to be construed as implying the claim that Thomas believed that he needed the premise, "immaterial entities exist," to establish his conclusion that the human soul is such an immaterial entity. Seemingly, he took the existence of such beings for granted and sought to establish that the human soul is such a being. But in my earlier analysis, I have held that there are no such independent arguments. Thomas' arguments for the subsistence of the human soul assume that immaterial entities exist, and this assumption is gratuitous unless it can be validated by the theistic arguments. Let us turn then to those arguments.

45. See *Summa Theologiae* Ia, 13, 12.

46. Ibid., Ia, 12 and 13.

47. See *Summa contra Gentiles* I, 3.

48. See *Summa Theologiae* Ia, 13, 6.

49. See, e.g., ibid., Ia, 13, 1 ad 2; 13, 3 ad 1; and 13, 5 ad 1.

Part III.   The Unity and Moral Worth of All Creation

1. I present these conceptions as viable, plausible alternatives to Thomas' understanding of God, creatures, and creaturely value discussed in earlier chapters. Primary sources include the following: Alfred North Whitehead, *Adventures of Ideas* (New York: The Free Press, 1967); *Modes of Thought* (New York: The Free Press, 1968); and *Process and Reality: An Essay in Cosmology*, corrected edition, ed. David Ray Griffin and Donald W. Sherburne (New York: The Free Press, 1978). See also the work of Charles Hartshorne, including *Creative Synthesis and Philosophic*

Method (LaSalle, Ill.: Open Court, 1970); *The Logic of Perfection and Other Essays in Neoclassical Metaphysics* (LaSalle, Ill.: Open Court, 1962); *A Natural Theology for Our Time* (LaSalle, Ill.: Open Court, 1967); and *Reality as Social Process* (New York: Hafner, 1971).

Chapter Five.   An Alternative Metaphysics

1. Though, to be sure, creatures may also be cared for for the sake of another and for the universe.

2. There are a number of other thinkers whose work in ecological ethics has been influenced by Whitehead's approach. John B. Cobb, Jr., for example, is a prominent ecological ethicist who takes his philosophical bearings from Whitehead. See, for example, his co-authored volume (with Charles Birch), *The Liberation of Life* (Denton, Tex.: Environmental Ethics Books, 1990), or his co-authored volume (with Herman Daly), *For the Common Good* (Boston: Beacon Press, 1994). These are, in my judgment, especially fine studies. Susan Buck-Armstrong's instructive essay, "Whitehead's Metaphysical System as a Foundation for Environmental Ethics," *Environmental Ethics* 8 (1986): 241–259, lays the basic groundwork for building an ecological ethic using Whitehead's insights. Andrew Kerr writes of the moral status of ecosystems from a Whiteheadian perspective in "Ethical Status of Ecosystems in Whitehead's Philosophy," *Process Studies* 24 (1995): 76–89. This essay is an excellent response to the critique that Whitehead's philosophy fails to be "holistic." Another fine article on this issue is John Cobb's "Deep Ecology and Process Thought," *Process Studies* 30 (2001): 112–131. Charles Birch's "Environmental Ethics in Process Thought," http://www.alfred.north.whitehead.com/AJPT/ajpt_papers/vol02/02_birch.htm, briefly but clearly outlines some of the fundamental insights of Whitehead's thought for an ecological ethic.

3. Whitehead, *Adventures of Ideas*, p. 158.

4. Whitehead distinguishes God from other actual entities by refusing to call him an "actual occasion."

5. Whitehead, *Process and Reality*, p. 75.

6. Ibid.

7. See Franklin I. Gamwell, *The Divine Good: Modern Moral Theory and the Necessity of God* (Dallas, Tex.: Southern Methodist University Press, 1996), p. 166.

8. See, e.g., ibid., p. 165.

9. Not that this would be any small task. Indeed, Whitehead thinks of it as impossible because of "weakness of insight and deficiencies of language." He holds that such an achievement can be approached only asymptotically (Whitehead, *Process and Reality*, p. 4).

10. Ibid., p. 3.

11. Ibid., p. 18, italics added; see also p. 110.

12. "The metaphysical characteristics of an actual entity—in the proper general sense of 'metaphysics'—should be those which apply to *all* actual entities" (ibid., p. 90, italics added).

13. This understanding of the concreteness of actual entities, and so the derivative nature of all other entities, is expressed in what Whitehead terms the "ontological principle." He holds that "it is a contradiction in terms to assume that some explanatory fact can float into the actual world out of nonentity. Nonentity must be nothingness" (ibid., p. 46). Therefore, "everything must be somewhere and 'somewhere' here refers to 'some actual entity'" (ibid., p. 46; see also p. 244). This is one articulation of the ontological principle. It can be stated simply as "no actual entity, then no reason" (ibid., p. 19). Or, again, "actual entities are the only *reasons*; so that to search for a *reason* is to search for one or more actual entities" (ibid., p. 24).

14. Ibid., p. 6.

15. Whitehead, *Modes of Thought*, p. 149.

16. Whitehead challenges this metaphysics on numerous grounds. Perhaps most fundamentally, he holds that it falls prey to the "fallacy of misplaced concreteness." Substance metaphysics mistakes an abstract character of composites, their enduring character, for the concrete character of final real things, which, as we will see, are characterized by becoming.

17. Whitehead, *Process and Reality*, p. 155.

18. Whitehead, *Adventures of Ideas*, p. 197.

19. Hartshorne, *Creative Synthesis and Philosophic Method*, p. 73.

20. Whitehead, *Process and Reality*, p. 18.

21. Ibid., p. 22. "Process is the growth and attainment of a final end" (ibid., p. 150).

22. Ibid., p. 23.

23. Ibid., p. 29.

24. As Whitehead puts it, "An actual entity is at once the subject experiencing and the superject of its experiences. It is subject-superject, and neither half of this description can for a moment be lost sight of" (ibid.).

25. Ibid., p. 23.

26. See Whitehead, *Adventures of Ideas*, p. 236.

27. See, e.g., Whitehead, *Process and Reality*, p. 154.

28. Ibid., p. 211.

29. "Each instance of concrescence is *itself* the novel individual 'thing' in question. There are not 'the concrescence' *and* 'the novel thing': when we analyze the novel thing we find nothing but the concrescence" (ibid.). The concrescence of an actual entity happens "all at once." This understanding entails an "epochal theory of time" in which, metaphysically, time occurs in droplets. The passage of physical time measures the transition between attained actuality and actuality in attainment, which Whitehead calls the macroscopic process. (See, e.g., ibid., pp. 214–215.) There is *concrescence* (or the microscopic process), which is "'the real internal con-

stitution of a particular existent,'" (ibid., p. 210) as well as *transition* (or the macro-scopic process) "from particular existent to particular existent" (ibid; see also p. 227 and p. 283). By holding that actual entities are droplets of experience, Whitehead overcomes Zeno's paradox in which nothing becomes because becoming is infi-nitely divisible (i.e., if becoming is infinitely divisible and what becomes later de-pends on what becomes earlier, then nothing can become). (See ibid., pp. 68–69.) If becoming occurs in droplets, then this problem is removed. The becoming of an actual entity spans a brief moment of time, perhaps a fraction of a second, but is actually undivided. "In every act of becoming there is the becoming of something with temporal extension; but . . . the act itself is not extensive, in the sense that it is divisible into earlier and later acts of becoming. . . . The creature is extensive but its act of becoming is not extensive" (ibid., p. 69).

30. Ibid., p. 40.

31. See ibid., p. 41.

32. Ibid., p. 24.

33. Ibid., p. 157.

34. None of this is to deny that we can consider sense data as qualities devoid of evaluative or emotional tone. Whitehead calls this "perception in the mode of pre-sentational immediacy." What he denies is that this is the *primitive* form of experi-ence. There is the more basic "perception in the mode of causal efficacy" in which the sensum is felt with emotion or subjective form, but only felt with some vague notion of the causal source of the feeling. It is felt in a certain way as from a certain place. Perception in the mode of presentational immediacy is a derivative and higher-order experience that depends upon this more primitive experience being massively simplified with its structural elements strongly emphasized. It presents the contemporary world in cross-section, so to speak, without any indication of past or future. "Hume's polemic respecting causation is, in fact, one prolonged, convincing argument that pure presentational immediacy does not disclose any causal influence" (Whitehead, *Process and Reality*, p. 123). But if this is taken as primitive experience, Whitehead holds that it leaves vast arenas of human experi-ence unaccounted for, such as reflex actions or the feeling of causal efficacy with its accompanying feeling tones. For example, an inhibition of familiar sensa can give rise to a multiple of causal feelings as when "in the silence, the irresistible causal ef-ficacy of nature presses itself upon us; in the vagueness of the low hum of insects in an August woodland, the inflow into ourselves of feelings from enveloping na-ture overwhelms us" (ibid., p. 176). What we inherit is not bare sensa, but actuali-ties (or actualized qualities) emotionally. To be sure, we interpret and transform the associated emotion, but this emotion does not originate with us. Whitehead does not claim that we are typically aware of the emotional tone of primitive feel-ings, though on the odd occasion we might be. As he puts it, "It must be remem-bered . . . that emotion in human experience, or even in animal experience, is not bare emotion. It is emotion interpreted, integrated, and transformed into higher

categories of feelings. But even so, the emotional appetitive elements in our conscious experience are those which most closely resemble the basic elements of all physical experience" (ibid., p. 163).

35. Ibid., p. 233.

36. Ibid., p. 177.

37. For an interesting article on the development of Whitehead's thought on subjectivity, see Lewis S. Ford, "Subjectivity in the Making," *Process Studies* 21 (1992): 1–24.

38. Whitehead, *Process and Reality*, p. 157.

39. Ibid., p. 159.

40. The "sensationalist principle," which accompanies the subjectivist principle most explicitly in the thought of Hume (and the basic content of which we have discussed above), is the understanding that "the primary activity in the act of experience is the bare subjective entertainment of datum, devoid of any subjective form of reception" (Whitehead, *Process and Reality*, p. 157). On my reading, this sensationalist principle simply makes more explicit the notion that the datum of experience, for these philosophers, can be analyzed solely in terms of universals. It is bare-sense datum, understood in terms of universals such as "greyness."

41. See ibid., pp. 157–160.

42. Ibid., p. 159.

43. See ibid.

44. Whitehead, *Modes of Thought*, p. 71. Or, again, "Subjective experiencing is the primary metaphysical situation which is presented to metaphysics for analysis" (Whitehead, *Process and Reality*, p. 160).

45. Whitehead, *Adventures of Ideas*, p. 184.

46. Whitehead, *Process and Reality*, p. 166.

47. Ibid., p. 160.

48. See ibid., p. 22.

49. Ibid., p. 23.

50. Ibid., p. 87. Whitehead holds that this doctrine of immanence is the only intelligible way to make sense of efficient causation.

51. Ibid., p. 166.

52. Ibid., p. 160.

53. Ibid., p. 166.

54. Ibid. We might note that the reformed subjectivist principle is an alternative formulation of ontological principle, with actual entities now understood to be subjects of experience: "nothing is to be received into the philosophical scheme which is not discoverable as an element in subjective experience" (ibid.). The ontological principle can be stated as "no actual entity, then no reason" (ibid., p. 19). All reasons, all explanations must ultimately be traceable to actual entities. Only actual entities are agents.

55. Ibid., p. 21.

56. Ibid.

57. Hartshorne, *Creative Synthesis and Philosophic Method*, p. 1.

58. See ibid., p. 3.

59. Another way of approaching Whitehead's notion that subjectivity or experience goes all the way down is the one favored by Hartshorne, who maintains that the denial of creativity or experience at any level of reality involves a wholly negative existential claim. Such claims are meaningless. Every meaningful existential claim must have some positive content. Every thought, every claim, must have some content, something which the thought is about. A sheerly negative existential claim purports to be a thought that has no content, and so is without meaning. Metaphysics has often introduced what Whitehead calls a "vacuous actuality," an actuality without experience, "a *res vera* devoid of subjective immediacy" (Whitehead, *Process and Reality*, p. 29). Whitehead takes repudiation of this notion to be central to his own project. To say the same thing, he takes the demonstration of the universality of subjectivity to be central to this project. The vacuous actuality is usually termed "mere matter."

Hartshorne holds, "Mere matter, as the zero of feeling and intrinsic value, is an absolute negation whose meaning is wholly parasitic on what it denies" (Hartshorne, *Creative Synthesis and Philosophic Method*, p. 143). We have no conceivable ground for limiting experience to our own kind. "The sheer absence of the psychical has no positive bearings" (ibid., p. 160). Hartshorne continues, "It tells me nothing about how . . . mindless bodies will behave. . . . Unless something is in the other bodies which could not be there if they had experiences, they do have them" (ibid., p. 160; see also p. 164). To deny the existence of experience at the level of organic unity (that is, when referring to an entity that is acted upon and responds in a unitary fashion) involves a sheerly negative proposition because it claims a mere absence that is not by implication also something positive. But, to repeat, since every thought must have content, to make a sheerly negative existential claim is not to have made any meaningful statement.

60. See Whitehead, *Process and Reality*, pp. 78–79.

61. Ibid., p. 53. Whitehead refers to such non-conscious human experience as dreaming or itching to support this claim, though it is also true that the claim is supported by his larger metaphysical scheme.

62. Ibid., p. 177.

63. Ibid.

64. Ibid., p. 115.

65. As Hartshorne points out, "The apparent inertness of a stone, or of water, tells us nothing as to the inactivity of its minute constituents. For the general situation is this: all concrete things . . . must react—if not as wholes then in their constituents—to their environments, they respond to what in effect are stimuli, and their responses become in turn stimuli to others" (Hartshorne, *Creative Synthesis and Philosophic Method*, p. 50). Modern physics confirms that minute particles do

indeed respond to their environment, and it is well known that plants and animals do so.

66. Ibid., p. 112, italics added.

67. Griffin, "Panexperientialist Physicalism and the Mind-Body Problem," *Journal of Consciousness Studies* 4 (1997): 248–268, see especially p. 264. See also Charles Hartshorne, "The Compound Individual," in *Philosophical Essays for Alfred North Whitehead* (London: Longmans, Green and Co., 1936), pp. 193–220.

68. Griffin, "Panexperientialist Physicalism and the Mind-Body Problem," p. 264. See also Hartshorne, "The Compound Individual."

69. Whitehead, *Process and Reality*, p. 53, italics added.

70. Alfred North Whitehead, *Science and the Modern World* (New York: The Free Press, 1967), p. 136.

71. See, e.g., Leemon B. McHenry, "Whitehead's Panpsychism as the Subjectivity of Prehension," *Process Studies* 24 (1995): 1–14, see especially pp. 6–8.

72. See, e.g., Thomas E. Hosinski, *Stubborn Fact and Creative Advance: An Introduction to the Metaphysics of Alfred North Whitehead* (Lanham, Md.: Rowman and Littlefield, 1993), p. 58.

73. Whitehead, *Adventures of Ideas*, p. 183. See also Whitehead, *Process and Reality*, p. 113.

74. See Whitehead, *Process and Reality*, p. 23.

75. Ibid., p. 164.

76. Ibid., p. 114. As Whitehead says, "In sense-reception the sensa are the definiteness of emotion: they are emotional forms transmitted from occasion to occasion" (ibid.). So the primitive form of experience is emotional.

77. Ibid., p. 23.

78. Ibid.

79. See ibid., p. 25. Still, one entity is not present in another *simpliciter*. Objectification entails elimination. "Objectification relegates into irrelevance, or into a subordinate relevance, the full constitution of the objectified entity. Some real component in the objectified entity assumes the role of being how that particular entity is a datum in the experience of the subject" (ibid., p. 62). The limitation whereby the actual entities felt are reduced to the perspective of one of their own feelings is imposed by the concrescing actualities past and the requirement that all the feelings felt in any incomplete phase be compatible or capable of integration in a later phase. (See ibid., p. 237.) Whitehead holds, "The many feelings, in any incomplete phase, are necessarily compatible with each other by reason of their individual conformity to the subjective aim evolved for that phase" (ibid., p. 224).

80. Ibid., p. 87.

81. Ibid., p. 25.

82. See ibid.

83. Ibid., p. 235.

84. Though any characteristic of an actual entity may be reproduced in a prehension, it is still only a subordinate part of the concrescing actual entity. "A reference to the complete actuality is required to give the reason why such a prehension is what it is in respect of its subjective form. This subjective form is determined by the subjective aim at further integration, so as to obtain the 'satisfaction' of the completed subject" (ibid., p. 19). The subjective forms are modified so that the subjective aim may be achieved. Certain prehensions may receive emphasis or be felt with increased intensity while others are relegated into relative triviality, all in service to the final goal of satisfaction. They become components in service to the whole and are modified according to the final end of the whole. Still, the fact that any concrescing subject must work from the data given in its actual world entails that the data limit the possibilities, even if the subjective forms of these data are also modified by the concrescing subject. As Whitehead puts it, "no feeling can be abstracted from its data, or its subject. It is essentially a feeling aiming at that subject, and motivated by that aim. Thus the subjective form embodies the pragmatic aspect of feeling; for the datum is felt with that subjective form in order that the subject may be the superject which it is" (ibid., p. 233).

85. Ibid., p. 27.

86. Beyond the broad agreement that God's primordial nature is the source of an actuality's initial aim, there is an important controversy among those who take their philosophical bearings from Whitehead. This controversy focuses especially on whether God is a single actuality in everlasting concrescence or a personally ordered society. For the purposes of this chapter, we do not need to enter this debate. The important point here is that for all the thinkers involved, there is an initial aim from God. So it is possible to speak of God's valuation as ordering the possibilities for a given concrescing occasion, either because this ordering (with appetition) is given in all its specificity or because of an entity's past and the gift of a general aim at beauty. For a cursory outline of this debate see Appendix B: God's Nature.

In the end, of course, my project does depend upon the anticipation that Whitehead's metaphysics, including its conception of God, can be given a coherent statement. In this larger sense, which goes beyond the present work, this controversy is important. For example, if each side offers convincing criticisms of the other side, then it opens the possibility that process metaphysics cannot finally be given a coherent formulation. In future work, I hope to take up this controversy and develop my own position. In the rest of this chapter, though I draw upon Whitehead's language, I try to do so in such a way that only those points that are crucial for this project, which do not happen to touch deeply on the noted controversy, are highlighted.

87. As interpreted either specifically with Whitehead or, with Hartshorne, as this valuation is determined by the entity's past coupled with the divine aim at intensity.

88. "[A]part from the intervention of God, there could be nothing new in the world, and no order in the world" (Whitehead, *Process and Reality*, p. 247).

89. Ibid., p. 248.

90. Ibid., p. 177.

91. See ibid., pp. 177–178.

92. Ibid.

93. "The defining characteristic is inherited throughout the nexus, each member deriving it from those members of the nexus which are antecedent to its own concrescence" (ibid., p. 34). So there is a defining characteristic shared by members of the society and the defining characteristic is due to the environment provided by the society. See ibid., p. 89.

94. See ibid., p. 90.

95. Ibid.

96. Ibid., p. 98.

97. Ibid.

98. Ibid.

99. Ibid.

100. Given our analysis to this point, it is obviously not possible simply to substitute the notion of "society" for that of "enduring substance."

101. "The societies in an environment will constitute its orderly element; and the non-social actual entities will constitute its element of chaos" (Whitehead, *Process and Reality*, p. 110).

102. Ibid., p. 105.

103. Ibid., p. 84.

104. For further discussion, see, e.g., Hartshorne, "The Aesthetic Matrix of Value," in *Creative Synthesis and Philosophic Method*, pp. 303–322.

105. Whitehead, *Adventures of Ideas*, p. 252.

106. "Whatever is a datum for a feeling has a unity as felt. Thus the many components of a complex datum have a unity: this unity is a 'contrast' of entities" (Whitehead, *Process and Reality*, p. 24).

107. Ibid., p. 228.

108. Whitehead, *Adventures of Ideas*, p. 258.

109. Whitehead, *Process and Reality*, p. 244.

110. Whitehead, *Adventures of Ideas*, p. 206.

111. If we consider a living creature, we see that its most immediate environment, its own body, organizes the initial data for the living occasions that its experience reaches a high level of intensity. Whitehead summarizes the point as follows: "*God's purpose in the creative advance is the evocation of intensities. The evocation of societies is purely subsidiary to this absolute end.* The characteristic of a living society is that a complex structure of inorganic societies is woven together for the production of a non-social nexus characterized by the intense physical experiences of its members. But such an experience is derivate from the complex order of the

material animal body, and not from the simple 'personal order' of past occasions with analogous experience. There is intense experience without the shackle of the past. This is the condition for spontaneity of conceptual reaction" (Whitehead, *Process and Reality*, p. 105, italics added. Note that the "non-social nexus" referred to is the living occasion [or occasions] itself. It is "non-social" in the sense that it cannot retain its general characteristic independent of the body, as, for example, a molecule of a bodily cell might.). The animal body orders and massively simplifies the welter of data received from the world. Detail is de-emphasized and structure is emphasized. It is only because of this ordering of the data that novelty and intense experience are possible.

112. Ibid., p. 115.

113. Ibid., p. 277.

114. Ibid., p. 102.

115. Ibid.

116. Indeed, Whitehead holds that "the primary meaning of 'life' is the origination of conceptual novelty—novelty of appetition" (ibid.). Or, again, "The essence of life is the teleological introduction of novelty, with some conformation of objectives. Thus novelty of circumstance is met with novelty of functioning adapted to steadiness of purpose" (Whitehead, *Adventures of Ideas*, p. 207).

117. Just as with the origination of novelty, so, too, can this coordination be understood to be what life is. "Life is the coordination of the mental spontaneities throughout the society" (ibid.).

118. Whitehead, *Modes of Thought*, p. 27.

119. See, e.g., ibid., p. 267.

120. Ibid., p. 261.

121. As Whitehead says, "The theory of judgment in the philosophy of organism . . . describes judgment as the subjective form of the integral prehension of the conformity, or of the non-conformity, of a proposition and an objectified nexus" (ibid., p. 190).

122. Whitehead, *Process and Reality*, p. 193.

123. Whitehead, *Modes of Thought*, p. 28.

124. Ibid., 26. Again, "the life of a human being receives its worth, its importance, from the way in which unrealized ideals shape its purposes and tinge its actions. The distinction between men and animals is in one sense only a difference of degree. But the extent of the degree makes all the difference. The Rubicon has been crossed" (ibid., p. 27). And, in fact, in *Modes of Thought*, Whitehead even categorizes the human body as its own distinct grade of aggregation of actualities. As noted, the categorization in *Process and Reality* sets the highest creaturely species of actuality as that which is the moment in the life history of a conscious society. Since, on Whitehead's account, there is not sharp separation between these species of actuality, one might well wonder why he does not categorize self-conscious actualities as a distinct species.

125. Whitehead, *Process and Reality*, p. 88.

126. Ibid., p. 105.

127. Ibid., p. 340, italics added.

128. Though Whitehead's understanding of God's nature would be profoundly challenged if it were not exemplified in some religious experience, this does not mean that it need be exemplified in all religious experience, any more than a true understanding of morality must be exemplified in all human purposes.

129. See Hosinski, *Stubborn Fact and Creative Advance*, pp. 185–187, for an interesting discussion on this matter.

130. Whitehead, *Process and Reality*, p. 343.

131. Ibid., p. 342.

132. Ibid., p. 343.

133. Ibid.

134. Since it is inevitable, it perhaps goes without saying that we are speaking of Whitehead's interpretation of that vision.

135. Whitehead, *Process and Reality*, p. 343.

136. Ibid.

137. Ibid.

138. Ibid.

139. Ibid., p. 345.

140. We here enter once again the controversy between those who take their philosophical bearings from Whitehead. For Whitehead, God's conceptual phase is the initial stage of God's concrescence followed by the physical pole. For worldly occasions, the order is reversed. Hartshorne's reformulation of God's nature as a personally ordered society makes the physical pole the initial phase, just as in worldly actualities. However this dispute is resolved, there is overall agreement on basic understanding of God's consequent nature.

141. "The completion of God's nature into a fullness of physical feeling is derived from the objectification of the world in God. He shares with every new creation its actual world; and the concrescent creature is objectified in God as a novel element in God's objectification of the world" (Whitehead, *Process and Reality*, p. 345).

142. Ibid.

143. The "prehension into God of each creature is directed with the subjective aim, and clothed with the subjective form" (ibid.).

144. Ibid.

145. Ibid., p. 346.

146. Ibid.

147. Hartshorne argues this in numerous places, especially with respect to human experience where the issue is raised to explicit awareness as the religious question of the meaning of existence. See, e.g., Charles Hartshorne, *Insights & Oversights of Great Thinkers: An Evaluation of Western Philosophy* (Albany: State University of New York Press, 1983), p. 217 and p. 360.

148. Whitehead, *Modes of Thought*, p. 111.

149. Ibid., p. 109

150. Ibid., p. 111, italics added.

Chapter Six.   Intrinsic Value and Moral Worth

1. With this principle, for example, the fact that inanimate objects are almost exclusively of instrumental value justifies treating them instrumentally. The triviality of the intensity of their subjective experience entails that any balancing of their intrinsic and instrumental values essentially means that these creatures are justifiably treated as instruments. Furthermore, for inanimate aggregates, such as rocks, their intrinsic value is merely the sum of the intrinsic value of the actualities that compose it, and these microscopic actualities are little affected by human action. Even here, however, solely instrumental value must be qualified. For instance, beautiful rock formations have their own special worth to God and thus should not, other things being equal, be destroyed.

2. See Charles Hartshorne, *The Divine Relativity: A Social Conception of God* (New Haven, Conn.: Yale University Press, 1948), chap. 1. See also the extended discussion between Arthur Lovejoy, Henry Veatch, and Anton Pegis cited in chap. 2, n. 120.

3. For a similar formulation, and a helpful discussion, see Birch and Cobb, *The Liberation of Life*, chap. 5.

4. See Holmes Rolston III, "Are Values in Nature Subjective or Objective?" *Environmental Ethics* 4 (1982): 125–151; and Holmes Rolston III, *Conserving Natural Value* (New York: Columbia University Press, 1994), p. 177. Indeed, Rolston, as a theist, is bound to find any such theory problematic.

5. Rolston, *Conserving Natural Value*, pp. 171–172; see also p. 177.

6. Ibid., p. 172.

7. Ibid., p. 173, italics added.

8. Holmes Rolston III, *Environmental Ethics: Duties to and Values in the Natural World* (Philadelphia: Temple University Press, 1988), p. 96, italics added.

9. Ibid., p. 174.

10. Rolston, "Are Values in Nature Subjective or Objective?" p. 146.

11. Rolston, *Environmental Ethics*, p. 109.

12. Rolston makes much of the genetic code in arguing for the intrinsic value of all creatures, arguing that it is a "propositional set" and a "normative set." See, e.g., ibid., p. 99. We do not need to enter into this portion of Rolston's discussion because it is not directly relevant to the critical discussion to come. However normative genes may be, they are normative only for the organism in question. It is difficult to see, without further argument, how this normativity is relevant to what is *morally* normative for human beings.

13. See, e.g., Rolston, *Environmental Ethics*, p. 109.

14. *Summa Theologiae* Ia, 5, 3.

15. *Summa contra Gentiles* IIIb, 112.

16. See, e.g., *Summa Theologiae* IaIIae, 64, 1; Ia, 96, 1; and *Summa contra Gentiles* IIIb, 112.

17. Rolston, *Environmental Ethics*, p. 96, italics added.

18. Rolston, *Conserving Natural Value*, p. 194.

19. See, e.g., ibid., pp. 107–108; and p. 194.

20. Consideration of Thomas' conception of reality exposes this hidden premise of the dominant paradigm.

21. Joel Feinberg, "The Rights of Animals and Unborn Generations," in *Philosophy and Environmental Crisis*, ed. William T. Blackstone (Athens: University of Georgia Press, 1974), p. 52.

22. Ernest Partridge, "Values in Nature: Is Anybody There?" *Philosophical Inquiry* 8 (1986): 96–110, see especially p. 103.

23. Elsewhere, I have examined Callicott's inchoate attempt to develop the outlines of a postmodern axiology. There, I argued that this attempt, while promising in many ways, fails because he remains convinced that value must be projected onto what he calls, in a merely verbal attempt to avoid Cartesian dualism, "erstwhile" objects from "erstwhile" subjects. That is, Callicot remains within the Modern mindset that he so roundly and frequently criticizes. See Francisco J. Benzoni, "Creatures as Creative: Callicott and Whitehead on Creaturely Value," *Environmental Ethics* 28 (2006): 37–56.

It also might be helpful to note Callicott's own ambiguous relationship to this Humean axiology. At times, Callicott seems explicitly to repudiate it. For example, in 1985, he states that "it is not consistent with a contemporary or post-revolutionary scientific world view"; moreover, it is "an insidious theoretical legacy of classical mechanics in a larger fabric which has succeeded and indeed transformed mechanism." See J. Baird Callicott, "Intrinsic Value, Quantum Theory, and Environmental Ethics," *Environmental Ethics* 7 (1985): 357–375. Reprinted in *In Defense of the Land Ethic: Essays in Environmental Philosophy* (Albany: State University of New York Press, 1989), pp. 157–174, especially p. 166. All page references to this article are to its reprinted version. He goes on to say that "the distinction between subject and object is untenable" (ibid., p. 167) and, in another article, that it rests on an obsolete worldview. See J. Baird Callicott, "Rolston on Intrinsic Value: A Deconstruction," *Environmental Ethics* 14 (1992): 129–143. Reprinted in *Beyond the Land Ethic: More Essays in Environmental Philosophy*, pp. 221–238, see especially p. 231. All page references to this article are to its reprinted version. It does not seem that there could be a clearer repudiation of an axiology than this. Thus, one might be excused for being a bit surprised when Callicott states, more than a decade later, "Regular readers of this journal know that I hold a subjectivist theory of value which I trace back to Hume" (J. Baird Callicott, "On Norton and the Failure of Monistic Inherentism," *Environmental Ethics* 18 [1996]: 219–221, especially p. 219). This ambiguity sometimes occurs within a single article. See, for example, J. Baird Callicott, "On the Intrinsic Value of Nonhuman Species," in *The Preservation of Species: The Value of Biological Diversity*, ed. Bryan G. Norton (Princeton, N.J.: Princeton University Press, 1986), pp. 138–172, see p. 133 and p. 151. Reprinted in *In Defense of the Land Ethic: Essays in Environmental Philosophy* (Albany: State University of New York Press, 1989), pp. 129–155. All page references to this article are to its reprinted version. Perhaps his current position is provided in the article in which he offers his critique of Rolston's position. There, Callicott states that, in addition to providing a non-anthropocentric value theory consistent with the metaphysical foundations of *postmodern* science, he also thinks that "it is important to offer a less elusive, tide-bucking nonanthropocentric value theory than Rolston's, based upon *modernist* orthodoxy, for unregenerate modernists, to whom values in nature without valuers seems less a heresy than an oxymoron" (Callicott, "Rolston on Intrinsic Value: A Deconstruction," p. 236, italics added).

Thus, Callicott continues to espouse the Humean subjectivist value theory not because he believes that it is correct, but because for "unregenerate modernists" it is the only way to provide adequate grounding for the moral intuition that nonhuman species have intrinsic value; never mind that "The Modern scientific world view is obsolete" (ibid., p. 231). It is rather puzzling to provide an obsolete, even false, value theory for an obsolete position. Still, because this theory continues to exert influence and because Callicott continues to defend it vigorously (apparently, within the confines of the "Modernist worldview"), an examination of it is useful. However, we will see that, even on its own Modernist grounds, the ethic fails because it does, in fact, collapse into relativism (from which it is saved only by covert appeal to transcendental standards of assessment, which appeal undermines the entire ethic). This discussion also affords us the opportunity to highlight the characteristics that a viable value theory must have, namely, a metaphysical understanding of the good and an understanding of subjectivity as characterizing all actual entities.

24. Callicott, "On the Intrinsic Value of Nonhuman Species," p. 138.

25. Callicott, "Intrinsic Value, Quantum Theory, and Environmental Ethics," p. 161.

26. Callicott, "On Norton and the Failure of Monistic Inherentism," p. 219. One might note that, in fact, there has been considerable slippage from the first to the second statement. After all, the first statement might be interpreted to mean that if something is a valuer, then it has value. Callicott interprets it to mean, in the second statement, that if something has value, then it is valued by a valuer.

27. J. Baird Callicott, "Introduction: Compass Points in Environmental Philosophy," in *Beyond the Land Ethic: More Essays in Environmental Philosophy* (Albany: State University of New York Press, 1999): 1–26, see p. 15.

28. Callicott, "On the Intrinsic Value of Nonhuman Species," p. 147.

29. Ibid., p. 133.

30. Ibid.

31. Ibid., first italics added.

32. See also J. Baird Callicott, "Moral Monism in Environmental Ethics Defended," *Journal of Philosophical Research* 19 (1994): 51–60. Reprinted in *Beyond the Land Ethic: More Essays in Environmental Philosophy* (Albany: State University of New York Press, 1999): 171–186, see especially p. 177. All page references to this article are to its reprinted version. This value theory, at least in the eyes of some, has some unlovely consequences, as the value of human beings must also be conferred. Consider the following: "To take a concrete example, consider a newborn infant. Let us assume, for the sake of clarity and simplicity, that the infant yet lacks self-consciousness and hence does not value itself and that there is no God who superordinately values it. According to Hume's classical subjectivist axiology, then, the value of the newborn infant of our example is wholly conferred upon it by its parents, other relatives, the family dog [though the implications of the dog's valuation is unclear], family friends, and perhaps impersonally and anonymously by some unrelated and unacquainted members of society" (Callicott, "Intrinsic Value, Quantum Theory, and Environmental Ethics," p. 161). Let us change the example slightly to clarify its implications. A newly impregnated woman is flying in a small aircraft over the Amazon forest. She was impregnated in a casual relationship with a man she barely knew and probably will never see again. He does not know that she is pregnant. Unfortunately, her plane crashes deep in the forest. She is the sole survivor. With the plane as her shelter, she manages to survive on the onboard provisions and by gathering food from the surrounding forest. Her attempts to contact the outside world are unsuccessful. After nine months and a difficult delivery, she gives birth to a baby boy. If this woman were to die tomorrow, Callicott's axiology would bind him to hold that the baby is quite literally without intrinsic value. What happens to this infant is, in his theory, quite literally a matter of indifference. Even without adding further detail, some may find this to be a disconcerting and, indeed, chilling conclusion—perhaps reason enough to reject this theory.

33. See, e.g., J. Baird Callicott, "Holistic Environmental Ethics and the Problem of Ecofascism," in *Beyond the Land Ethic: More Essays in Environmental Philosophy* (Albany: State University of New York Press, 1999), pp. 59–75, see p. 69.

34. See, e.g., Callicott, "Holistic Environmental Ethics and the Problem of Ecofascism"; or Callicott, "On the Intrinsic Value of Nonhuman Species." For a thoughtful critique of this reading of Hume, see Y. S. Lo, "A Humean Argument for the Land Ethic?" *Environmental Values* 10 (2001): 523–539; and Y. S. Lo, "Non-Humean Holism, Un-Humean Holism," *Environmental Values* 10 (2001): 113–123.

35. J. Baird Callicott, "Can a Theory of Moral Sentiments Support a Genuinely Normative Environmental Ethic?" *Inquiry* 35 (1992): 183–198. Reprinted in *Beyond the Land Ethic: More Essays in Environmental Philosophy* (Albany: State University

of New York Press, 1999), 99–116, see p. 106. All page references to this article are to its reprinted version.

36. Callicott, "On the Intrinsic Value of Nonhuman Species," p. 153; see also p. 150.

37. Callicott, "Can a Theory of Moral Sentiments Support a Genuinely Normative Environmental Ethic?" p. 108. He maintains, "The moral sentiments are both natural and universally distributed among human beings as I mentioned before. In other words, like physical features—the placement of the eyes in the head, two arms, two legs, an opposed thumb, and so forth—the moral sentiments are only slightly variable psychological features common to all people. Just as there are people, to be sure, who are physically freakish or maimed, so there may be people who, because of congenital defect of the vagaries of life, are lacking one, several, or all the moral sentiments to one degree or another. Still, we can speak of normal and even correct moral judgments, the exceptions notwithstanding, just as we can speak of physical normality and even correct bodily proportions and conditions. Hume's ethical subjectivism, therefore, does not necessarily imply that right and wrong, good and evil, virtue and vice are, so to speak, existentially indeterminate, nor does his theory collapse into an emotive relativism." (J. Baird Callicott, "Hume's Is/Ought Dichotomy and the Relation of Ecology to Leopold's Land Ethic," *Environmental Ethics* 4 (1984): 173–184. Reprinted in *In Defense of the Land Ethic: Essays in Environmental Philosophy* (Albany: State University of New York Press, 1989), pp. 117–127, see p. 121. All page references to this article are to its reprinted version.

38. See, e.g., Callicott, "Moral Monism in Environmental Ethics Defended," p. 183; or Callicott, "Can a Theory of Moral Sentiments Support a Genuinely Normative Environmental Ethic?" p. 111.

39. Callicott, "Can a Theory of Moral Sentiments Support a Genuinely Normative Environmental Ethic?" p. 109.

40. Callicott also puts the point in terms of "values" or "ends." "We are moved to act exclusively by 'passions,' that is, by feelings, our values among them. . . . Values—whether selfish or unselfish—determine our ends, empirically informed reason our means" (J. Baird Callicott, "Just the Facts, Ma'am," *Environmental Professional* 9 [1987]: 279–288. Reprinted in *Beyond the Land Ethic: More Essays in Environmental Philosophy* [Albany: State University of New York Press, 1999], pp. 79–97, see p. 86. All page references to this article are to its reprinted version.). Callicott goes on to maintain that our values are fixed by evolution. "Darwin's biosocial account of the origin of moral values explains how values in general, and moral values in particular, have become more or less fixed, standardized by natural selection. . . . If you care about yourself, wish others well, and delight in social prosperity, you have the 'right' values, but not because your values correspond to any moral facts. Rather, one may be said to have the right values in the same sense that one may be said to have the right number of fingers if one has five on each hand.

Values, like physical features, have been normalized, standardized by natural selection" (ibid., p. 87). Values, then, are not radically relative because there is a norm of normalcy, a consensus of which values are the "right" ones to have. And this consensus is an empirical matter that is the result of evolution.

41. See, e.g., Kristin Shrader-Frechette, "Biological Holism and the Evolution of Ethics," *Between the Species* 6 (1990): 185–192; and Kristin Shrader-Frechette, "Individualism, Holism, and Environmental Ethics," *Ethics and the Environment* 1 (1996): 55–69.

42. Callicott, "Can a Theory of Moral Sentiments Support a Genuinely Normative Environmental Ethic?" p. 109.

43. Ibid., p. 101.

44. See, e.g., ibid., p. 105.

45. Although it was Kant who first gave rigorous philosophical formulation to this understanding of normative force, at least some pre-Kantian ethical theories employed such an understanding. Thomas Aquinas' moral theory is one such example.

46. Callicott, "Can a Theory of Moral Sentiments Support a Genuinely Normative Environmental Ethic?" p. 112.

47. Ibid., p. 111.

48. Ibid., p. 113.

49. The following comment of Callicott's (which is on Leopold's position but is obviously shared by Callicott himself) indicates the propriety of using the term "fixed by." "A land ethic . . . is not only 'an ecological necessity,' but an 'evolutionary possibility' because a moral response to the natural environment—Darwin's social sympathies, sentiments, and instincts translated and codified into a body of principles and precepts—would be *automatically* triggered in human beings by ecology's social representation of nature. . . . Therefore, the key to the emergence of a land ethic is, simply, universal ecological literacy" (J. Baird Callicott, "The Conceptual Foundations of the Land Ethic," in *Companion to a Sand County Almanac: Interpretive and Critical Essays,* ed. J. Baird Callicott [Madison: University of Wisconsin Press, 1987], pp. 186–217. Reprinted in J. Baird Callicott, *In Defense of the Land Ethic: Essays in Environmental Philosophy* [Albany: State University of New York Press, 1989], pp. 75–99, see p. 82, italics added; see also pp. 81–82. All page references to this article are to its reprinted version.).

50. Further, such relativism suffers from self-referential problems insofar as it explicitly denies but implicitly affirms a universal moral law. The cultural relativist affirms the following claim: all moral norms are completely culturally bound. If the moral law is understood to be the norm according to which all other norms are evaluated, then this affirmation is itself the moral law and is not itself wholly culturally bound. On the contrary, it is the norm by which all other norms are to be assessed. So the cultural relativist explicitly denies that there is a universal

moral law while implicitly affirming such a law, thus rendering the position self-referentially incoherent.

51. Callicott, "Can a Theory of Moral Sentiments Support a Genuinely Normative Environmental Ethic?" p. 113.

52. As Callicott puts it in relation to Leopold's land ethic, "while human nature changes very slowly, our *ideas* about who we are, what sort of world we live in, and our relationship to the natural environment change rapidly and not at all arbitrarily or blindly. They change in response to scientific discovery and to intra- and inter-cultural critical reflection and debate" (ibid., p. 114). So, if these ideas change in accord with rational discussion across cultures rather than arbitrarily or blindly, then, to restate the point, there must be principles in accordance with which argument across cultures can be assessed.

Conclusion

1. The conception of the divine individual as wholly perfect and utterly in control also serves to shield us from the threat of meaninglessness that we perhaps fear above all. It provides the comforting story that, in the end, it is all taken care of for us. We need only to find our way along the path that God has predetermined for us in order to enjoy eternal bliss. But this very conception of God, derived from Greek metaphysics, is fraught with internal contradictions (such as the attempt to relate the eternal and temporal, the unchanging and the changing, and so on) and is inconsistent with the Christian vision as revealed in the person of Jesus Christ (for example, it cannot truly make sense of Jesus' suffering *as a revelation of the divine nature*, and, indeed, it cannot truly make any meaningful sense of the notion that God loves the world). Nor does it lend itself to opening our hearts to the plight of the least ones. If God, after all, cannot be affected by their plight, why, then, should we be so affected? To be sure, there is much more to say about this matter. But one must ask if this endless conversation is not simply seeking to build Ptolemaic ellipses around a conception that is simply not worth salvaging.

2. Another way of addressing this issue is to attempt to remove a commonly perceived roadblock to the reception of this vision—the fear that one group will impose (or attempt to impose) its vision of the good on everyone else. A discussion of the nature of democracy could go some way toward addressing these concerns by articulating an understanding of deliberative democracy in which public space is opened up for *rational* persuasion. This discussion could also provide the forum for articulating a critique of the commitment of liberal democracies to expansionist economics in the face of mounting evidence that such expansion undermines our ecological security. The primary purpose of the democratic state could then be seen not as working to ensure the continuous expansion of access to economic

goods and services, but rather working to ensure the continuous expansion of freedom. These are some directions suggested by the present work that need to be pursued.

Appendix A.   Spiritual Change and Materiality

1. Note that it is not necessary to specify that the thing known is material in the case of material cognizers because such cognizers are only suited to know such entities.

2. *Summa Theologiae* Ia, 78, 3.

3. *Disputed Questions on Truth*, 26, 3 ad 4.

4. Ibid.

5. *Summa Theologiae* Ia, 85, 2 ad 1.

6. See Lonegran, *Verbum: Word and Idea in Thomas*, p. 149.

7. *Summa contra Gentiles* I, 51 and 52.

8. See Pasnau, *Theories of Cognition in the Later Middle Ages*, pp. 188–191.

9. In what follows, I use the term "intelligible species" in the usual sense to mean the form by which the intellect understands, rather than the universal understood. This is in accord with the distinction Thomas makes, for example, in *Questions on the Soul*, 2, 5, where he says, "universals, with which the sciences deal, are that which is known through intelligible species; they are not the intelligible species themselves. . . . For an intelligible species is that by which the intellect understands, not that which the intellect understands."

10. Thomas' explanation of the immaterial existence of things in the soul is consistent with this analysis. The senses acquire sensible species "free from matter," or immaterially. This is to say, they receive sensible forms in an intentional manner that does not cause the sense organs to receive the naturally existing form. But because it is received into a material organ and materiality is the principle of individuation, the sensible species must be an individual species or a species that is the likeness of a particular. This could only be true if the sensible species produces (or, more accurately, is itself) some sort of *material modification* in the sense organ. (See, for example, *Questions on the Soul*, 13.)

11. The exterior senses have two limitations that, absent the interior senses, would render them of little use. First, they do not themselves distinguish between objects of different senses. For this, the interior sense of "common sense" is necessary. Without the common sense, we could not distinguish whiteness from sweetness, whereas the common sense knows both at once. By the common sense, we perceive that we see or hear, etc. Second, the exterior senses are informed only as long as the sensible object is present. They do not themselves manipulate or retain the impression. This is necessary, for example, in order that an animal be moved to

seek something that is absent. (See *Summa Theologiae* Ia, 78, 4.) To accomplish this, the interior senses of imagination, memory, and the cogitative power are needed.

12. *Summa Theologiae* Ia, 78, 4.

13. *Commentary on Aristotle's 'De Anima'* III. L.5:C 644.

14. *Summa Theologiae* Ia, 12, 9 ad 2. See also ibid., IaIIae, 173, 2.

15. For our purposes, it is the imagination that is of special significance. It is from the phantasm that the intellect abstracts the intelligible species by which it understands. The phantasm itself, since it is in a corporeal organ, is a likeness of a singular that is "here and now." The same thing is true for the phantasm as was true for the likeness impressed upon the exterior senses. The interior sensitive powers are in potency to receive the individual forms of sensible things. Therefore, they are capable of particular knowledge of any sensible thing and so of all sensible things.

16. *Summa Theologiae* Ia, 56, 2 obj 3.

17. Ibid., Ia, 56, 2 ad 3.

18. Ibid., Ia, 56, 2, italics added. We might note here that each angel is its own species. Every created thing is placed in its species according to its form. With material things, there can be many individuals of the same species because material things are individuated by matter. Since angels are immaterial, every individual must be its own species; both the species and the individuation must be by way of form.

19. Ibid., italics added.

Appendix B.   God's Nature

1. Whitehead, *Process and Reality*, p. 31.

2. Hartshorne maintains that in Whitehead's philosophy "an actuality is a novel synthesis of many antecedent actualities, themselves syntheses of their predecessors, each new actuality adding itself to the previous 'many,' thus forming a new plurality to be subsequently synthesized, and so on forever. If then God were a concrete singular, he would be but an episode in cosmic becoming" (Charles Hartshorne, "Whitehead and Ordinary Language," in *Whitehead's Philosophy: Selected Essays, 1935–1970* [Lincoln: University of Nebraska Press, 1972], p. 177). As a merely concrete singular, rather than a personally ordered society, God could not affect the concrescence of worldly occasions because no occasion can prehend an entity that has not completed its concrescence. God would be "but an episode in cosmic becoming" rather than the primordial ground of order and novelty.

3. Hartshorne, *Creative Synthesis and Philosophic Method*, p. 59.

4. Ibid., p. 62.

5. Ibid., p. 63.

6. For a summary of this issue, see, e.g., Lewis S. Ford, "Whitehead's Differences from Hartshorne," in *Two Process Philosophers: Hartshorne's Encounter with Whitehead*, ed. Lewis S. Ford (Tallahassee, Fla.: American Academy of Religion, 1970), pp. 58–83; and David Ray Griffin, "Hartshorne's Differences from Whitehead," in ibid., pp. 35–57. See also Leonard Eslick, "Divine Causality," *The Modern Schoolman: A Quarterly Journal of Philosophy* 62 (May 1985): 233–247.

7. This position seems to be confirmed by Hartshorne's statement: "All God can directly give us is the beauty of his ideal for us, an ideal to which we cannot simply not respond, but to which our response has to be partly self-determined, and it has to be influenced by past creaturely responses in our universe. 'Persuasion' is the ultimate power; now even God can simply coerce" (Hartshorne, *Creative Synthesis and Philosophic Method*, pp. 239–240). It seems to me that Whitehead could fully agree with this statement. However, for Whitehead, the content of the ideal is those eternal objects that are directly relevant to the concrescing entity in all their specificity, whereas, for Hartshorne, such specificity is unnecessary—all that is needed to the past of the actuality in question and the initial aim to maximize unity in diversity. As Hartshorne puts it, "The only definiteness a particular instance of creative experience presupposes is that of previous experiences, including divine experiences" (ibid., p. 62).

8. See, e.g., Lewis S. Ford, "God as a Temporally-Ordered Society: Some Objections," *Tulane Studies in Philosophy* 34 (1986): 41–52; and Lewis S. Ford, "Is Process Theism Compatible with Relativity Theory?" *Journal of Religion* 48 (April 1968): 124–135.

9. Hartshorne, *Creative Synthesis and Philosophic Method*, p. 124. See also Hartshorne, *A Natural Theology for Our Time*, pp. 93–97.

Bibliography

Aertsen, Jan. "The Convertibility of Being and the Good in St. Thomas Aquinas." *The New Scholasticism* 59 (1985): 449–470.

———. "Good as Transcendental and the Transcendence of the Good." In *Being and Goodness: The Concept of the Good in Metaphysics and Philosophical Theology*, edited by Scott MacDonald, 56–73. Ithaca: Cornell University Press, 1991.

———. "Thomas Aquinas on the Good: The Relation between Metaphysics and Ethics." In *Thomas' Moral Theory: Essays in Honor of Norman Kretzmann*, edited by Scott MacDonald and Eleonore Stump, 235–253. Ithaca and London: Cornell University Press, 1998.

Annice, Sister M. "Historical Sketch of the Theory of Participation." *The New Scholasticism* 26 (1952): 46–79.

Attfield, Robin. *The Ethics of Environmental Concern*. New York: Columbia University Press, 1983.

Barad, Judith. "Thomas' Inconsistency on the Nature and Treatment of Animals." *Between the Species: A Journal of Ethics* 4 (Spring 1988): 102–111.

Benzoni, Francisco J. "Creatures as Creative: Callicott and Whitehead on Creaturely Value." *Environmental Ethics* 28 (2006): 37–56.

Birch, Charles. "Environmental Ethics in Process Thought." http://www.alfred .north.whitehead.com/AJPT/ajpt_papers/vol02/02_birch.htm.

Birch, Charles, and John B. Cobb, Jr. *The Liberation of Life*. Denton, Tex.: Environmental Ethics Books, 1990.

Bourke, Vernon. "Is Thomas Aquinas a Natural Law Ethicist?" *The Monist: An International Quarterly Journal of General Philosophical Inquiry* 58 (1974): 52–66.

Brown, Lester, et al. *The State of the World*. New York: W. W. Norton and Company, 1997.

Brown, Warren S., Nancey Murphy, and H. Newton Murphy, eds. *Whatever Happened to the Soul? Scientific and Theological Portraits of Human Nature.* Minneapolis: Fortress Press, 1998.

Buck-Armstrong, Susan. "Whitehead's Metaphysical System as a Foundation for Environmental Ethics." *Environmental Ethics* 8 (1986): 241–259.

Buersmeyer, Keith. "Predication and Participation." *The New Scholasticism* 51 (1981): 35–51.

Business Week. (Data from the UN Population Fund.) October 25, 1999.

Callicott, J. Baird. *Beyond the Land Ethic: More Essays in Environmental Philosophy.* Albany: State University of New York Press, 1999.

———. "Can a Theory of Moral Sentiments Support a Genuinely Normative Environmental Ethic?" *Inquiry* 35 (1992): 183–198. Reprinted in *Beyond the Land Ethic: More Essays in Environmental Philosophy*, 99–116. Albany: State University of New York Press, 1999.

———. "The Conceptual Foundations of the Land Ethic." In *Companion to a Sand County Almanac: Interpretive and Critical Essays,* edited by J. Baird Callicott, 186–217. Madison: University of Wisconsin Press, 1987. Reprinted in *In Defense of the Land Ethic: Essays in Environmental Philosophy*, 75–99. Albany: State University of New York Press, 1989.

———. *In Defense of the Land Ethic: Essays in Environmental Philosophy.* Albany: State University of New York Press, 1989.

———. "Introduction: Compass Points in Environmental Philosophy." In *Beyond the Land Ethic: More Essays in Environmental Philosophy*, 1–26. Albany: State University of New York Press, 1999.

———. "Moral Monism in Environmental Ethics Defended." *Journal of Philosophical Research* 19 (1994): 51–60. Reprinted in *Beyond the Land Ethic: More Essays in Environmental Philosophy*, 171–186. Albany: State University of New York Press, 1999.

———. "On the Intrinsic Value of Nonhuman Species." In *The Preservation of Species: The Value of Biological Diversity*, edited by Bryan G. Norton, 138–172. Princeton, N.J.: Princeton University Press, 1986. Reprinted in *In Defense of the Land Ethic: Essays in Environmental Philosophy*, 129–155. Albany: State University of New York Press, 1989.

———. "On Norton and the Failure of Monistic Inherentism." *Environmental Ethics* 18 (1996): 219–221.

———. "Rolston on Intrinsic Value: A Deconstruction." *Environmental Ethics* 14 (1992): 129–143. Reprinted in *Beyond the Land Ethic: More Essays in Environmental Philosophy*, 221–238. Albany: State University of New York Press, 1999.

Christian, William. *An Interpretation of Whitehead's Metaphysics.* New Haven, Conn.: Yale University Press, 1959.

Cobb, John B., Jr. "Deep Ecology and Process Thought." *Process Studies* 30 (2001): 112–131.

Daly, Herman E., and John B. Cobb, Jr. *For the Common Good: Redirecting the Economy toward Community, the Environment, and a Sustainable Future.* Boston: Beacon Press, 1994.

Deely, John N. "The Immateriality of the Intentional as Such." *The New Scholasticism* 42 (1968): 293–308.

Drum, Peter. "Thomas and the Moral Status of Animals." *American Catholic Philosophical Quarterly* 64, no. 4 (Autumn 1992): 483–488.

Eslick, Leonard. "Divine Causality." *The Modern Schoolman: A Quarterly Journal of Philosophy* 62 (May 1985): 233–247.

Fabro, Cornelio. "The Intensive Hermeneutics of Thomistic Philosophy: The Notion of Participation." *The Review of Metaphysics* 27 (1974): 449–491.

Feinberg, Joel. "The Rights of Animals and Unborn Generations." In *Philosophy and Environmental Crisis*, edited by William T. Blackstone. Athens: University of Georgia Press, 1974.

Ford, Lewis S. "God as a Temporally-Ordered Society: Some Objections." *Tulane Studies in Philosophy* 34 (1986): 41–52.

———. "Is Process Theism Compatible with Relativity Theory?" *Journal of Religion* 48 (April 1968): 124–135.

———. "Subjectivity in the Making." *Process Studies* 21 (1992): 1–24.

———. "Whitehead's Differences from Hartshorne." In *Two Process Philosophers: Hartshorne's Encounter with Whitehead*, edited by Lewis S. Ford, 58–83. Tallahassee, Fla.: American Academy of Religion, 1970.

Foster, David R. "Thomas' Arguments for Spirit." *American Catholic Philosophical Quarterly* 65 (1991): 235–252.

French, William. "Christianity and the Domination of Nature." Ph.D. dissertation, University of Chicago, 1985.

Gamwell, Franklin I. *The Divine Good: Modern Moral Theory and the Necessity of God.* Dallas, Tex.: Southern Methodist University Press, 1996.

Gilson, Etienne. *The Christian Philosophy of St. Thomas Aquinas.* Notre Dame, Ind.: University of Notre Dame Press, 1956.

Goudie, Andrew. *The Human Impact on the Natural Environment.* 5th edition. Cambridge, Mass.: The MIT Press, 2001.

Green, Joel B., ed. *What about the Soul? Neuroscience and Christian Anthropology.* Nashville: Abingdon Press, 2004.

Griffin, David Ray. "Hartshorne's Differences from Whitehead." In *Two Process Philosophers: Hartshorne's Encounter with Whitehead*, edited by Lewis S. Ford, 35–57. Tallahassee, Fla.: American Academy of Religion, 1970.

———. "Panexperientialist Physicalism and the Mind-Body Problem." *Journal of Consciousness Studies* 4 (1997): 248–268.

Hammond, Allen L., et al., eds. *World Resources 1994–95: A Guide to the Global Environment.* New York and Oxford: Oxford University Press, 1994.

Hartshorne, Charles. *Creative Synthesis and Philosophic Method.* LaSalle, Ill.: Open Court, 1970.

———. *The Divine Relativity: A Social Conception of God.* New Haven, Conn.: Yale University Press, 1948.

———. *Insights & Oversights of Great Thinkers: An Evaluation of Western Philosophy.* Albany: State University of New York Press, 1983.

———. "The Compound Individual." In *Philosophical Essays for Alfred North Whitehead,* 193–220. London: Longmans, Green and Co., 1936.

———. *The Logic of Perfection and Other Essays in Neoclassical Metaphysics.* LaSalle, Ill.: Open Court, 1962.

———. *A Natural Theology for Our Time.* LaSalle, Ill.: Open Court, 1967.

———. *Reality as Social Process.* New York: Hafner, 1971.

———. "Whitehead and Ordinary Language." In *Whitehead's Philosophy: Selected Essays, 1935–1970.* Lincoln: University of Nebraska Press, 1972.

Hosinski, Thomas E. *Stubborn Fact and Creative Advance: An Introduction to the Metaphysics of Alfred North Whitehead.* Lanham, Md.: Rowman and Littlefield, 1993.

Jeeves, Malcom, ed. *From Cells to Souls—And Beyond: Changing Portraits of Human Nature.* Grand Rapids, Mich.: Eerdmans, 2004.

John, Sister Helen James. "Participation Revisited." *The Modern Schoolman: A Quarterly Journal of Philosophy* 39 (1962): 154–165.

Kenny, Anthony. *Thomas on Mind.* London and New York: Routledge, 1993.

Kerr, Andrew. "Ethical Status of Ecosystems in Whitehead's Philosophy." *Process Studies* 24 (1995): 76–89.

Kretzmann, Norman. "Philosophy of Mind." In *The Cambridge Companion to Thomas,* edited by Norman Kretzmann and Eleonore Stump, 128–159. Cambridge and New York: Cambridge University Press, 1993.

Le Blanc, Jill. "Eco-Thomism." *Environmental Ethics* 21, no. 3 (Fall 1999): 293–306.

Lindbeck, George. "Participation and Existence in the Interpretation of St. Thomas Aquinas I." *Franciscan Studies* 17 (1957): 1–22.

———. "Participation and Existence in the Interpretation of St. Thomas Aquinas II." *Franciscan Studies* 17 (1957): 107–125.

Linzey, Andrew. *Christianity and the Rights of Animals.* New York: Crossroad, 1987.

Lo, Y. S. "A Humean Argument for the Land Ethic?" *Environmental Values* 10 (2001): 523–539.

———. "Non-Humean Holism, Un-Humean Holism." *Environmental Values* 10 (2001): 113–123.

Lonegran, Bernard J. *Verbum: Word and Idea in Thomas.* Notre Dame, Ind.: University of Notre Dame Press, 1967.

Lovejoy, Arthur O. "Analogy and Contradiction: A Surrejoinder." *Philosophy and Phenomenological Research* 7, no. 4 (June 1947): 626–634.

———. "The Duality of the Thomistic Theology: A Reply to Mr. Veatch." *Philosophy and Phenomenological Research* 7, no. 3 (March 1947): 413–438.

———. "Necessity and Self-Sufficiency in the Thomistic Theology: A Reply to President Pegis." *Philosophy and Phenomenological Research* 9, no. 1 (September 1948): 71–88.

McHenry, Leemon B. "Whitehead's Panpsyschism as the Subjectivity of Prehension." *Process Studies* 24 (1995): 1–14.

McInerny, Ralph M. *Ethica Thomistica: The Moral Philosophy of Thomas Aquinas.* Revised edition. Washington, D.C.: The Catholic University of America Press, 1997.

———. "Saint Thomas on De hebdomadibus." In *Being and Goodness*, edited by Scott MacDonald, 74–97. Ithaca: Cornell University Press, 1991.

The Millennium Assessment Synthesis Report. www.milleniumassessment.org .2005.

Murphy, Nancey. "Physicalism without Reductionism: Toward a Scientifically, Philosophically, and Theologically Sound Portrait of Human Nature." *Zygon* 34, no. 4 (December 1999): 551–571.

Northcott, Michael. *The Environment and Christian Ethics.* Cambridge and New York: Cambridge University Press, 1996.

Novak, Joseph A. "Thomas and the Incorruptibility of the Soul." *History of Philosophy Quarterly* 4 (1987): 405–421.

Owens, Joseph. *An Interpretation of Existence.* Milwaukee: Bruce Publishing Co., 1968.

Partridge, Ernest. "Values in Nature: Is Anybody There?" *Philosophical Inquiry* 8 (1986): 96–110.

Pasnau, Robert. "Thomas and the Content Fallacy." *The Modern Schoolman: A Quarterly Journal of Philosophy* 75 (1998): 293–314.

———. *Theories of Cognition in the Later Middle Ages.* Cambridge and New York: Cambridge University Press, 1997.

Pegis, Anton. "*Principale Volitum*: Some Notes on a Supposed Thomistic Contradiction." *Philosophy and Phenomenological Research* 9, no. 1 (September 1948): 51–70.

———. *St. Thomas and the Problem of the Soul in the Thirteenth Century.* Toronto: Pontifical Institute of Mediaeval Studies, 1978.

Peterson, Anna. *Being Human: Ethics, Environment, and Our Place in the World.* Berkeley and Los Angeles: University of California Press, 2001.

Porter, Jean. *The Recovery of Virtue: The Relevance of Thomas for Christian Ethics.* Louisville, Ky.: Westminster/John Knox Press, 1990.

Population Reference Bureau.www.prb.org, 2005.

Ramussen, Larry. *Earth Community, Earth Ethics.* Maryknoll, N.Y.: Orbis, 1996.

Robb, James H. "Introduction." In Thomas Aquinas, *Questions on the Soul*, translated by James H. Robb. Milwaukee: Marquette University Press, 1984.

Rolston, Holmes, III. "Are Values in Nature Subjective or Objective?" *Environmental Ethics* 4 (1982): 125–151.

———. *Conserving Natural Value*. New York: Columbia University Press, 1994.

———. *Environmental Ethics: Duties to and Values in the Natural World*. Philadelphia: Temple University Press, 1988.

Santmire, Paul. *The Travail of Nature: The Ambiguous Ecological Promise of Christian Theology*. Philadelphia: Fortress Press, 1985.

Shrader-Frechette, Kristin. "Biological Holism and the Evolution of Ethics." *Between the Species* 6 (1990): 185–192.

———. "Individualism, Holism, and Environmental Ethics." *Ethics and the Environment* 1 (1996): 55–69.

Simon, Yves. *Introduction à l'ontologie du Connaître*. Paris, 1934.

Singer, Peter. *Animal Liberation*. New York: Random House, 1975.

Tardiff, Andrew. "A Catholic Case for Vegetarianism." *Faith and Philosophy: Journal of the Society of Christian Philosophers* 15, no. 2 (1998): 210–222.

te Velde, Rudi A. *Participation and Substantiality in Thomas Aquinas*. Revised from the Dutch with the help of Anthony P. Runia. Leiden: E. J. Brill, 1995.

Thomas Aquinas. *An Exposition of the 'On the Hebdomads' of Boethius*. Translated by Janice L. Schultz and Edward A. Synan. Washington, D.C.: The Catholic University of America Press, 2001.

———. *Commentary on Aristotle's 'De Anima.'* Translated by Kenelm Foster and Silvester Humphries. Notre Dame, Ind.: Dumb Ox Books, 1994.

———. *Commentary on Aristotle's 'Nicomachean Ethics.'* Translated by C. I. Litzinger. Notre Dame, Ind.: Dumb Ox Books, 1993.

———. *Commentary on the Metaphysics of Aristotle*. Translated by John P. Rowan. Chicago: Regnery, 1961.

———. *Disputed Questions on Truth*. Vol. 1 translated by Robert William Mulligan. Vol. 2 translated by James V. McGlynn. Vol. 3 translated by Robert W. Schmidt. Chicago: Regnery, 1952–1954.

———. *The Division and Methods of the Sciences, Questions V–VI of the Commentary on Boethius' De Trinitate*. Translated by Armand Maurer. Toronto: Pontifical Institute of Mediaeval Studies, 1953.

———. *On Spiritual Creatures*. Translated by M. C. Fitzpatrick. Milwaukee: Marquette University Press, 1951.

———. *On the Power of God*. Translated by English Dominicans. London: Burns, Oates, and Washbourne, 1932–1934.

———. *Questions on the Soul*. Translated by James H. Robb. Milwaukee: Marquette University Press, 1984.

———. *Scriptum in IV Sententiarum*. Edited by Pierre Mandonnet and M. F. Moos. Paris: Lethielleux, 1933.

———. *Summa contra Gentiles*. Translated by English Dominicans. London: Burns, Oates, and Washbourne, 1934.

———. *Summa Theologiae*. Translated by English Dominicans. New York: Christian Classics, 1981.

Veatch, Henry. "A Note on the Metaphysical Grounds for Freedom, with Special Reference to Professor Lovejoy's Thesis in 'The Great Chain of Being.'" *Philosophy and Phenomenological Research* 7, no. 3 (March 1947): 391–412.

———. "A Rejoinder to Professor Lovejoy." *Philosophy and Phenomenological Research* 7, no. 4 (June 1947): 622–625.

Weisheipl, James. *Friar Thomas d'Aquino: His Life, Thought, and Works*. Washington, D.C.: The Catholic University of America Press, 1974.

Whitehead, Alfred North. *Adventures of Ideas*. New York: The Free Press, 1967.

———. *Modes of Thought*. New York: The Free Press, 1968.

———. *Process and Reality: An Essay in Cosmology*. Corrected edition. Edited by David Ray Griffin and Donald W. Sherburne. New York: The Free Press, 1978.

———. *Science and the Modern World*. New York: The Free Press, 1967.

Wippel, John. "Thomas Aquinas and the Axiom 'What Is Received Is Received According to the Mode of Knower.'" In *A Straight Path: Studies in Medieval Philosophy and Culture, Essays in Honor of Arthur Hyman*, edited by Ruth Link-Salinger et al., 279–289. Washington, D.C.: The Catholic University of America Press, 1988.

———. "Thomas Aquinas and Participation." In *Studies in Medieval Philosophy*, edited by John Wippel, 117–158. Washington, D.C: The Catholic University of America Press, 1987.

———. "Thomas Aquinas on Creatures as Causes of *Esse*." *International Philosophical Quarterly* 40, no. 2 (June 2000): 197–213.

Index

actuality
  relationship to perfection, 24,
    25–26, 42–43, 44
  Thomas on, 3, 5, 12, 18–19, 24,
    25–29, 39–40, 42–43, 44, 45,
    85–86, 100–101, 120, 122, 129,
    163–64, 184, 194n.15, 196nn.24,
    37, 199n.61, 202n.14, 207n.79
  Whitehead on actual entities/
    occasions, 130–56, 159, 188–89,
    219n.4, 220nn.13, 24, 221n.34,
    222n.54, 224n.79, 225nn.84, 86,
    230n.23, 237n.2
angels, 94, 104–5, 118, 186–87, 213n.26,
  237n.18
Annice, Sr. M., 196n.46
Anselm, St., 70
Aristotle
  on change, 31
  on definitions, 23
  on efficient causality, 31, 32
  on form, 22, 30, 81–82, 148, 194n.15,
    212n.6, 218n.43
  on goodness, 21–23, 24, 29, 30, 43,
    195n.22, 197n.52
  on justice, 66, 70, 209n.83
  Nichomachean Ethics, 23
  on Plato, 23, 30, 31, 77–78, 87, 91,
    197n.52

  on possible intellect, 86
  on received and recipient, 82–83,
    97–98, 110, 112
  on the soul, 78, 80, 81–82, 123
  on species, 15
  on substantial form, 148
Attfield, Robin, 192n.1, 193n.10
Augustine, St., 77
Averroës, 77
Avicenna, 77

Barad, Judith, 192n.1
being
  as act of being (*actus essendi*), 25, 39
  essential vs. accidental, 26–27
  of God, 5, 7–8, 22, 30, 34, 35–38,
    39–40, 122, 129, 145, 163–64,
    200n.72
  relationship to intrinsic goodness,
    3, 4, 5, 11–13, 15, 16, 17, 21–29, 31,
    37, 38–40, 44, 162–63, 169, 179,
    196n.37, 199n.61
  scale/hierarchy of, 29, 30, 43–46,
    202nn.8, 14, 203n.16
  Thomas on, 3, 4, 7–8, 20, 22–29,
    30, 34, 35–38, 39, 44, 60–61,
    194nn.12, 24, 196n.37, 197n.52,
    199n.61, 200n.72, 201n.80
  as transcendental, 22, 29

Birch, Charles, 219n.2
Boethius
  on goodness, 21, 26, 31–32, 39
  on participation, 21
  Thomas' commentary on *On the
    Hebdomads,* 21, 23, 32, 39
Bourke, Vernon, 59
Brown, Warren S., 192n.2
Buck-Armstrong, Susan, 219n.2
Buersmeyer, Keith, 196n.46

Callicott, J. Baird
  on culture and ethics, 174–76,
    234n.50, 235n.52
  on Darwinian evolution, 172,
    173–74, 176, 233n.40
  and Hume's theory of moral
    sentiments, 172–74, 176, 177,
    230n.23, 232n.32, 233n.37,
    234n.49
  on intrinsic value/goodness, 8–9,
    125, 162, 165–67, 171–77,
    231n.26, 232n.32, 233n.40,
    234n.49
  on Leopold's land ethic, 172,
    234n.49, 235n.52
  on reason and moral judgments,
    171, 174, 175, 176
  and relativism, 171, 173, 174–75, 177,
    230n.23, 233n.37, 234n.50
change
  Thomas on material change, 83–85,
    96, 113–16, 184, 185, 236n.10
  Thomas on spiritual/intentional
    change, 83–85, 89, 90–91, 96,
    100, 103, 113–16, 184–85, 186–87,
    236n.10
  Whitehead on becoming, 132–33,
    143–44, 220nn.16, 29
  See also efficient causality; final
    causality
Cobb, John B., Jr., 219n.2

cognition, 82–92
  act of understanding/intellect in
    act, 89–92, 94–97, 98, 100–101,
    104, 107–8, 111, 116, 183, 184,
    214nn.39, 43, 49, 215n.53
  of contraries, 95, 103, 109, 112–16
  the inner word in, 90, 92, 99, 100,
    112, 216n.11
  and intentionality, 82, 83, 84, 85,
    89, 90–91, 96, 113–16, 183–87,
    213n.21, 217n.29
  knowledge of human soul, 75, 86,
    90, 123
  knowledge of immaterial entities,
    97–123, 186–87, 217n.37
  role of form in, 75, 79, 83–85, 86–92,
    105–6, 107–8, 110–12, 184–85,
    217n.28
  role of intelligible species in, 7, 83,
    87–92, 95–96, 98, 99–107, 108,
    111–12, 116, 184, 185, 214nn.39,
    49, 215nn.53, 55, 56, 236n.9,
    237n.15
  role of interior senses/sensitive
    powers in, 96, 97, 183–84,
    185–86, 236n.11, 237n.15
  role of spiritual change in, 83–85,
    89, 90–91, 100, 103, 113–16,
    184–85, 186–87, 236n.10
  role of universals in, 12, 85–86,
    87–89, 90–92, 93, 94, 97–116, 117,
    123, 128, 185, 215nn.53, 55, 216n.8,
    217n.28
  of singulars, 104–5, 107, 109, 117,
    217n.29, 236n.10, 237n.15
  See also sense perception
consciousness
  relationship to intensity of feeling,
    145
  relationship to subjectivity, 8–9,
    140–41, 146, 166, 170, 176,
    223n.61

self-consciousness, 155, 156, 163, 164, 166, 227n.124, 232n.32
Whitehead on, 128, 135, 136, 137, 153, 154–55, 156, 159, 163, 164, 166, 227n.124
contraries, 95, 103, 109, 112–16

Daly, Herman, 219n.2
Darwin, Charles: on evolution of ethics, 173–74, 176, 233n.40, 234n.49
Descartes, René, 4, 130
mind-matter dualism of, 132
and subjectivist principle, 136
subjectivist turn of, 136, 137
Dioum, Baba, 179
diversity of creatures
relationship to perfection, 43, 49
Thomas on, 12, 13–14, 15, 43, 49–51, 52–54, 56, 164, 193n.11, 205n.36
Whitehead on, 164
dualism
of mind and matter, 132, 137, 141, 149
Whitehead on, 131–32, 134, 137, 149

ecological problems
carbon dioxide, 1
consumption in industrialized countries, 181–82, 191n.3, 235n.2
and democracy, 235n.2
ecosystem change, 1–2, 11, 165, 178
extinction of species, 1, 4, 11, 15–16
global warming, 1
and perfection of universe, 15–16
population growth, 1
rainforest destruction, 1, 11
relationship to moral worth of creatures, 2, 3, 14–15
efficient causality
Aristotle on, 31, 32
and modern science, 128

Thomas on, 20, 31–40, 42, 56–57, 120, 194n.10, 201n.80
Whitehead on, 138, 139, 140–41, 221n.34, 222n.50
essence
vs. accident, 19–20, 26–27, 35, 149
of God, 30, 34, 35–38, 39–40, 120, 121, 145, 200n.72, 201n.80
of human beings, 20, 198n.58, 205n.57
of material vs. immaterial entities, 117–18
Thomas on, 19–20, 26–27, 35–40, 44–45, 87, 88–89, 91, 108, 120, 121, 132, 147, 194n.12, 198n.58
Whitehead on, 149

Fabro, Cornelio, 196n.46
Feinberg, Joel, 170
final causality
final end of human beings, 5–6, 13–14, 41, 42–46, 51–52, 54, 57–58, 63, 123, 129, 202n.1, 204n.17
final end of non-rational creatures, 5–6, 13–14, 15, 41–46, 51–52, 54, 57–58, 129, 202n.1
final perfection of the universe, 5–6, 13–14, 15–16, 41, 51–52, 54, 55–56, 57–58, 123, 128, 129, 179–81
God as final cause, 41, 42–44, 129, 156, 196n.44
Ford, Lewis S., 222n.37
form
Aristotle on, 22, 30, 81–82, 148, 194n.15, 212n.6, 218n.43
contrary forms, 95, 103, 109, 112–16
human soul as, 7, 75, 78–82, 94, 118, 123, 212nn.6, 14, 218n.43
intentional vs. natural existence of, 84, 85, 89, 96, 113–16, 183–85, 186–87, 213n.21, 217n.29

form (*cont.*)
    Plato on, 22, 23, 30–31, 87, 197n.52,
        198n.58
    role in cognition, 75, 79, 83–85,
        86–92, 105–6, 107–8, 110–12,
        184–85, 217n.28
    substantial vs. accidental, 19–20
    Thomas on, 18–20, 21, 22, 30–31,
        32–35, 38, 39, 44, 57, 75, 79–82,
        83–85, 95–96, 98, 100, 107–12,
        184–85, 186–87, 194nn.8, 12,
        15, 198n.58, 199n.63, 200nn.67,
        72, 202n.14, 214n.41, 236n.9,
        237nn.15, 18
formal causality
    God as exemplary cause, 38, 39, 42,
        53, 201n.80
    Thomas on, 19–20, 31–32, 35, 38, 39,
        42, 53, 57, 201n.80
fortitude, 207n.79
Foster, David R., 215n.1, 216nn.2, 4
freedom
    freedom/slavery dichotomy, 14, 16,
        41, 48–49, 73–74, 123, 155–56,
        204n.24
    of God, 211n.120
    of human beings, 14, 16, 41, 48–49,
        73–74, 123, 139–40, 155–56,
        180–82, 192n.1, 203n.16,
        204nn.17, 24
    and universals, 14, 16, 64
    Whitehead on, 128, 139–40, 151–52,
        153, 155
French, William, 50–51

Gamwell, Chris, 213n.21, 217n.26
God
    as actual entity, 131, 159, 188–89,
        225n.86, 237n.2
    being of, 5, 7–8, 22, 30, 34, 35–38,
        39–40, 122, 129, 145, 163–64,
        200n.72

    consequent nature of, 145, 156,
        157–60, 180, 228nn.128, 140
    as Creator, 17, 21, 22, 29, 31, 32–40,
        42–44, 46, 70–73, 117, 140,
        156, 200n.75, 201n.80,
        211n.120
    creatures loved and cared for by, 41,
        127, 130, 145, 161, 178–79, 180, 181,
        235n.1
    divine justice vs. human justice, 6,
        42, 70–73
    and end times/final perfection of
        the universe, 5–6, 13–14, 15–16,
        41, 51–52, 54, 55–56, 57–58, 123,
        128, 129, 179–81
    essence of, 30, 34, 35–38, 39–40, 120,
        121, 145, 200n.72, 201n.80
    eternal law of, 42, 58, 60, 63, 67–68,
        205n.57, 210n.114
    as exemplary cause, 38, 39, 42, 53,
        201n.80
    as experiencing the world, 127, 129,
        156, 157–61, 163, 164, 178–79, 180,
        181, 188, 189–90, 228nn.141, 143,
        229n.1, 235n.1, 238n.7
    as final cause, 41, 42–44, 129, 156,
        196n.44
    freedom of, 211n.120
    goodness of, 5, 22, 30, 34, 37–38,
        39, 42–43, 52, 120–21, 129, 145,
        164, 197n.52, 200n.72, 202n.11,
        211n.120
    ideas/intellect of, 53, 71, 195n.22,
        201n.80
    imitation of, 37–38, 201n.80
    as immaterial, 7–8, 94, 104–5,
        120–23, 200n.72, 218n.44
    knowledge of, 12, 192n.1, 204n.17
    love for, 62, 204n.17
    and meaning of existence, 156, 157,
        161, 181, 228n.147, 235n.1
    necessary existence of, 145

omnipotence of, 120, 180–81,
   211n.120, 235n.1
omniscience of, 145
participation in, 3, 5, 16, 21–22,
   29–40, 196n.46
perfection of, 37, 38, 42–43, 121, 129,
   180–81, 235n.1
as personally ordered society, 189,
   225n.86, 228n.140, 237n.2
primordial nature of, 145, 156, 159,
   188–90, 225n.86, 228n.140,
   237n.2, 238n.7
proofs of existence of, 7, 120–23,
   218n.44
providence of, 6, 11, 15–16, 41, 46,
   47–48, 49, 51, 53–54, 58, 63, 72,
   127, 128, 193n.11
rationality of, 63, 71
relationship to ecological ethic, 125,
   129, 180–81
as revealed by Jesus, 158–59, 160–61,
   178–79, 235n.1
simplicity of, 22, 36, 37, 38, 71, 120,
   200n.72, 201n.80
species preserved in existence by,
   15, 53–54, 205n.41
subjective aim of, 145–46, 149, 150,
   157, 160, 189–90, 225nn.86, 87,
   226nn.88, 111, 228n.143,
   238n.7
as Triune, 120
as truth, 22
as Unmoved Mover, 120–21
will of, 71, 118, 193n.13, 211n.120
wisdom of, 71, 120–21, 160
goodness
   as accidental, 26–27, 43, 199n.61
   and analogical predication,
      197n.52
   Aristotle on, 21–23, 24, 29, 30, 43,
      195n.22, 197n.52
   Boethius on, 21, 26, 31–32, 39

   as convertible with being, 3, 4, 5,
      11–13, 15, 16, 17, 21–29, 31, 37,
      38–40, 44, 162–63, 169, 179,
      196n.37, 199n.61
   of God, 5, 22, 30, 34, 37–38, 39,
      42–43, 52, 120–21, 129, 145,
      164, 197n.52, 200n.72, 202n.11,
      211n.120
   hierarchy/grades of, 12–13, 29, 30,
      43–46, 49–50, 52, 54, 193n.11,
      202nn.11, 14, 203n.16,
      209n.83
   ontological goodness vs. moral
      worth, 3, 4, 5, 11–13, 15, 16, 22, 27,
      28–29, 30, 40, 44, 162–63, 169
   participated goodness, 3, 5, 16,
      21–22, 29–40, 196n.46
   Plato on, 21–22, 23, 30–31, 34,
      197n.52
   as substantial/essential, 17, 21, 26–27,
      32, 37, 38–40, 43, 199n.61
   as transcendental, 22, 23, 24, 28, 29,
      196n.37
   See also instrumental value/
      goodness; intrinsic value/
      goodness; perfection
Green, Joel B.: What about the Soul?,
   192n.2
Griffin, David Ray, 224nn.67, 68

Hartshorne, Charles, 218n.1, 225n.87
   on actual entities, 132
   on category of the ultimate,
      188–89
   on creativity, 139, 223n.59, 238n.7
   on God's primordial nature, 188–90,
      228n.140, 237n.2, 238n.7
   on matter, 223n.59
   on meaning of existence, 228n.147
   on mind-matter dualism, 141
   on response of concrete things to
      environment, 223n.65

human beings
  essence of, 20, 198n.58, 205n.57
  final end of, 5–6, 13–14, 41, 42–46,
    51–52, 54, 57–58, 63, 123, 129,
    202n.1, 204n.17
  freedom of, 14, 16, 41, 48–49, 73–74,
    123, 139–40, 155–56, 180–82,
    192n.1, 203n.16, 204nn.17, 24
  inclinations of, 61–62, 64
  moral worth of, 3, 4–5, 6, 8, 11–13,
    15, 22, 50, 123, 139, 162–63, 169
  as part of nature, 4, 5, 8, 128, 131–32,
    142, 155–56, 178–79, 181–82,
    227n.124
  perfection of, 5–6, 24–26, 41, 51–52,
    55–56, 60–62, 64, 128, 129
  as rational, 12, 14, 16, 35, 41, 44,
    46–49, 54, 55, 59–63, 64, 69, 72,
    73, 128, 140, 155–56, 171, 192n.1,
    203n.16, 205n.57, 207n.79,
    210n.103, 212n.14
  relationship between parents and
    children, 69–70
  relationship to God, 69–70, 205n.51
  as self-conscious, 155, 156, 163, 164,
    166, 232n.32
  as separate from nature, 2, 4–5, 7, 12,
    13–14, 16, 41, 46–49, 69, 73–74,
    79, 94, 123, 128, 129, 155–56,
    162–63, 179, 181, 192n.1, 193n.4,
    204n.17
  will of, 71, 72–73, 128, 207n.79
  See also human intellect; human soul
human intellect, 85–92, 213nn.19, 21
  act of understanding, 89–92, 94–97,
    98, 100–101, 104, 107–8, 111, 116,
    183, 184, 214nn.39, 43, 49, 215n.53
  agent intellect, 87–89, 90–91, 117
  contraries known by, 95, 109, 112–16
  first principles of practical vs.
    speculative intellect, 60–61
  and inner word, 90, 92, 99, 100, 112,
    216n.11
  and intelligible species, 7, 83, 87–92,
    95, 98, 99–107, 108, 111–12, 116,
    184, 185, 214nn.39, 49, 215nn.53,
    55, 56, 236n.9, 237n.15
  possible intellect, 86–87, 88, 89,
    90–91, 92, 100–101, 105, 113–16,
    117, 214n.41
  potential to know all things of, 93,
    94–97
  and virtue, 65, 207n.79
  See also cognition
human soul
  Aristotle on, 78, 80, 81–82, 123
  as entity, 7, 12, 18, 20, 69, 75, 78–79,
    90, 91, 93–116, 122, 123, 193n.6,
    212nn.6, 14, 218n.43
  as form, 7, 20, 75, 78–82, 94, 97, 118,
    122, 123, 212nn.6, 14, 218n.43
  freedom of, 41, 46–47, 48–49,
    64, 72, 73–74, 192n.1, 203n.16,
    204nn.17, 24
  as immaterial, 12, 69, 80, 86, 92,
    93–123, 216n.8, 217n.28, 218n.44
  as immortal, 6, 7, 12, 41, 46–47, 49,
    58, 72, 73, 78, 79, 80, 81–82, 92,
    93–116, 156, 180, 192n.1, 204n.17,
    205n.51
  knowledge of, 75, 86, 90, 123
  and nonreductive physicalism,
    192n.2
  Plato on, 77–78, 123
  relationship to body, 7, 78–79,
    80–82, 91, 94–97, 118, 123,
    205n.51, 212n.14, 215nn.56–58
  sensitive appetite of, 23–25, 61–62,
    65, 195n.22, 207n.79
  Thomas on, 4–8, 11, 12, 14, 15, 16, 18,
    20, 41, 45, 46–49, 55, 58, 69,
    73–74, 75, 77–82, 93–116, 127,
    155–56, 179, 193n.6, 205n.51,
    212nn.6, 14, 218n.44
Hume, David
  on causality, 221n.34

Dialogues, 158
and sensationalist principle,
222n.40
and subjectivist principle, 136,
222n.40
theory of moral sentiments, 172–74,
176, 230n.23, 232n.32, 233n.37

immaterial entities
angels as, 94, 104–5, 118, 186–87,
213n.26, 237n.18
God as immaterial, 7–8, 94, 104–5,
120–23, 200n.72, 218n.44
human soul as immaterial, 12,
69, 80, 86, 92, 93–123, 216n.8,
217n.28, 218n.44
intelligible species as immaterial,
102–6, 108–9
knowledge of, 116–23, 186–87, 217n.37
vs. material entities, 7–8, 20, 94,
116–23, 131–32, 147, 155–56, 163,
183, 218nn.42, 44, 236n.1
ontological immateriality, vs.
representative immateriality,
7, 75, 93–94, 97, 98–101, 103–9,
111–12, 114–17, 118, 119, 122, 123,
217nn.21, 29
universals as, 92, 97–117
instrumental value/goodness
defined, 3
of non-human creatures, 5, 6, 8,
11, 12–14, 16, 41–42, 44–52, 54,
56–63, 58, 63, 72–73, 127, 128, 163,
167, 179, 191n.4, 193n.7, 203n.16,
205n.53, 209n.83, 229n.1
Thomas on, 5, 6, 11, 12–14, 16, 28–29,
41–42, 44–52, 54, 56–63, 72–73,
127, 128, 169, 179, 191n.4, 193n.7,
203n.16, 205n.53, 209n.83
intentionality, 82, 83, 89, 90–91, 183–87
intentional vs. natural existence, 84,
85, 89, 96, 113–16, 183–85, 186–87,
213n.21, 217n.29

intrinsic value/goodness
Callicott on, 8–9, 125, 165–67,
171–77, 231n.26, 232n.32, 233n.40,
234n.49
defined, 3
hierarchy of, 125, 130, 142, 147, 156,
163, 166–67, 179, 193n.5, 229n.1
of non-human creatures, 5, 8–9, 125,
127, 129, 142, 162–63, 165–77, 182,
229n.1
relationship to being, 3, 4, 5, 11–13,
15, 16, 17, 21–29, 31, 37, 38–40, 44,
162–63, 169, 179, 196n.37,
199n.61
relationship to God's experience,
129, 130
relationship to human valuation,
8–9, 165–67, 171–77
relationship to moral worth, 3, 5,
8, 11–13, 15, 16, 17, 22, 30, 40, 44,
162–63, 167–77
relationship to subjectivity, 8–9,
129, 142, 150, 162–63, 165–67, 168,
169–77
Rolston on, 8–9, 125, 162, 165–71,
176–77, 229nn.4, 12, 230n.23
Thomas on, 3, 4, 5, 11–13, 15, 16, 17,
21–29, 31, 37, 38–40, 162–63, 169,
179, 196n.37, 199n.61
Whitehead on, 8, 9, 125, 129, 135,
142, 145–46, 150–51, 152–53, 156,
159, 160, 161, 162–63, 166–67, 182,
225nn.86, 87, 230n.23

Jeeves, Malcolm: *From Cells to Souls—
And Beyond,* 192n.2
Jesus Christ, 158–59, 160–61, 178–79,
235n.1
John, Sr. Helen James, 196n.46
justice
Aristotle on, 66, 70, 209n.83
commutative justice, 67–68,
210n.103

justice (*cont.*)
    distributive justice, 67–70, 210n.108
    general/legal justice, 68, 209n.83
    as giving each its due, 42, 58, 66–67,
        68–71, 72, 210n.103
    human justice vs. divine justice, 6,
        42, 70–73
    relationship to equality, 65, 66–71,
        209n.89, 210nn.103, 108
    Thomas on, 6, 42, 58–59, 65–73,
        207n.79, 208n.81, 209nn.83, 89,
        210nn.103, 108, 211n.120

Kant, Immanuel, 171, 174, 234n.45
Kenny, Anthony: *Thomas on Mind*,
    194n.15, 212nn.6, 11, 218n.43
Kerr, Andrew, 219n.2
Kretzmann, Norman, 212n.11

Leopold, Aldo, 172, 234n.49, 235n.52
Lindbeck, George, 196n.46
Linzey, Andrew, 193n.7
love
    vs. fear, 181
    for God, 62, 204n.17
    of neighbor, 62, 181
Lovejoy, Arthur O., 211n.120

McInerny, Ralph M., 196n.46
meaning of existence
    and God, 156, 157, 161, 181, 228n.147,
        235n.1
    Hartshorne on, 228n.147
    Whitehead on, 156, 157, 161
moral worth
    defined, 3, 191n.4
    of human beings, 3, 4–5, 6, 8, 11–13,
        15, 22, 50–51, 123, 139, 162–63, 169
    of non-human creatures, 2, 5, 8,
        12–14, 15, 16, 50–58, 116, 123, 125,
        127, 128, 156, 167–76, 179, 182,
        191n.4

vs. ontological goodness, 3, 4, 5,
    11–13, 15, 16, 22, 27, 28–29, 30, 40,
    44, 162–63, 169, 179
relationship to creativity and
    freedom, 139
relationship to ecological problems,
    2, 3, 14–15
relationship to intrinsic value/
    goodness, 3, 5, 8, 11–13, 15, 16,
    17, 22, 30, 40, 44, 162–63,
    167–77
relationship to subjectivity, 8, 139,
    142, 166–67
Thomas on, 4–5, 6, 7, 8, 11–12, 13–15,
    16, 22, 27, 28–29, 30, 42, 43–44,
    45–46, 54, 58, 59, 62–63, 65, 73,
    79, 94, 127, 139, 162–63, 169, 179,
    191n.4, 230n.20
Murphy, H. Newton, 192n.2
Murphy, Nancey: *Whatever Happened
    to the Soul?*, 192n.2

natural law
    first principle of practical reason,
        59–61, 62
    precepts of, 6, 59–64, 205n.57
    relationship to God's eternal law,
        42, 58, 60, 63, 67–68, 205n.57,
        210n.114
    relationship to reason, 59–60, 63,
        205n.57
    Thomas on, 6, 42, 58–63, 67–68,
        205n.57, 209n.83, 210n.114
negative existential claims, 164–65,
    223n.59
Novak, Joseph A., 216n.8

Origen, 43, 49, 50, 52

participation
    first mode of, 198n.58
    as on-going, 34

participated goodness, 3, 5, 16,
    21–22, 29–40, 196n.46
    second mode of, 198n.58, 199n.61
    third mode of, 32–33, 199n.61
Partridge, Ernest, 170
Pasnau, Robert, 213n.19, 216n.4
Pegis, Anton C., 211n.120
perfection
    of creatures, 5–6, 24–26, 27–29, 35,
        41, 42–45, 55–56, 60–62, 63, 64,
        67–68, 128, 129, 199n.61, 202nn.3,
        8, 14, 203n.16
    vs. desirability, 61
    of God, 37, 38, 42–43, 121, 129,
        180–81, 235n.1
    hierarchy/grades of, 44–45, 202n.14,
        203n.16
    of human beings, 5–6, 24–26, 41,
        51–52, 55–56, 60–62, 64, 128, 129
    relationship to actuality, 24, 25–26,
        42–43, 44
    relationship to diversity, 43, 49
    relationship to form, 198n.58
    of subsistence, 79
    of the universe, 5–6, 11, 12, 13–14,
        15–16, 30, 41, 43, 44–45, 49–58,
        63, 94, 117–19, 123, 128, 129,
        179–80, 202n.8, 205n.41, 209n.83
    See also goodness; intrinsic value/
        goodness
Peterson, Anna, 12, 193nn.4–6
    Being Human, 192n.2
Plato
    Aristotle on, 23, 30, 31, 77–78, 87, 91,
        197n.52
    on forms, 22, 23, 30–31, 87, 197n.52,
        198n.58
    on goodness, 21–22, 23, 30–31, 34,
        197n.52
    on principle that like knows like,
        98, 107
    on the soul, 77–78, 123

Porter, Jean, 209n.89
potentiality
    Thomas on, 18–19, 26, 42–43, 44,
        83, 85–87, 93, 94–97, 100–101,
        113, 114, 115, 120, 122, 129, 184,
        194n.15, 199n.61, 202n.14,
        207n.79, 237n.15
    Whitehead on, 159, 188
propositions, 90, 92, 155, 215n.53,
    227n121
    negative existential propositions,
        164–65, 223n59
prudence, 207n.79

rationality
    of God, 63, 71
    of human beings, 12, 14, 16, 35, 41,
        44, 46–49, 54, 55, 59–63, 64,
        69, 72, 73, 128, 140, 155–56, 171,
        192n.1, 203n.16, 205n.57, 207n.79,
        210n.103, 212n.14
    relationship to moral judgments,
        171, 174, 175, 176
    Thomas on, 5, 6, 11–12, 14, 16, 20,
        35, 41, 44, 46–49, 54, 55, 59–63,
        64, 71, 73, 128, 155–56, 171,
        203n.16
    Whitehead on, 137, 155–56, 171
Rolston, Holmes, III
    on genetic code, 229n.12
    on intrinsic value/goodness, 8–9,
        125, 162, 165–71, 176–77, 229nn.4,
        12, 230n.23
    on systemic value, 167, 168
    vs. Thomas, 169

Santmire, Paul, 193n.7
science, modern, 128, 135, 140, 165, 190,
    223n.65, 230n.23
sense perception
    role of sensible species in, 184–85,
        236n.10

sense perception (*cont.*)

Thomas on, 83, 84, 85, 86, 88, 90,
91, 93, 95–97, 106, 109, 111, 114,
115, 117, 118, 183–86, 213n.26,
215nn.56, 58, 236nn.10, 11

Whitehead on, 135, 143, 221n.34,
222n.40, 224n.76

Simon, Yves, 85

Singer, Peter, 193n.7

species

Aristotle on, 15

diversity of, 15, 43, 49–51, 52–54,
56, 164, 193n.11,
205n.36

extinction of, 1, 4, 11, 15–16

as preserved by God, 15, 53–54,
205n.41

Thomas on, 11, 12–13, 15, 19, 23, 30,
33–34, 38, 43, 44–45, 49–51,
52–54, 56, 132, 164, 193n.11,
194n.1, 198n.58, 200n.67,
201n.80, 205nn.36, 39, 41, 57,
237n.18

Whitehead on, 164

subjectivity

evolution of moral sentiments,
173–74, 176, 233n.40, 234n.49

Hume's theory of moral sentiments,
172–74, 176, 230n.23, 232n.32,
233n.37

reformed subjectivist principle, 138,
222n.54

relationship to consciousness,
8–9, 140–41, 146, 166, 170, 176,
223n.61

relationship to intrinsic goodness/
value, 8–9, 129, 142, 150, 162–63,
165–67, 168, 169–77

relationship to moral worth, 8, 139,
142, 166–67

subjectivist principle, 136,
222n.40

substance

first substance vs. second substance,
194n.1

immaterial substances, 7–8, 131–32,
194n.4, 200n.72

material substances, 18–19, 131–32,
194n.4, 200n.72

Thomas on, 17–20, 75, 78–82, 91,
117–18, 130, 131–33, 147, 194n.1,
197n.52, 198n.58

Whitehead on, 131–32, 142, 148–49,
220n.16

Tardiff, Andrew, 193n.9

temperance, 207n.79

te Velde, Rudi, 196n.46

Thomas Aquinas

on accidents, 18, 35, 130, 132,
197n.52, 198n.58

on actuality, 3, 5, 12, 18–19, 24,
25–29, 39–40, 42–43, 44, 45,
85–86, 100–101, 120, 122, 129,
163–64, 184, 194n.15, 196nn.24,
37, 199n.61, 202n.14, 207n.79

on analogical predication, 7, 34,
120–22, 197n.52, 200nn.70, 72

on angels, 94, 104–5, 118, 186–87,
213n.26, 237n.18

on being, 3, 4, 7–8, 20, 22–29, 30,
34, 35–38, 39, 44, 60–61, 122,
194nn.12, 24, 196n.37, 197n.52,
199n.61, 200n.72, 201n.80

on the categories, 17–18, 23,
197n.52

on charity, 73

on the cogitative power, 96, 186,
236n.11

on common good, 68, 69, 209n.83

on the common sense, 96, 236n.11

on contingent beings, 35–36,
200n.75

on definitions, 23

on diversity of creatures, 12, 13–14,
    43, 49–51, 52–54, 56, 164, 193n.11,
    205n.36
on efficient causality, 20, 31–40, 42,
    56–57, 120, 194n.10, 201n.80
on end times/final perfection of the
    universe, 5–6, 13–14, 15–16, 41,
    51–52, 54–58, 94, 123, 128, 129
on equality, 65, 66–70, 209n.89,
    210nn.103, 108
on equivocal predication, 197n.52
on essence, 19–20, 26–27, 35–40,
    44–45, 87, 88–89, 91, 108, 120,
    121, 132, 147, 194n.12, 198n.58
on evil, 61, 195n.22, 196n.37
on faith, 120
on final causality, 5–6, 13–14, 15–16,
    27–29, 31, 41, 42–46, 51–52,
    54, 55–58, 63, 123, 128–29, 164,
    194n.10, 196n.44, 204n.17
on final end of human beings,
    5–6, 13–14, 41, 42–46, 51–52, 54,
    57–58, 63, 123, 129, 202n.1
on final end of non-rational
    creatures, 5–6, 13–14, 15, 41–46,
    51–52, 54, 57–58, 129, 202n.1
on form, 18–20, 21, 22, 30–31, 32–35,
    38, 39, 44, 57, 75, 79–82, 83–85,
    95–96, 98, 100, 107–12, 184–85,
    186–87, 194nn.8, 12, 15, 198n.58,
    199n.63, 200nn.67, 72, 202n.14,
    214n.41, 236n.9, 237nn.15, 18
on formal causality, 19–20, 31–32,
    35, 38, 39, 42, 53, 57,
    201n.80
on genus, 23, 33–34, 117–18, 194n.1,
    198n.58, 200n.67, 205n.57
on God as Creator, 17, 21, 22,
    31, 32–40, 42–44, 70–73, 117,
    200n.75, 211n.120
on God as exemplary formal cause,
    38, 39, 42, 201n.80
on God as final cause, 41, 42–44,
    129, 196n.44
on God as immaterial, 7–8, 94,
    104–5, 120–23, 200n.72, 218n.44
on God's being, 7–8, 22, 30, 34,
    35–38, 39–40, 122, 163–64
on God's essence, 35–38, 39–40,
    120, 121
on God's eternal law, 42, 58, 60, 63,
    67–68, 205n.57, 210n.114
on God's goodness, 5, 22, 30, 34,
    37–38, 39, 42–43, 52, 120–21, 129,
    164, 197n.52, 200n.72, 202n.11,
    211n.120
on God's ideas/intellect, 53, 71,
    195n.22, 201n.80
on God's perfection, 37, 38, 42–43,
    129, 163–64
on God's providence, 6, 11, 15–16, 41,
    46, 47–48, 49, 51, 53–54, 58, 63,
    72, 127, 128, 193n.11
on God's rationality, 63, 71
on God's simplicity, 22, 36, 37, 38, 71,
    120, 200n.72, 201n.80
on God's will, 71–73, 117, 193n.13,
    211n.120
on habituation, 64, 71, 207n.79
on human appetite, 23–25, 61–62,
    65, 195n.22, 207n.79
on human freedom, 14, 16, 41,
    48–49, 73–74, 123, 139, 155–56,
    204n.24
on human perfection, 5–6, 24–26,
    41, 51–52, 55–56, 60–62, 64,
    128, 129
on human soul, 4–8, 11, 12, 14, 15,
    16, 18, 20, 41, 45, 46–49, 55, 58,
    69, 73–74, 75, 77–82, 93–116,
    127, 155–56, 179, 193n.6, 205n.51,
    212nn.6, 14, 218n.44
on imagination, 96, 185–86, 236n.11,
    237n.15

Thomas Aquinas (*cont.*)

on immaterial vs. material entities, 7–8, 20, 94, 116–23, 131–32, 147, 155–56, 163, 183, 218nn.42, 44, 236n.1

on immortality, 6, 7, 12, 41, 46–47, 49, 58

on instrumental value/goodness, 5, 6, 11, 12–14, 16, 28–29, 41–42, 44–52, 54, 56–63, 72–73, 127, 128, 169, 179, 191n.4, 193n.7, 203n.16, 205n.53, 209n.83

on intentionality, 82, 83–85, 89, 90–91, 96, 100, 103, 113–16, 183–87, 213n.21, 217n.29, 236n.10

on interior senses, 96, 97, 183–84, 185–86, 236n.11, 237n.15

on intrinsic goodness and being, 3, 4, 5, 11–13, 15, 16, 17, 21–29, 31, 37, 38–40, 162–63, 169, 179, 196n.37, 199n.61

on justice, 6, 42, 58–59, 65–73, 207n.79, 208n.81, 209nn.83, 89, 210nn.103, 108, 211n.120

vs. Kant, 234n.45

on matter, 18–19, 20, 33, 45, 57, 75, 79, 80, 81–82, 83–85, 86–87, 94, 96, 98, 102–3, 106, 107, 109, 110–11, 112–16, 184, 185, 194nn.5, 8, 12, 15, 198n.58, 200n.72, 202n.14, 205n.51, 212n.14, 236n.10, 237n.18

on memory, 96, 186, 236n.11

on moral worth, 4–5, 6, 7, 8, 11–12, 13–15, 16, 22, 27, 28–29, 30, 42, 43–44, 45–46, 54, 58, 59, 62–63, 65, 73, 79, 94, 127, 139, 162–63, 169, 179, 191n.4, 230n.20

on motion, 120, 122

on natural law, 6, 42, 58–63, 67–68, 205n.57, 209n.83, 210n.114

on one as transcendental, 22, 23

on participated goodness, 3, 5, 16, 21–22, 29–40, 196n.46

on perfection of creatures, 5–6, 24–26, 27–29, 35, 41, 42–45, 55–56, 60–62, 63, 64, 67–68, 128, 129, 199n.61, 202nn.3, 8, 14, 203n.16

on perfection of the universe, 5–6, 11, 12, 13–14, 15–16, 30, 41, 43, 44–45, 49–58, 63, 94, 117–19, 123, 128, 129, 179–80, 202n.8, 205n.41, 209n.83

on the pleasant, 28, 207n.79

on potentiality, 18–19, 26, 42–43, 44, 83, 85–87, 93, 94–97, 100–101, 113, 114, 115, 120, 122, 129, 184, 194n.15, 199n.61, 202n.14, 207n.79, 237n.15

on principle and term of an action, 107, 108–9

on principle of individuation, 19, 98, 102–3, 106, 110, 194n.8, 236n.10, 237n.18

on principle that like knows like, 98, 107

on proofs of God's existence, 7, 120–23, 218n.44

on rationality, 5, 6, 11–12, 14, 16, 20, 35, 41, 44, 46–49, 54, 55, 59–63, 63, 64, 71, 73, 128, 155–56, 171, 203n.16

on sense perception/sense knowledge, 83, 84, 85, 86, 88, 90, 91, 95–97, 106, 109, 111, 114, 115, 117, 118, 183–86, 213n.26, 215nn.56, 58, 236nn.10, 11

on sensitive souls, 45, 202n.14, 213n.19

on sin, 61–63, 68

on species of creatures, 11, 12–13, 15, 19, 23, 30, 33–34, 38, 43, 44–45, 49–51, 52–54, 56, 132, 164,

193n.11, 194n.1, 198n.58, 200n.67,
    201n.80, 205nn.36, 39, 41, 57,
    237n.18
on spiritual/intentional change,
    83–85, 89, 90–91, 96, 100, 103,
    113–16, 184–85, 186–87,
    236n.10
on substance, 17–20, 75, 78–82, 91,
    117–18, 130, 131–33, 147, 194n.1,
    197n.52, 198n.58
on substantial goodness, 21, 26–27,
    32, 37, 38–40, 43, 199n.61
on transcendentals, 22, 23, 24, 28,
    29, 30, 196n.37
on treatment of animals, 45–46,
    47–48, 57, 63, 67–68, 169, 191n.4,
    193n.9, 202n.14
on truth, 22, 23
on universals, 7, 12, 14, 16, 19, 49,
    64, 85–86, 87–89, 90–92,
    97–116, 117, 123, 128, 130, 155,
    192n.1, 203n.16, 215nn.53, 55,
    56, 60, 216nn.8, 11, 217n.28,
    236n.9
on univocal predication, 18, 20, 31,
    120, 122, 197n.52, 200n.72
on univocal vs. non-univocal
    causes, 33–34, 199n.63
on vegetative souls, 45, 202n.14
on virtue, 6, 28, 58–59, 60, 62,
    63–73, 207n.79, 208n.81
vs. Whitehead, 4, 8, 125, 128–29,
    130, 131–33, 139, 147, 155–56,
    162–65, 182
See also cognition; human intellect
Thomas Aquinas, works of
commentary on Boethius' On
    the Hebdomads, 21, 23, 32, 39,
    195n.18, 196n.46, 198n.58
Commentary on the Metaphysics
    of Aristotle, 194nn.1, 3, 10, 15,
    215n.60, 217n.34, 218n.42

Disputed Questions on Truth, 21, 23,
    25, 60, 103–4, 197n.52, 211n.120,
    215n.53
On Spiritual Creatures, 194n.8
On the Power of God, 54–56,
    199n.63, 205n.51
Questions on the Soul, 78–79, 81–82,
    94–101, 105–6, 212n.14, 236n.9
Scriptum in IV Sententiarum,
    205n.57
Summa contra Gentiles, 47–48, 121,
    200n.72, 201n.80, 202nn.8, 14,
    204n.17, 214n.49, 217n.33
Summa Theologiae, 23–24, 102,
    120–21, 197n.52, 202n.14, 205n.57,
    209n.83, 212nn.6, 14, 213n.19,
    214n.43, 217nn.27, 30, 35, 37
truth, 22, 23, 155

universals
as immaterial entities, 92, 97–117,
    118
vs. intelligible species, 98, 99–100,
    101–6, 107–9, 111–12, 116, 215n.55,
    216n.11, 236n.9
ontological immateriality vs.
    representative immateriality
    of, 75, 93–94, 97, 98–101, 103–9,
    111–12, 114–17, 118, 119, 122, 123,
    217nn.21, 29
vs. particulars, 49, 104–5, 107, 109,
    217n.29
role in cognition, 12, 85–86, 87–89,
    90–92, 93, 94, 97–116, 117, 123,
    128, 185, 215nn.53, 55, 216n.8,
    217n.28
as second substances, 194n.1,
    215n.60
and subjectivist principle, 136
Thomas on, 7, 12, 14, 16, 19, 49, 64,
    85–86, 87–89, 90–92, 97–116, 117,
    123, 128, 130, 155, 192n.1, 203n.16,

universals (*cont.*)
       215nn.53, 55, 56, 60, 216nn.8, 11,
       217n.28, 236n.9
    as what many share, 92, 215n.60
    Whitehead on, 128, 130, 136, 141, 155,
       188, 189, 222n.40, 238n.7

Veatch, Henry, 211n.120
virtue
    intellectual vs. moral virtues, 65,
       207n.79
    and rational appetite, 65, 207n.79
    relationship to habituation, 64, 71,
       207n.79
    and sensitive appetite, 65, 207n.79
    Thomas on, 6, 28, 58–59, 60, 62,
       63–73, 207n.79, 208n.81

Whitehead, Alfred North
    on actual entities/occasions, 130–56,
       159, 188–89, 219n.4, 220nn.13,
       24, 221n.34, 222n.54, 224n.79,
       225nn.84, 86, 230n.23, 237n.2
    on beauty, 8, 129, 144–45, 146,
       149–50, 153, 163
    on becoming, 132–33, 143–44,
       220nn.16, 29
    on concrescence, 134, 137–38,
       140–41, 142, 143–46, 148, 149,
       151, 153, 154–55, 159–60, 188–89,
       220n.29, 224n.79, 225n.86,
       228nn.140, 141, 237n.2, 238n.7
    on conformal phase of
       concrescence, 141, 143, 145, 146,
       151, 154–55, 159–60
    on consciousness, 128, 135, 136, 137,
       153, 154–55, 156, 159, 163, 164, 166,
       227n.124
    on creativity, 8, 128, 129, 139–41,
       152–53, 170–71, 226n.111
    on degrees of freedom and
       creativity, 140–41
    on diversity of species, 164

    on dualism, 131–32, 134, 137, 149
    and ecological ethics, 8, 125, 129,
       142, 162–65
    on efficient causality, 138, 139,
       140–41, 221n.34, 222n.50
    on essence and accident, 149
    on freedom, 128, 139–41, 151–52,
       153, 155
    on God as actual entity, 131, 159,
       188–89, 225n.86, 237n.2
    on God as revealed by Jesus, 158–59,
       160–61
    on God's consequent nature, 145,
       156, 157–60, 180, 228nn.128, 140
    on God's experience/prehension of
       the world, 127, 129, 156, 157–61,
       163, 164, 178–79, 180, 188, 189,
       228nn.141, 143
    on God's primordial nature, 145,
       156, 159, 188–90, 225n.86,
       228n.140, 237n.2
    on God's relation to creatures, 144,
       145–46, 156, 157–60, 178–79, 180
    on God's subjective aim, 145–46,
       149, 150, 157, 160, 225nn.86, 87,
       226nn.88, 111, 228n.143, 238n.7
    on gradations of actual entities/
       occasions, 147–48, 151–56, 163,
       166–67
    on human beings as part of nature,
       4, 131–32, 142
    influence of, 219n.2
    on intensity of feeling/subjective
       experience, 144–45, 146, 148,
       149–51, 152, 154, 155, 156, 157, 163,
       225n.87, 226nn.106, 111, 229n.1
    on judgment, 154, 227n.121
    on living societies, 152–53,
       227nn.116, 117, 124
    on meaning of existence, 156, 157,
       161
    on mental/conceptual pole, 145, 146,
       150, 152, 159, 160, 188, 228n.140

on metaphysical characteristics,
130–31, 137–38, 219n.9, 220n.12
on microscopic vs. macroscopic
level, 140, 220n.29
on negative prehensions, 134, 143, 151
on novelty, 145, 149, 150, 151–54, 155,
156, 226n.88, 111, 227nn.116, 117,
237n.2
on objectification, 137–38, 143,
224n.79, 228n.141
on the ontological principle,
220n.13, 222n.54
on order in nature, 145, 146–48, 149,
150–51, 153, 156, 226nn.88, 100,
111, 237n.2
on past actual entities, 134–35,
137–38, 143–44, 151, 159, 162–63,
164–65, 224n.79, 237n.2
on the physical pole, 143, 145, 150,
151, 153, 159–60, 188, 228n.140
on positive prehensions/feelings,
134–35, 143, 151
on potentiality, 159, 188
on prehension, 134, 143, 145, 154,
225n.84, 227n.121, 228n.143
on principle of relativity, 137–38, 159
on rationality, 137, 155–56, 171
on reformed subjectivist principle,
138, 222n.54
on satisfaction of completed
subject, 132, 149, 153, 189, 225n.84
on self-consciousness, 155, 156, 163,
164, 166, 227n.124
on sense perception, 135, 143,
221n.34, 222n.40, 224n.76
on societies, 146, 147–49, 150–51,
152–53, 154–55, 225n.86,
226nn.93, 100, 101, 111,
227nn.116, 117, 124

on solipsism of the present
moment, 136, 149
on subjective aims/final causality,
128–29, 133, 139, 144–46, 149,
150, 152–53, 154, 156, 157–60,
163, 164, 171, 220n.21, 224n.79,
225nn.84, 86
on subjective form/feeling-tone,
134–35, 143, 154, 159–60, 221n.34,
224n.76, 225n.84, 227n.121,
228n.143
on subjectivist principle, 136
on subjectivity/actual entities as
subjects of experience, 8, 9,
129, 132–33, 134–42, 162–63,
164–65, 170–71, 176, 177, 220n.24,
222n.44, 223nn.59, 61, 229n.1,
230n.23
on subjects as superjects, 133,
138–39, 220n.24, 225n.84
on substance metaphysics, 131–32,
142, 148–49, 220n.16
on supplemental phase of
concrescence, 141, 146, 151,
153
vs. Thomas, 4, 8, 125, 128–29, 130,
131–33, 139, 147, 155–56, 162–65,
182
on time, 220n.29
on universals/eternal objects,
128, 130, 136, 141, 155, 188, 189,
222n.40, 238n.7
on value, 8, 9, 125, 129, 135, 142,
145–46, 147, 150–51, 152–53, 156,
159, 160, 161, 162–63, 166–67, 182,
225nn.86, 87, 230n.23
Wippel, John, 196n.46, 200n.72

Zeno's paradox, 220n.29

Francisco J. Benzoni

is visiting assistant professor of business ethics at the

Fuqua School of Business, Duke University.